Byzanz und die euromediterranen Kriegskulturen

Band 1

Herausgegeben vom
Graduiertenkolleg 2304

Johannes Pahlitzsch / Jörg Rogge (eds.)

Victors and Vanquished in the Euro-Mediterranean

Dealing with Victory and Defeat in the Middle Ages

With 16 figures

V&R unipress

Mainz University Press

Deutsche
Forschungsgemeinschaft

Bibliografische Information der Deutschen Nationalbibliothek
Die Deutsche Nationalbibliothek verzeichnet diese Publikation in der Deutschen
Nationalbibliografie; detaillierte bibliografische Daten sind im Internet über
https://dnb.de abrufbar.

**Veröffentlichungen der Mainz University Press
erscheinen bei V&R unipress.**

© 2024 Brill | V&R unipress, Robert-Bosch-Breite 10, D-37079 Göttingen, ein Imprint der Brill-Gruppe
(Koninklijke Brill NV, Leiden, Niederlande; Brill USA Inc., Boston MA, USA; Brill Asia Pte Ltd,
Singapore; Brill Deutschland GmbH, Paderborn, Deutschland; Brill Österreich GmbH, Wien,
Österreich)
Koninklijke Brill NV umfasst die Imprints Brill, Brill Nijhoff, Brill Schöningh, Brill Fink, Brill mentis,
Brill Wageningen Academic, Vandenhoeck & Ruprecht, Böhlau und V&R unipress.
Wo nicht anders angegeben, ist diese Publikation unter der Creative-Commons-Lizenz
Namensnennung-Nicht kommerziell-Keine Bearbeitungen 4.0 lizenziert (siehe https://creative
commons.org/licenses/by-nc-nd/4.0/) und unter dem DOI 10.14220/9783737014779 abzurufen.
Jede Verwertung in anderen als den durch diese Lizenz zugelassenen Fällen bedarf der vorherigen
schriftlichen Einwilligung des Verlages.

Umschlagabbildung: Manasses-Chronik, Eroberung von Preslav durch Ioannes Tzimiskes und von
Pliska durch Basileios II., Miniatur auf Blatt 183, Entnommen aus: Ivan Dujčev, Die Miniaturen der
Manasses-Chronik, Sofia / Leipzig 1965, S. 66.
Druck und Bindung: CPI books GmbH, Birkstraße 10, D-25917 Leck
Printed in the EU.

Vandenhoeck & Ruprecht Verlage | www.vandenhoeck-ruprecht-verlage.com

ISSN 2941-9174
ISBN 978-3-8471-1477-2

Contents

Johannes Pahlitzsch
Byzantium's Place in the Euro-Mediterranean Cultures of War 7

I Remembering Victory and Defeat

Athina Kolia-Dermitzaki
The Rhetoric of Victory in Byzantine Texts of the 10th to 12th Centuries:
Historiography and Panegyrics in a Comparative Context 27

Tristan Schmidt
The Merciful Emperor, the Tame Barbarian, and the Ideal of Imperial
Victory in Times of Failure. Border Warfare in 11th and 12th Century
Byzantium 55

Alexandra Vukovich
Victory and Defeat Liturgified. The Symbolic World of Martial Ritual in
Early Rus 83

II Practices of Celebrating Victory and Triumphs

Jörg Rogge
After the Battle. Triumphs and Victory Celebrations in Late Medieval
England 115

Klaus Pietschmann
Musical Echoes of Victory and Defeat in Fifteenth-Century Court
Culture 125

III The Culture of Dealing with the Vanquished

Thomas Scharff
Ad internitionem delevit. How Victorious Franks Treated their Defeated
Enemies 141

Michael J. Decker
The Wars of John II Komnenos and the Decline of Byzantium in the
East 159

Graham A. Loud
Victors and Vanquished in Norman Italy 183

Thomas Dittelbach
The Acculturation of Conflict. The Norman Conquest of Islamic Sicily
under the Rule of Homage and Fealty 199

List of Figures 221

Johannes Pahlitzsch

Byzantium's Place in the Euro-Mediterranean Cultures of War

The significance of Byzantium for Europe's cultural history is indisputable.[1] Nevertheless, interdisciplinary projects have not to date examined this central question systematically. Indeed, as far as the general public in Western Europe is concerned, Byzantium remains a huge blank space.[2] And even in cross-cultural research project Byzantium is at best a marginal phenomenon. The reason for this is that Byzantium is not seen as part of our own (Western) 'European' culture, but rather as something exotic and remote. The DFG-funded Mainz Research Training Group (RTG) 2304 for doctoral students, "Byzantium and the Euro-Mediterranean Cultures of War. Exchange, Differentiation and Reception" (https://grk-byzanz-wars.uni-mainz.de/), makes a substantial contribution in closing this research lacuna with its program of research and study. The RTG approaches a concrete research topic, the Euro-Mediterranean cultures of war and Byzantium's entanglements with them, and in this way aims to contribute to the rehabilitation of Byzantium from its still-marginal status within Western scholarship through an interdisciplinary approach.

Our approach is based on the concept of cultural transfer and transculturality, which postulates that first a cultural encounter takes place, which then leads to communication and finally to cultural exchange between members of different cultural groups. In this sense, this model presupposes the existence of distinct 'cultures' and thus seems to contradict more recent ideas of transculturality that are more interested in the interweaving of different cultural traditions in the social space[3] and thus maintain that cultures are not homogenous units but always hybrid and themselves subjected to constant development processes.[4]

---

1 Auzépy, Byzance en Europe; Altripp, Byzanz in Europa; Kolovou, Byzanzrezeption in Europa; Speer, Knotenpunkt Byzanz; Gastgeber / Daim, Byzantium as Bridge. I would like to thank Dr. Miriam Salzmann and Dr. Max Ritter for their support in writing this paper.
2 Cameron, Absence of Byzantium; idem, Byzantine Matters.
3 Christ, et al., Transkulturelle Verflechtungen, 72–73.
4 This idea of transculturality was developed for the modern era by Welsch, Transkulturalität; and id., Transculturality. For criticism on his ideas, see Abu-Er-Rub, et al., Introduction,

Doubtlessly, this concept of transculturality has contributed to a more nuanced view of contact and exchange in the historical cultural sciences. However, it should be remembered that social groups always construct their own identities in contrast to other groups by postulating certain cultural differences. These constructed cultures, as 'collective imaginations', are part of historical practice and thus shape the cultural and social world.⁵ This raises the question as to how viable the concept of transculturality is in practical use, when all cultures are hybrid, entangled, shared or fluid, to use some of the current buzzwords.⁶

In particular, the applicability of this concept – initially developed for modern societies – to premodern cultures needs to be further critically developed.⁷ Michael Borgolte has pointed out that in the Middle Ages, when connections and communication over long distances were more limited, the assumption of the existence of a fundamental hybridity of cultures must not necessarily apply to the same degree. Borgolte calls for differentiation, so as not to succumb to tautology and fall into heuristic dead ends. He argues that it is in fact the historian's task to define supposedly universal phenomena and processes more closely along epoch-specific lines.⁸

The task of historical research is not only to determine "what actually happened (wie es eigentlich gewesen),"⁹ but also to identify the ideas and concepts that can be grasped in the sources and to question how they are constructed. In this sense, the concept of differing 'cultures' or 'cultural systems' becomes more relevant. The study of cultural contact, exchange and transfer must therefore equally and simultaneously involve the concepts of transculturality and interculturality, the latter of which is based on the existence of demarcated cultures. Current cultural transfer research is, thus, not only multilinear (rather than based on linear teleological concepts), but also multi-perspectival.¹⁰ Against this background, cultural encounter and cultural transfer are to be understood as models, whereby 'culture' represents, on the one hand, a heuristically-necessary

---

XXV–XXVI. The following is based on Pahlitzsch, Cultural Encounters, 83–84. For more recent overviews from an archaeological point of view see Müller / Meier, Inklusion – Exklusion and Nakoinz / Knitter, Modelle der Transkulturalität.

5 Mersch, Transkulturalität, 247; Christ, et al., Transkulturelle Verflechtungen, 76, where the question is also raised whether a world without cultural identities and thus also without cultural otherness would even be imaginable.

6 Abu-Er-Rub, et al., Introduction, XXVI, draw attention to the problem that "ostensibly, there is a paradox at the heart of transculturality: in order to point to the transcultural, one first has to assume separate cultures, while simultaneously negating their existence."

7 Mersch, Transkulturalität, 245–246.

8 Borgolte, Mittelalter in der größeren Welt, 43.

9 Ranke, Geschichten, VI.

10 Pahlitzsch, Cultural Encounters, 84; Trakulhun, Bewegliche Güter, 79–83. For a broader understanding of cultural transfer, see also Christ, et al., Transkulturelle Verflechtungen, 60.

construct that should not be confused with what actually exists,[11] while on the other hand a specific 'culture', such as the construct of a certain social group, could become an actual historical reality.

To examine the significance of Byzantium for the history and cultural development of the Euro-Mediterranean does not include the assumption of Byzantium's predominance. Instead, we are more concerned with examining how Byzantium was integrated within the processes of exchange and entanglement that shaped the Euro-Mediterranean. Owing to its geographical location, the Byzantine Empire was not only in constant contact with its neighbours, be it the Latin and Slavic world or the Near East, but often also involved in conflicts with them. The Research Training Group thus concentrates specifically on the entanglement between Byzantium and other cultures of war, including reciprocal, though not always intentional, exchange and cultural differentiation.

We define cultures of war, and we are aware that this is a construct, both as the forms and practices of war and as the norms, interpretations and reflections relating to war. Thus, both the practices and the theory of war can be subsumed in this term. As of today, scholars have scarcely reflected upon cultures of war as a defined heuristic concept. Our Research Training Group therefore carries out fundamental research by supplying an empirically-tested definition of cultures of war. Though the field of "New Military History" has examined social and cultural aspects of war for some decades now, historians in this discipline usually still understand battle and the battlefield as the core of their research.[12] They usually do not speak of *culture of war*, but of *military culture*.[13] Our understanding of cultures of war differs from this approach to include all forms of thought and action concerned with war. Recently, Yannis Stouraitis has published the *Companion to the Byzantine Culture of War*, which collects numerous fundamental studies on Byzantium's cultures of war between the 4th century and 1204.[14] Despite its title, however, the *Companion* does not define its understanding of "culture of war". Though it seems to follow a similar concept of culture of war as it has been developed in the Research Training Group, it does not reflect the use of the term.[15]

---

11 Borgolte, Mittelalter in der größeren Welt, 41–43; Barzen, et al., Kontakt und Austausch, 202.
12 Hoffenaar, New Military History, 8–9; Keegan, Face of Battle, 29; Lynn, Embattled, 784; id., Battle, xv; Morillo, Typology, 41; Morillo, What is Military History?.
13 Wilson, Defining Military Culture, 14. Other scholars apply the term *culture of war* solely to the concepts of war held by a certain population, as for instance in studies on the German war culture during the First World War, Audoin-Rouzeau, Von den Kriegsursachen zur Kriegskultur, 210–214; Lynn, Battle, 331.
14 Stouraitis, Companion to the Byzantine Culture of War.
15 The structuring of the volume in two parts, the first on the "Mentality of War" and the second on "Warfare as Socio-Political Praxis" corresponds to the basic division of the Research

There is no doubt that war is an anthropological constant, whereby the reasons for war remain essentially the same, despite all changes in weapons, tactics, equipment and the state of civilization. War significantly influenced and shaped medieval societies and concerns contact and exchange as well as contention and differentiation with others per se.[16] The cultures of war which arose as a result developed not only in opposition to, but also under the influence of other cultures. It is for this reason that we have decided on a comparative, transcultural, synchronic and diachronic examination of Euro-Mediterranean cultures of war as our research topic.

In order to ascertain the degree of the entanglement of Byzantium's culture of war with other Euro-Mediterranean cultures of war over the *longue durée*, our research concept considers the reception of Byzantine traditions in post-Byzantine periods. The transcultural comparison with phenomena similar to those in Byzantium is also integrated within our research program.[17] In this way we can ascertain specific characteristics of the compared cultures of war as well as other common features which cannot so easily be ascribed to immediate processes of transfer or reception. This leads us to consider deeper cultural entanglements on a less-evident level and the possible common origins of these cultures, for example in the ancient world. For that reason we include Roman cultures of the Imperial period and Late Antiquity in our research program since ancient traditions continued to have an effect in Byzantium and the Euro-Mediterranean. Indeed, the Byzantines themselves continually referred to real or constructed ancient traditions.

Given this background, four aspects for the analysis of cultural exchange have emerged from the various dissertation projects conducted by the Research Training Group. First, we focus on various **ancient and late antique traditions** that were influential for later periods, such as the legitimation of war and rule or warfare and war technology.[18] For example, Florian Groll's dissertation project

---

Training Group's research program into the two research fields "expressional forms" and "interpretative concepts".

16 McMillan, War, 1, 14–20, 41–60.
17 Drews / Oesterle, Vormoderne Globalgeschichten, 11; Borgolte, Perspektiven europäischer Mittelalterhistorie, 24; Rexroth, Vergleich, 371–372.
18 In the context of the Research Training Group, these topics are studied on the philological-historical level by Florian Groll, cf. below note 19; Manuel Krumbiegel, Die Bedeutung und Funktionen von Kampf- und Kriegsmetaphorik in den Schriften des Evagrius Ponticus (Diss. Johannes Gutenberg-Universität (JGU) Mainz, in preparation); Michael Rapp, (K)eine Sprache des Friedens? – Die Verwendung von Kriegsmetaphorik in den Werken Tertullians (Diss. JGU Mainz, in prep.); Sophia Ulrich, Die Kriegshistoriographie des Orosius (Diss. JGU Mainz, 2023); on the iconographic level by Julia Sophia Hanelt, Geprägte Gelübde – Untersuchungen zu den Votaprägungen anlässlich der Regierungsjubiläen der römischen Kaiser von Antoninus Pius bis Carus (Diss. JGU Mainz, 2023), Philipp Hanelt, Untersuchungen zu

examines the military representation and legitimization of the ruling family at the time of the first emperors, Augustus and Tiberius (31 BC–37 AD). The conduct of war was seen increasingly as the task of the whole imperial family from the late Augustan period. This signalled that the ruling dynasty could guarantee a secure, militarily-successful future in the face of the death of the aging emperor. Presenting the family members as triumphant in a military context is also increasingly discernible within later Roman imperial dynasties.[19]

Second and third, various historical, archaeological, art historical and musicological projects from 6–7th c. North Africa to St. Petersburg in the 18th century examine **processes of cultural transfer** in the Euro-Mediterranean space between Byzantium and other societies, as well as **post-Byzantine reception.** They discuss the legitimacy of war with reference to crusader ideology[20], concepts of identity and alterity, as well as the construction of images of the Other in ideological and literary discourses, and, *inter alia*, Byzantium as an orientalising motive in the construction of identities.[21]

As far as material culture is concerned, the appropriation of foreign objects (e.g. weapons or dress accessories) into a specific material culture and a change in burial custom regarding grave goods is discussed, for example by Regina Maria Molitor's project, who examines the Byzantine border region on the Lower Danube, a zone of contact with the "barbarian" world, from the 4th–7th century. The project analyses male burials and the custom of putting weapons in graves as a means of self-representation in the context of a frontier society with a strong military identity. This is an important contribution to understanding the processes of exchange and transfer between the Byzantine and the "barbarian" cultures of war in Late Antiquity.[22]

Kavalleriedarstellungen in der Spätantike im Osten des Imperium Romanum (Diss. JGU Mainz, 2023); and Katharina Schoneveld, cf. below note 23.
19 Florian Groll, Sieg und Familie im frühen Patriziat. Eine Studie zur militärischen Repräsentation der Verwandten des Augustus (Diss. JGU Mainz, 2022). See also Hanelt, (Bild-)Semantik von Jubiläumsvota.
20 Lorenz Kammerer, Die gelehrte Auseinandersetzung mit den Kreuzzügen anlässlich des Zweiten Hussitenkrieges 1467 (Diss. JGU Mainz, in prep.); Oana-Andreea Chiriluş, Moldavian and Wallachian Perceptions, Attitudes and Reactions to the Ottoman Threat during the 15th–16th Centuries (Diss. JGU Mainz, in prep.).
21 Sophia Sonja Guthier, Waräger und Ostslaven als Bedrohung von Byzanz in der russischen Textkultur des 18. und 19. Jahrhunderts (Diss. JGU Mainz, 2023); Bart Peters, Recollecting Conflict. Depictions of War in the Narratives of Early Medieval Southern Italy (Diss. JGU Mainz, in prep.); Gwendolyn Döring, "Ch'al Impero Bizantin / Torni d'Austria un Costantin." Untersuchungen zur Rezeption byzantinischer Herrscherpersönlichkeiten und kriegerischer Auseinandersetzungen im italienischen Musiktheater der Frühen Neuzeit am Beispiel Konstantins des Großen (Diss. JGU Mainz, in prep.).
22 Regina Maria Molitor, Kriegertum in Grenzgesellschaften – Waffengräber des 4.–7. Jh. an der byzantinischen Donaugrenze (Diss. JGU Mainz, in prep.). Philipp Margreiter, Africam de-

Katharina Schoneveld investigated how ancient military knowledge was absorbed by the Byzantine Empire from the 10th century on the basis of Byzantine military manuals and in particular of technical drawings of siege engines and artillery. She examines the development of the drawings in the manuscripts and explores how the drawings were integrated into the transfer of knowledge as a means of visual reinforcement. The Western European reception of these Byzantine manuscripts is also considered, tracing connections to 14th and 15th century "machine books".[23]

Fourthly, Helen Wiedmaier and Christos Zafeiropoulos have undertaken **transcultural comparisons** of notions of combatant groups and individuals between the late medieval West and Byzantium. Wiedmaier analyses how battles were described and how men were depicted as combatants in late medieval historiography, referring to several select 14th c. descriptions of battles such as those of Gammelsberg (1313), Morgarten (1315), Mühldorf (1322) or Sempach (1386).[24] Similarly, Zafeiropoulos examines the descriptions of Byzantine combatants, from the emperor, generals and officers down to the common soldier and their various functions in the historiography and rhetoric of the 13th and 14th century. It becomes evident that Byzantine orators followed a tradition based on the treatise of the rhetorician Menander of Laodicea (3rd century CE), who instructs panegyrists to portray the emperor as a competent warrior and as a victorious leader of the army. Historians, on the other hand, did not employ specific models for their descriptions.[25] The construction of combatants in both Byzantium and the West are largely congruent, as these two studies ascertain. Moreover, *topoi* played a far greater role than descriptions of 'real' persons for the depiction of combatants. Although specific transfer cannot be determined, the Byzantine and Latin texts are perceptibly influenced by classical models and biblical texts.

A framework based on the results of the projects to date thus begins to emerge. Beyond isolated individual cases, a larger spatio-temporal correlation is recognisable and we can begin to understand the various forms and ways in which Byzantine cultures of war were entangled with the cultures of war of the wider Euro-Mediterranean. Panagiotis Agapitos has been developing a comparable concept in the framework of his five-year Gutenberg Research Fellowship at

---

fendere. Byzantinische Fortifikationen in der nordafrikanischen Region Thugga im 6. und 7. Jahrhundert (Diss. JGU Mainz, in prep.), deals also with a border region.

23 Katharina Schoneveld, Illustrationen zur Kriegstechnik in byzantinischen Handschriften; ead., Manuscript Illuminations.

24 Helen Wiedmaier, Kämpfer auf dem Schlachtfeld – Kämpfer in den Texten; ead., Sinnstiftung; ead., Antlitz der Erde.

25 Christos Zafeiropoulos, Descriptions of Byzantine Combatants in Byzantine Written Sources during the Reign of the First Palaiologan Emperors (1259–1328) (Diss. JGU Mainz, 2022).

Mainz University. In his project "A Narrative History of Byzantine Literature, AD 1050–1500", Agapitos proposes to set Byzantine literature in a so-called Medieval Eurasian literary supersystem that roughly corresponds to our Euro-Mediterranean space. Within this literary system Agapitos finds regional peculiarities of narrative as well as transregional patterns of storytelling that cannot be explained by the traditional recourse to the direct imitation of models from other literatures.[26]

The basic connectivity of the Euro-Mediterranean space, despite all differences, rests to a certain extent on the fact that these areas had been, in the main, part of the Roman Empire or within its sphere of influence. This quite evidently made the development of more deeply-entrenched entanglements on various levels easier, even if it is almost impossible to define the original agents contributing to this process. An appropriate scholarly model for this type of entanglement is the 'rhizome', a term originally designating a rootstalk/rootstock that spreads underground from which offshoots sprout in different places. In this endlessly interwoven nexus of connections, the resulting entanglements and cultural congruencies cannot in all their complexity be reduced to single causes.[27] So while this model defies easy explanations of cultural exchange as something that is set in motion by a specific individual transferring objects, ideas or knowledge from A to B, and while it leaves many questions unanswered, it deepens our understanding of the complex and in fact in most cases untraceable ways of cultural transfer and entanglement.[28]

As for such rhizomatic entanglements (*rhizomatische Geflechte*) in the framework of the Euro-Mediterranean cultures of war, we have discerned three especially-tangible lines of tradition from antiquity that were used as points of reference both in Byzantium and the West and continued to be effective in the Middle Ages and the Early Modern period: early Christian discourses on the

---

26 The lecture by Agapitos, Byzantine Literature within a Medieval Eurasian Literary Supersystem: Amorous Tales and the Practice of Narrative Fiction (held on 19 March 2021 at the Center for Medieval Studies of the University of Toronto, and as yet unpublished), is a case study to argue for the existence of a Medieval Eurasian literary supersystem. I would like to thank the author for providing me with his script.
27 Christ, et al., Transkulturelle Verflechtungen, 183–185.
28 Christ, et al., Transkulturelle Verflechtungen, 77: "Eine transkulturelle Geschichtsforschung versteht in diesem Sinne die neue Begrifflichkeit nicht nur als kategoriale Benennung, sondern insbesondere als Anregung, ihre Untersuchungsobjekte neu zu konstituieren, dynamische Beziehungsgeflechte und prozessuale Veränderungen in den Blick zu nehmen, anstatt vornehmlich nach Übertragungen zwischen zwei oder mehreren autonom definierten Einheiten zu suchen." ("In this sense, transcultural historical research understands the new terminology not only as a categorical designation, but especially as a stimulus to reconstitute its objects of investigation, to take a look at dynamic networks of connections and processual changes, instead of primarily searching for transmissions between two or more autonomously-defined entities.").

legitimacy of war and how it was viewed, which were of great importance for later attitudes to war in Byzantine society and in the Latin West; Roman traditions of legitimizing a ruler through his triumphs, which we find in various media; and finally Roman military technological know-how, evident e. g. in the construction of fortresses and military manuals.

Thus, the investigation of cultural transfer reveals manifold areas, forms and paths of entanglement, as well as modes of differentiation between Byzantium and other Euro-Mediterranean war cultures: from cultural exchange instigated by individual actors in various border regions, to cultural contacts on a broader scale and conflicts in which Byzantium appeared as an opponent or an ally, to the transfer of knowledge, even though specific paths of communication can no longer be traced.

Byzantine cultures of war continued to be influential in the Euro-Mediterranean space after the fall of the Byzantine empire in 1453. We can identify discourses intended to strengthen and form identities or rather differentiation in various contexts. One decisive factor seems to be whether the population was aware of a historical connection to Byzantium, as for example in Southeastern Europe or in Russia. Despite, or perhaps because of, the basic acknowledgement of such an historical connection, distinctions between these people and their Byzantine heritage could be drawn which helped to shape their own identity (for example in early modern Russia). Indeed, in the Balkans Byzantium remained a living tradition, which was implicated in issues such as ethnogenesis and collective identity. As a historiographical construct, it was exposed to political and ideological deployment.[29] Where Byzantium was considered exotic and foreign, it was easier to adopt its traditions or history to undergird certain claims to hegemony (for example the Habsburgs in the 18th century). These reception processes show how the heritage of the Byzantine cultures of war can be implemented for current discourse.

In essence, for Euro-Mediterranean cultures of war, as indeed for cultures in general, it can be said that they always remain hybrid and are prone to continual processes of change, both intentional and unconscious. Byzantium was, however, an integral element of the Euro-Mediterranean space. Our investigations show that Byzantine culture participated in the process of exchange in various, not always evident, ways and was integrated in the nexus of Euro-Mediterranean cultures of war. Byzantium played a special role in the mediation of ancient and Near Eastern knowledge, which was creatively transformed in this process.

The present collection of articles originates from the inaugural conference of the Research Training Group in October 2018 entitled "Victors and Vanquished

---

29 Mishkova, The Afterlife of a Commonwealth; Kusber, Byzantinische Autokratie; Maner / Zelepos, Antike und Byzanz.

in the Euro-Mediterranean. Cultures of War in the Middle Ages" held at the Leibniz Institute for European History and the Johannes Gutenberg-University in Mainz, on 18–20 October 2018. It was sponsored by the Leibniz-Science-Campus Mainz/Frankfurt "Byzantium between Orient and Occident". In order to facilitate a fruitful discussion and start a concise transcultural comparison, various regions were included, Latin Europe as well as the Slavic world and Byzantium. Experts from disciplines that principally work with texts, as well as those that analyze material culture and musicologists participated.

The goal of the conference, as of this book, is to analyze Euro-Mediterranean cultures of war and the place Byzantium had in them in a comparative perspective on the basis of three concrete sets of topics: 1) remembering victory and defeat, 2) practices of celebrating victory and triumphs and 3) the culture of dealing with the vanquished.

The first section deals with different strategies of or rather narratives about coping with victory and defeat. Questions of the legitimation of authority, for instance in historiography, panegyric, pictorial representations and architecture are closely linked to it. Accordingly, Athina Kolia-Dermitzaki in her paper "The Rhetoric of Victory in Byzantine Texts of the 10th to 12th Centuries: Historiography and Panegyrics in a Comparative Context" explores how Byzantine authors depicted and enhanced military victories in their texts. Kolia-Dermitzaki seeks to demonstrate that the writers, certain reservations notwithstanding, draw a picture that corresponds to reality. More specifically, the proximity of the events described to the delivery of an oration can be seen as a factor forcing orators to present actual facts. Kolia-Dermitzaki underlines that the related events were not fictions aimed at entertaining their readers, but rather narratives based on reality, colored perhaps by an author's personal experience or perception. She does not believe that the rhetoric of victory underwent any significant change during the period under consideration. As for the factors which Byzantine authors consider decisive for the positive outcome of a campaign, battle, or siege, following leitmotifs are discernible: bravery and valor moderated by prudence (in order to avoid excessive aggression); wisdom and sagacity; large and well-organized expeditionary forces; honorable fighting; sharp-minded stratagems; the art of diplomacy. Among the positive effects of military success, the most common ones mentioned are the capture of booty and prisoners the liberation of Byzantine prisoners of war, and the provisioning of the army, while rhetoric also pays some attention to more long-term positive effects of victories.

Tristan Schmidt investigates dealings with victory and defeat in his paper "The Merciful Emperor, the Tame Barbarian, and the Ideal of Imperial Victory in Times of Failure. Border Warfare in 11th and 12th Century Byzantium", Schmidt presents several cases in which Byzantine authors depict imperial military policy towards various (semi-)nomadic groups threatening the border regions of the empire (Pechenegs, Turks, Cumans). Due to the flexible tactics, mobility and political fragmentation of these groups, decisive victories and sustainable agreements were hard to achieve. Hence, the imperial encomiasts had to go to certain lengths to fulfill the requirements of the traditional depiction of the emperor as an undisputed victor and replace an ambiguous reality with a rhetorically constructed certainty. This could be achieved through references to former military successes or to the general capability of the emperor and his army, intended to distract attention from the lack of current proof, as well as representing negotiations with the enemy as though the emperor held a strong position, even if this was not in fact the case. In stark contrast to panegyrics, historiography took a much more critical stance towards imperial policy and addressed the problem of the elusive nomadic enemies in a more open and practical way. It is remarkable though that both genres share a number of motifs, albeit treated in a different way, which allows Schmidt to use the notion of a "quasi-dialogue" of texts. This mainly concerns the discussion of the sustainability of the achieved military successes and the possibility of transforming the perceived "barbaric" nature of the (allegedly) defeated enemy in order to eliminate any threats in the future. Both Kolia-Dermitzaki and Schmidt therefore show that dealing with the vanquished (which is the topic of the third part of this volume) was an integral part of presenting the ruler's victoriousness.

Alexandra Vukovich analyses several characteristic aspects of the ideology of rulership in early Rus in the $11^{th}/12^{th}$ century in her paper on "Victory and Defeat Liturgified: The Symbolic World of Martial Ritual in Early Rus". This ideology was intertwined with both religious and military spheres: the ruler was personally and principally involved in war, whereas any military victory and the outcome of conflicts in general were interpreted by contemporary chronicles as fundamentally providential events. Actions attributed to princes in battle and after a victory, such as acclamations, liturgical invocations, receiving a blessing or oathtaking by "kissing the Cross", are represented clearly as ritual acts of a highly personalized nature, accompanied by descriptions of divine intercession ultimately defining which side was going to be victorious. Apart from this "liturgization" and ritualization of warfare, the princes of Rus also integrated symbols of victorious rulership and divine intercession into their personal iconographies, e.g. images on seals and coins, in church decoration, and especially through consistent association with their patron saints. A prince's legitimacy and authority depended on the superiority of his military might, military victories being an indicator of the divine confirmation *par excellence*. In contradiction to moral injunctions against violence, chronicle narratives liturgically and ritually validate military violence, celebrating victories against both pagans and other princes (mostly blood relatives) with similar religious connotations. Vukovich therefore shows how the rulers of Rus took up various strands of tradition: while edificatory literature focusses on iconic rulership based on Byzantine ideals, pre-Christian ideals of rulership and local practices were also used.

The second section deals with practices of celebrating victory and triumphs, which represent a means of direct communication between rulers, the army and the populace. In this context the participants express their gratitude to the army, the generals, the ruler or another higher authority, and it is here that the embedding of the martial in each individual culture is expressed. Jörg Rogge takes up this idea in his article on "After the Battle. Triumphs and Victory Celebrations in Late Medieval England". He studies a number of examples of celebrations of victory in Medieval Europe from mid-11th to the late 15th century. Except for one episode which took place in the Holy Roman Empire, all his examples are drawn from the history of the British Isles. Rogge underlines that none of the studied cases show any signs of a direct influence from the antique model of a Roman triumph. Moreover, there is in general no evidence of an exclusively secular triumph or celebration of a victory before 1500. The celebrations described always had a strong liturgical connotation, each of the so-called soldier kings setting his gratefulness to God in the foreground. All the ceremonies analyzed by the author clearly underline the connection between the personal piety of the ruler and his military superiority against his enemies. This military superiority, in the view of the victors, was based on the legitimacy of their reasons for war, and confirmed by the fact that God apparently helped the victorious king to fulfill his duty on the battlefield.[30] As for the essence of the celebrations themselves, they comprised immediate actions on the battlefield, a public demonstration and communication of the victory, a liturgical thanksgiving for God's help and secular festivities with wine, singing and tournaments. The *topoi* that these texts describe, and the general reasons for victory on the battlefield, can be found similarly in Byzantine historiography and rhetoric (cf. Kolia-Dermitzaki). Zafeiropoulos in his above-mentioned dissertation clearly shows their employment of ancient texts and models.

Klaus Pietschmann demonstrates the strong connection between the military sphere and church ritual in his study of "Musical Echoes of Victory and Defeat in Fifteenth Century Court Culture". He investigates the way military motifs were used in the late medieval music composed in courtly contexts. The first example presented is Guillaume Dufay's *Lamentatio Sanctae Matris Ecclesiae Constantinopolitanae* on the occasion of conquering Constantinople. In it, the composer draws an analogy between the fall of Constantinople and the biblical destruction of Jerusalem, at the same time achieving a "liturgification" as he places the composition on the same level as the lamentation over Christ's death on the cross during Holy Week. In addition, the lamentation implicitly addresses the sover-

---

30 For Byzantium compare Stephenson, Imperial Theology of Victory.

eign of every court at which it is performed with a call for a crusade. A similar intertwining of eschatological and worldly levels of meaning can be found in around 40 mass compositions of the 15th and 16th century based on the melody of a martial French chanson *L'homme armé*. With simple words and a catchy melody this chanson sings of an armed warrior, his fearsome appearance, and military mobilization in general. Thus, by employing this melody in the composition of a mass, the military sphere is implicitly evoked and transported into the rite of the mass, among others delivering a reference to the crusades. Overall, it can be stated that military victories and defeats usually did not echo in courtly music of the 15th century, the examples analyzed being rare exceptions which transcend sorrow and introduce a theological level, thus calling for a crusade only in an implicit manner and conceiving a possible victory as primarily spiritual in nature, not military.

The treatment of prisoners of war, the enemy dead and the subjected population likewise belongs to the frame of inquiry. Here, practices are of special importance. Thomas Scharff in his paper "*Ad Internitionem Delevit*. How Victorious Franks Treated Their Defeated Enemies" relies on 9th and 10th century sources. Numerous examples demonstrate a wide range of possible forms of treatment. One possibility was to pursue the vanquished who attempted to flee the battlefield, slaughtering those who failed to escape and taking their weapons and armor as booty. Then again pursued enemies could be captured rather than massacred, although killing or mutilation might still occur sometime after the battle. On the other hand, prisoners could be spared altogether and set free, after taking an oath of loyalty to the victor or after a ransom had been paid. Finally, the vanquished might simply be spared and released out of charity or for other reasons. In some cases, a certain sort of proto-chivalric behavior meant that a few ringleaders of the defeated army were released, whilst common warriors were not covered by the merciful attitude. As for the background of particular decisions, Scharff suggests the point of being captured during or after the battle, the nature of the war and the quality of the opponents as criteria for differentiation. Commenting on this last factor, he uses the distinction between intra- and transcultural wars, which can be subdivided again into intercultural and subcultural wars.[31] The author also remarks on a certain difference between the behavior of the Carolingian and Ottonian rulers, leading to the suggestion that the political, cultural, and social conditions of the state in question should also be considered. In conclusion, Scharff underlines the possibility of distortion since most authors aimed at characterizing the victorious ruler in accordance with a certain agenda, not necessarily in accordance with actual events.

---

31 Morillo, Typology; Kortüm, Kriegstypus und Kriegstypologie.

Under the title "The Wars of John II Komnenos and the Decline of Byzantium in the East" Michael J. Decker investigates the emperor's motives for his military campaigns in Cilicia and Syria (1137–38 and 1142–43) and the reasons for his ultimate failure. Describing the interactions of different powers in the region at the time, he carefully reconstructs the events of the campaign. Decker underlines the thorough preparations for the campaign during the years 1135–36, the (supposedly) considerable size of the forces assembled, and the return for the second campaign: these can be seen as indicators that the emperor regarded this direction as a priority even as he was facing tumult inside and outside the Empire. Decker argues that John was planning to obtain direct control of the prosperous and prestigious city of Antioch, then held by Prince Raymond of Poitiers. According to Decker, at the begin of the second campaign the emperor was set on claiming the Crusader-held city as his own as the first campaign had demonstrated that the Franks of Antioch were not trustworthy allies: Raymond had in fact agreed to become a vassal of the emperor, as had Joscelin II of Courtenay, Count of Edessa, but it seems that both princes had primarily hoped the emperor would fail in Syria and that they would be spared the subjection to him. They therefore failed to prove themselves as useful.

Graham A. Loud goes beyond the immediate consequences of military defeat in his article "Victors and Vanquished in Norman Italy" and analyses the specifics of the Norman conquest of southern Italy. Contrary to the takeover of England and the displacement of the local Anglo-Saxon elite, which took around a decade, in Italy the whole process lasted around ninety years. According to Loud, the principal reason for the slow pace was the small number of the incomers. This limitation made it necessary for the Normans to "infiltrate" local society and to rely on local allies rather than establishing their own prowess. There is indeed evidence of violence and bloodshed as the events progress, but at the same time sources show part of the local aristocracy allying with the conquerors and providing military assistance. Moreover, once in control, the Normans sought conciliation with the local population through intermarriage and inclusion of the traditional elite into the new order of power, preserving some of their pre-conquest wealth. This mainly concerned the Lombards, but also some of the Greek and Arab-speaking (both Muslim and Christian) populations. As disastrous and traumatic as some experiences of this conquest certainly were, in general the dichotomy of Norman vs. non-Norman seems to have ceased to matter by 1130, despite the fact that religious, cultural, and linguistic differences still had relevance.

Thomas Dittelbach, finally, investigates the cultural consequences of the Norman conquest on the subjected, non-Norman population of Southern Italy in his paper on "The Acculturation of Conflict. The Norman Conquest of Islamic Sicily under the Rule of Homage and Fealty". He refers to an interweaving of the culture of the victorious minority, in this case the Normans, and the vanquished majority, in this case the Muslim, Byzantine, and Jewish populations of Sicily. The author represents the Normans as understanding the necessity of allying with the dominant ethnic and political groups of the conquered region and indeed achieving certain success, even though they were not able to sustain this policy in the long term. On the one hand, the Normans applied the pyramid of feudal social relations to the whole of the multicultural Sicilian population, their "tribal identity" serving as the ultimate foundation of their acculturation strategies. On the other hand, the Normans adopted a number of elements characteristic for the courts of either contemporary or earlier Muslim dynasties, namely the Fatimids in Cairo and the Abbasids in Bagdad. With the backing of the papal authority Duke Robert Guiscard intended from the very start to create "a modern feudal state on Islamic soil", with the Norman ruler a vassal of the Pope, and the local population groups his own vassals.

The articles in this volume demonstrate, as do the projects of our Research Training Group, the manifold entanglements of the Euro-Mediterranean cultures of war and the integral role Byzantium played within this broad cultural setting. These entanglements could take many forms and show varying structures and developments, be it the profound 'rhizomatic' entanglement of reference to and transformation of ancient traditions in various areas, or direct contacts, exchanges and differentiation between different population groups. Though many of these complex processes remain as yet uncharted our transcultural approach contributes to a deeper understanding of the Euro-Mediterranean cultures.

Bibliography

Literature

Abu-Er-Rub, Laila / Brosius, Christiane / Meurer, Sebastian / Panagiotopoulos, Diamantis / Richter, Susan, Introduction, in: Engaging Transculturality. Concepts, Key Terms, Case Studies, ed. Laila Abu-Er-Rub / Christiane Brosius / Sebastian Meurer / Diamantis Panagiotopoulos / Susan Richter, Abingdon 2020, XXIII–XLI.

Altripp, Michael, Byzanz in Europa. Europas östliches Erbe. Akten des Kolloquiums "Byzanz in Europa" vom 11.–15. Dezember 2007 in Greifswald, Turnhout 2011.

Audoin-Rouzeau, Stéphane, Von den Kriegsursachen zur Kriegskultur: neuere Forschungstendenzen zum Ersten Weltkrieg in Frankreich, in: Neue politische Literatur 39 (1994), 203–217.

Auzépy, Marie-France (ed.), Byzance en Europe, Saint-Denis 2003.

Barzen, Rainer / Bulgakova, Victoria / Frederek Musall / Pahlitzsch, Johannes / Schorkowitz, Dittmar, Kontakt und Austausch zwischen Kulturen des europäischen Mittelalters. Theoretische Grundlagen und methodisches Vorgehen, in: Mittelalter im Labor. Die Mediävistik testet Wege zu einer transkulturellen Europawissenschaft, ed. Michael Borgolte / Juliane Schiel / Bernd Schneidmüller / Annette Seitz (Europa im Mittelalter 10), Berlin 2008, 195–209.

Borgolte, Michael, Perspektiven europäischer Mittelalterhistorie an der Schwelle zum 21. Jahrhundert, in: Das europäische Mittelalter im Spannungsbogen des Vergleichs: zwanzig internationale Beiträge zu Praxis, Problemen und Perspektiven der historischen Komparatistik, ed. Michael Borgolte (Europa im Mittelalter 1), Berlin 2001, 13–27.

Borgolte, Michael, Mittelalter in der größeren Welt: eine europäische Kultur in globaler Perspektive, in: Historische Zeitschrift 295 (2012), 35–61.

Cameron, Averil, The Absence of Byzantium, in: Nea Hestia (2008), 4–58.

Cameron, Averil, Byzantine Matters, Princeton 2014.

Christ, Georg / Saskia Dönitz / Daniel König / Şevket Küçükhüseyin / Margit Mersch / Britta Müller-Schauenburg / Ulrike Ritzerfeld / Christian Vogel / Julia Zimmermann, Transkulturelle Verflechtungen. Mediävistische Perspektiven, Göttingen 2016.

Drews, Wolfram / Oesterle, Jenny R., Vormoderne Globalgeschichten: eine Einführung, in: Transkulturelle Komparatistik. Beiträge zu einer Globalgeschichte der Vormoderne, ed. Wolfram Drews / Jenny R. Oesterle, Leipzig 2008, 8–14.

Gastgeber, Christian / Daim, Falko (ed.), Byzantium as Bridge Between West and East, Proceedings of the International Symposium, Vienna 2012 (Veröffentlichungen zur Byzanzforschung 36), Vienna 2015.

Hanelt, Julia Sophia, Die (Bild-)Semantik von Jubiläumsvota – Eine numismatische Ursprungssuche in augusteischer Zeit, in: Augustus immortalis. Aktuelle Forschungen zum Princeps im interdisziplinären Diskurs, Beiträge des interdisziplinären Symposions an der Humboldt-Universität zu Berlin, 25.–27. Oktober 2019, ed. Jessica Bartz / Martin Müller / Rolf Frank Sporleder, Berlin 2020, 89–96.

Hoffenaar, Jan, "New" Military History, in: Handbook of Military Sciences, ed. Anders Sookermany, Cham 2021, 1–14.

Keegan, John, The Face of Battle, New York 1976.

Kolovou, Foteini (ed.), Byzanzrezeption in Europa: Spurensuche über das Mittelalter und die Renaissance bis in die Gegenwart (Byzantinisches Archiv 24), Berlin 2012.

Kortüm, Hans-Henning, Kriegstypus und Kriegstypologie: Über Möglichkeiten und Grenzen einer Typusbildung von "Krieg" im Allgemeinen und vom "mittelalterlichen Krieg" im Besonderen, in: Formen des Krieges. Von der Antike bis zur Gegenwart, ed. Dietrich Beyrau / Michael Hochgeschwender / Dieter Langewiesche (Krieg in der Geschichte 37), Paderborn 2007, 71–98.

Kusber, Jan, Die "byzantinische Autokratie" als "travelling concept": Das Beispiel Russland, in: Byzanz und seine europäischen Nachbarn: Politische Interdependenzen und kulturelle Missverständnisse, ed. Ludger Körntgen / Jan Kusber / Johannes Pahlitzsch / Filippo Carlà-Uhink (Byzanz zwischen Orient und Okzident 17), Mainz 2020, 139–149.

Lynn, John A., The Embattled Future of Academic Military History, in: Journal of Military History 61 (1997), 777–789.

Lynn, John A., Battle: A History of Combat and Culture, Boulder 2003.

Maner, Hans-Christian / Zelepos, Ioannis (ed.), Antike und Byzanz als historisches Erbe in Südosteuropa (19.–21. Jahrhundert) (Südosteuropa-Jahrbuch 45), Berlin / Bern / Brussels 2020.

McMillan, Margaret, War. How Conflict Shaped Us, London 2020.

Mersch, Margit, Transkulturalität, Verflechtung, Hybridisierung – "Neue" epistomologische Modelle in der Mittelalterforschung, in: Transkulturelle Verflechtungsprozesse in der Vormoderne, ed. Wolfram Drews / Christian Scholl (Das Mittelalter, Beihefte, 3), Berlin 2016, 239–251.

Mishkova, Diana, The Afterlife of a Commonwealth: Narratives of Byzantium in the National Historiographies of Greece, Bulgaria, Serbia and Romania, in: Entangled Histories of the Balkans, vol. 3: Shared Pasts, Disputed Legacies, ed. Roumen Daskalov / Alexander Vezenkov (Balkan Studies Library 16), Leiden 2015, 118–273.

Morillo, Stephen, A General Typology of Transcultural Wars: The Early Middle Ages and Beyond, in: Transcultural Wars from the Middle Ages to the 21st Century, ed. Hans-Henning Kortüm, Berlin 2006, 29–42.

Morillo, Stephen, What is Military History?, Cambridge / Malden MA 2006.

Müller, Ulrich / Meier, Thomas, Inklusion – Exklusion. Transkulturalität im Raum. Eine Einführung, in: Exklusion – Inklusion. Transkulturalität im Raum, mit Beiträgen der Jahrestagung 2018 in Kiel, ed. Thomas Meier / Ulrich Müller / Winfried Schenk (Siedlungsforschung 37), Bonn 2020, 13–42.

Nakoinz, Oliver / Knitter, Daniel, Modelle der Transkulturalität, in: Exklusion – Inklusion. Transkulturalität im Raum, mit Beiträgen der Jahrestagung 2018 in Kiel, ed. Thomas Meier / Ulrich Müller / Winfried Schenk (Siedlungsforschung 37), Bonn 2020, 43–62.

Pahlitzsch, Johannes, Cultural Encounters and Transfer. The Case of Pious Foundations in the Islamicate World, in: The Routledge Companion to Cultural History in the Western World, 1250–2000, ed. Alessandro Arcangeli / Jörg Rogge / Hannu Salmi, London / New York 2020, 83–95.

Ranke, Leopold von, Geschichten der romanischen und germanischen Völker von 1494 bis 1535, vol. 1, Leipzig, Berlin 1824.

Rexroth, Frank, Der Vergleich in der Erforschung des europäischen Mittelalters: Versuch eines Resümees, in: Das europäische Mittelalter im Spannungsbogen des Vergleichs: zwanzig internationale Beiträge zu Praxis, Problemen und Perspektiven der historischen Komparatistik, ed. Michael Borgolte (Europa im Mittelalter 1), Berlin 2001, 371–380.

Schoneveld, Katharina, Illustrationen zur Kriegstechnik in byzantinischen Handschriften: Transfer und Adaption antiken Wissens in Byzanz (Byzanz und die euomediterranen Kriegskulturen 2), Göttingen 2024.

Schoeneveld, Katharina, Manuscript Illuminations in Military Manuals, in: Military Manuals in the Medieval Mediterranean and Beyond, ed. Conor Whately (submitted for publication).

Speer, Andreas (ed.), Knotenpunkt Byzanz. Wissensformen und kulturelle Wechselbeziehungen (Miscellanea Mediaevalia 36), Berlin 2012.

Stephenson, Paul, The Imperial Theology of Victory, in: Companion to the Byzantine Culture of War, ed. Yannis Stouraitis, Leiden 2018, 23–58.

Stouraitis, Yannis (ed.), A Companion to the Byzantine Culture of War, ca. 300–1204 (Brill's Companions to the Byzantine World 3), Leiden 2018.

Trakulhun, Sven, Bewegliche Güter: Theorie und Praxis der Kulturtransferforschung, in: Musik-Sammlungen: Speicher interkultureller Prozesse, vol. A, ed. Erik Fischer, Stuttgart 2007, 72–94.

Welsch, Wolfgang, Was ist eigentlich Transkulturalität?, in: Hochschule als transkultureller Raum? Kultur, Bildung und Differenz in der Universität, ed. Lucyna Darowska / Thomas Lüttenberg / Claudia Machol Bielefeld 2010, 39–66.

Welsch, Wolfgang, Transculturality – the Puzzling Form of Cultures Today, in: Spaces of Culture: City, Nation, World, ed. Mike Featherstone / Scott Lash, London 1999, 194–213.

Wiedmaier, Helen, Kämpfer auf dem Schlachtfeld – Kämpfer in den Texten. Schlachtenschilderungen in den historiografischen Quellen des 14. und beginnenden 15. Jahrhunderts (Byzanz und die euromditerranen Kriegskulturen 3), Göttingen 2024.

Wiedmaier, Helen, Sinnstiftung nach der Schlacht bei Mühldorf – die Darstellung der Besiegten in der Historiografie des 14. Jahrhunderts, in: Eroberte im Mittelalter, ed. Rike Szill / Andreas Bihrer (Europa im Mittelalter 3), Berlin 2023, 411–428.

Wiedmaier, Helen, "Sie bedeckten das Antlitz der Erde wie Heuschrecken." Die Konstruktion von Männern als Besiegte im 14. Jahrhundert, in: Geschichte wird von den Besiegten geschrieben. Darstellung und Deutung militärischer Niederlagen in Antike und Mittelalter, ed. Manuel Kamenzin / Simon Lentzsch (Krieg und Konflikt 19), Frankfurt / New York 2023, 95–118.

Wilson, Peter H., Defining Military Culture, in: The Journal of Military History 72 (2008), 11–41.

1   Remembering Victory and Defeat

Athina Kolia-Dermitzaki

The Rhetoric of Victory in Byzantine Texts of the 10th to 12th Centuries: Historiography and Panegyrics in a Comparative Context

The theoretical approach to war and peace in the Middle Ages, and more particularly in Byzantium, has been a subject of study since the early 1990s. Both medievalists and Byzantinists have turned to the study of war ideology, the existence or absence of a legal framework regulating its declaration and rules of conduct (*jus belli – jus ad bellum*), its effects on societal organization and development, as well as to the economy, and the attitude of the Church towards war. Furthermore, scholars of Byzantium have begun to show interest in the perception of war by contemporaries, the development of military technology, the fate of non-combatants and prisoners of war in general, the ideological background, the relation between "just" and "holy" war, how they were perceived by the Byzantines[1] etc.

Interest in the above-mentioned issues led to the organization of scholarly conferences where these subjects were discussed: Byzantium at War (9th–12th c.) in 1996, Byzantine War Ideology between Roman Imperial Concept and Christian Religion, in 2011, Histories of War in South-Eastern Europe: An Approach in the Longue Durée. A Centenary since the Balkan Wars of 1912–13, in 2013, Common Men and Women at War, 300–1500 AD, in 2014 Violence in war was the subject of a two-day conference in 2014 in Paris (La violence des soldats dans les récits de guerre, de l'Antiquité à l'époque contemporaine)[2] while in 2016. During the last

---

1 The first scholar to exhibit interest in the way war was conducted and the notion of "just war" in Byzantium was the eminent jurist, Georgios Michaelides-Nouaros, Professor of Civil Law at the University of Athens; in 1961 he published a study on the Taktika of Leo VI (Ὁ βυζαντινὸς δίκαιος πόλεμος κατὰ τὰ Τακτικὰ τοῦ Λέοντος τοῦ Σοφοῦ) and highlighted – among other things – the key elements of military tactics from the standpoint of the law. The most recent study dealing with the issues of war and peace as viewed from a legal perspective is that of Pitsakis, Guerre et paix en droit byzantin, 203–231; it is an interesting article, although the author's point of view regarding the issue of "holy war" in Byzantium is based mainly on the particular emphasis he placed on the study of canon law and its interpretation. He did not interpret – though he did not ignore – testimonies from other sources.
2 For the Proceedings see: Tsiknakes (ed.), Τὸ εμπόλεμο Βυζάντιο (9ος–12ος αι.); Koder / Stouraitis (ed.), Byzantine War Ideology; Kolia-Dermitzaki et. al. (ed.), Ιστορίες πολέμου στη νοτιοανατολική Ευρώπη; Cosme / Couvenhes et al. (ed.), Le récit de guerre.

International Congress of Byzantine Studies in Belgrade, a thematic session on War and peace in Byzantium: Changes and turning-points in the Middle and Late Byzantine period (7th–15th centuries) was organized by the author of the present paper.[3] Lastly, a series of annual conferences on Medieval Culture and War for Postgraduates and early career researchers should be mentioned, which have been held since 2016 in Leeds, Lisbon, Brussels and Athens. In spite of the rich bibliography on the above-mentioned subjects, a large number of issues are in need of further investigation, reassessment or a new approach.

In the present paper the way in which historiographers as well as panegyrists of the tenth to the twelfth century display and promote military victories in their texts will be examined and analyzed. The questions posited are the following: a) Do the sources under consideration describe a sanitized or a realistic version of the outcome of the army's combat operations? b) Do the narratives of these two very different literary genres overlap and, if so, to what degree? c) Do authors of the tenth century face/present victory in a manner that differs from that of eleventh and twelfth century authors, given the monumental changes that had taken place on the political, economic and social level?

To begin with, we should note the issues of reliability that the two aforementioned types of sources (and not only they, of course) present. A serious question modern research has been posing for the past two decades, one that we must touch upon here, is the issue of an authors' impartiality when composing their text, and the extent to which they interfere with it or not. Modern researchers approach works of historiography with particular skepticism – due to the Byzantines' different perception of the history-writing process and a lack of specific methodological rules – and consider the degree to which these works can be viewed as literary texts whose main purpose was to please their readers or listeners. Ralph-Johannes Lilie in his study of whether the descriptions of events mentioned in the works of tenth-twelfth century historiographers correspond to reality or constitute inventions on the part of the authors, notes that the latter clearly seek to "entertain" their readers or listeners. They frequently embellish their narrative with incidents and characterizations, their purpose being to showcase the character of the persons involved or to recapture the milieu in which the events took place. Indeed, these events are often completely fictional,

---

3 For the abstracts of the session see Kolia-Dermitzaki, War and Peace in Byzantium, 477–485. In this session Dr. Nike Koutrakou presented a paper that would have been equally at home in the present conference, since she covered the interesting topic of how the Byzantine government managed defeat ("Managing the other face of Byzantine war: was there a mode of presenting and accepting defeat?") based on tenth and eleventh century historiographers. See the abstract, as above, 481, and the publication Koutrakou, The Other Face of War in Byzantium, 1541–1564.

without even a kernel of actual fact in them.⁴ This complete lack of a core of reality is in my opinion an exaggerated assumption: after all, accepting this view would lead to the conclusion that the entire historiographical production of the Byzantines was a work of fiction that had nothing to do with reality. This would be a gross overstatement, since most historical descriptions are accurate and the facts correctly presented, even if they had gone through a process of literary treatment.⁵

The same holds true – perhaps to an even greater extent – for panegyrics.⁶ The composition and delivery of these orations took place almost exclusively during official court ceremonies in the presence of the emperor, to whom most of them were addressed, or before the populace to celebrate an event of cardinal importance (for example the termination of a war) or during religious festivities. Added to the exaggerated literary expressions or descriptions used by the orators, all these considerations definitely make scholars justifiably suspicious as to whether the events to which they refer are real or simply figments of the speaker's imagination. However, orators usually refer to events that took place only a year or two before the speech was delivered, thus they were addressed to an audience familiar with those events.⁷ The orator, therefore, may embellish them in a way that exaggerates the promotion of actions and persons, but he is always obligated to base his version on a core of actual events. At any rate, modern scholars can look beyond the events and – by reading between the lines – may trace veiled personal views, as well as more widespread mentalities.⁸

The study of the sources (both historiography and rhetoric) brought to light the existence of specific elements embedded in the description of victorious

---

4 See Lilie, Reality and Invention, with thorough relevant bibliography in the footnotes. See also the brief but informative introduction by Macrides, Editor's Preface, IX–XII. For a slightly different position, see Treadgold, Early Byzantine Historians, 350–379; Idem, Middle Byzantine historians, 457–487; Cf. Macrides, The Historian in the History; Nilsson, To Narrate the Events of the Past. For the most recent views on this issue, see Neville, Why did the Byzantines Write History?, 265–276; Treadgold, Unwritten Rules, 277–292; Kaldellis, The Manufacture of History, 293–306.
5 This is the final conclusion of Lilie, Reality and Invention, 209–210, as well. Cf. McGrath, Warfare as Literary Narrative.
6 On Byzantine rhetoric see Hunger, Literatur der Byzantiner, 67–157. Particularly on encomia and funeral orations/monodies, see 120–145. See also Jeffreys, Rhetoric in Byzantium, especially the contributions by Martha Vinson, Dimiter Angelov, Wolfram Hörandner and Jakov Ljubarskij. For a first approach to the rhetoric of war, see Kolia-Dermitzaki, Το εμπόλεμο Βυζάντιο στις ομιλίες και επιστολές, 213–238.
7 Dennis, Imperial Panegyric, 131–140. On this issue, see also Lilie, Reality and Invention, 205–206.
8 See Ljubarskij Jakov, How Should a Byzantine Text be Read, 55–72; Kolia-Dermitzaki, Το εμπόλεμο Βυζάντιο στις ομιλίες και επιστολές. See also, Wirth, Kaiser Manuel I. Komnenos, for parallel passages from historiographers and rhetors which confirm this point of view and the ascertainment that their texts complement each other quite often.

operations and contributing – according to the authors – to the positive outcome of a campaign, a battle, or even a siege. At the same time, this study helped to form an idea regarding the authors' attitude towards the means employed by the victorious Byzantines to reach the desired outcome: conquering the enemy.

The first element one comes across in rhetoric of victory is bravery[9], the valor shown by Byzantines, but also a measured aggressiveness in battle, a show of a sharp mind combined with prudence. I will mention two illuminating examples: Eustathios Argyros, *patrikios* and *hypostrategos ton Anatolikon*, "who belonged to the most noble and illustrious family of the Argyroi, campaigned victoriously against the Ismaelites and put them to flight, not once but many times, honored and gifted with strength and power, wisdom and valor and prudence, a sound mind and a sense of justice" according to the Continuator of Theophanes.[10] Another passage that displays a similar perception, though referring to the conflict between Romanos Diogenes and the entire family of Michael VII Doukas after the former's defeat in Mantzikert (August 1071), may be found in the Chronographia of Michael Psellos. The passage refers to Konstantinos Doukas (son of the Caesar Ioannes Doukas[11]) who was initially given the task of dealing with Diogenes and defeated him in battle: "very active and of sharp and wonderful mind, excellent in knowing what needed to be done and in interpreting the facts".[12]

Synesis (wisdom, sagacity) and *phronesis/sophrosyne* (prudence) are mental virtues also highly valued by orators – apart from the obvious one, bravery. Several examples support this statement. I shall limit myself to two instances from two monodies by Michael Italikos regarding members of the Komnenoi family: one written in 1131 for the *sebastokrator* Andronikos Komnenos, son of the emperor Alexios I,[13] and one composed in 1142 for the *sebastokrator* An-

---

9 On the issue of bravery in war, see Maniati-Kokkini, Η επίδειξη ανδρείας στον πόλεμο.

10 Theophanes Continuatus, 368$_{21}$–369$_5$ "ὃς τῆς καλλίστης καὶ ἀγαθῆς γενεᾶς τῶν Ἀργυρῶν ἐκπεφώνηται τοῖς Ἰσμαηλίταις κατεστράτει καὶ ἔτρεπεν οὐχ ἅπαξ ἀλλὰ καὶ πολλάκις, ῥώμῃ καὶ ἰσχύϊ καὶ συνέσει καὶ ἀνδρείᾳ καὶ φρονήσει καὶ σωφροσύνῃ καὶ δικαιοσύνῃ τετιμημένος καὶ ἐπειλημμένος". The author refers to the 904 campaign against the Arabs of Tarsos and Mompsuestia. See Vannier, Familles byzantines, 22–24; Cheynet / Vannier, Les Argyroi, 59–60 with an explanation for the title ὑποστράτηγος; Tougher, Leo VI, 210–213, 217–218.

11 On Konstantinos Doukas see Polemis, The Doukai, 59–60.

12 Michael Psellos, Chronographia, ed. Reinsch, vol. I, book VII, § 154, 276$_2$–277$_4$ [Michel Psellos, Chronographie, ed. Renaud, vol. II, book VII, § 33, p. 167$_{3-5}$] ("οὗτος δὲ καὶ τὴν χεῖρα δραστήριος· καὶ τὴν σύνεσιν ὀξὺς καὶ θαυμάσιος· γνῶναί τε τὰ δέοντα καὶ ἑρμηνεῦσαι ἐπιφανέστατος"). For some more indicative examples among others, see Leon Diakonos, Historia, tr. Talbot / Sullivan 18$_{14-16}$, for Leon Phokas; Anna Komnene, Alexias, XIV, ch. 1, § 3, 425$_{31}$, for Eumathios Philokales; Michael Attaleiates, 24$_{5-8}$, for Ioannes Batatzes.

13 Michel Italikos, Lettres et discours, no 3, 82–88. For Andronikos Komnenos, son of Alexios I, see ibid., 31–34; Skoulatos, Les personnages byzantins, no 12, 16–19; Varzos, Η γενεαλογία των Κομνηνών, no 35, 229–237. Cf. Kolia-Dermitzaki, Ο στρατός και ο στρατιώτης, 198.

dronikos Komnenos, son of John II Komnenos.[14] In both monodies the deceased are praised for their conduct in warfare as warriors and leaders. The first, the son of Alexios I, is daring, courageous, full of prowess and prudence, an inspired warrior;[15] the second, the son of Ioannes Komnenos, demonstrated military and strategic skills, and exhibited wisdom and prudence par excellence.[16]

At this point a remark is in order. When comparing references by historians (and more so of orators) to the army's contribution to victory, we will notice that references to the contribution made by their leaders (generals and other military commanders), are more numerous and often more expansive than those to the group of warriors as such. This observation could mean that the authors were more interested in the leader than in the rank-and-file soldier. There are two reasons behind this preference: the first is linked to the fact that the leader bears the ultimate responsibility for the outcome of a battle or a war. That much is clearly stated by Michael Attaleiates: "[...] if someone should lay down as a general rule that the final result [of a battle], whether for better or for worse, should be attributed to the commander, he would not altogether fall short of a true and accurate judgement".[17] The second reason is that the personality of a leader and his actions[18] (viewed in either a positive or a negative light) attract the attention of the author and his readers far more than the faceless soldier and by extension the army can, more so when the military leader comes from a "noble lineage" (a feature that was at a premium during the period in question) or is a person recognized for his successes or military skills.[19] Nevertheless, we often come across references to the army (and soldiers as a group), whose bravery and valor, contribute to victory.[20]

---

14 Michel Italikos, Lettres et discours, no 11, 130–134. For Andronikos Komnenos, son of John II Komnenos, see ibid., 34–38; Varzos, Η γενεαλογία των Κομνηνών, no 76, 357–361. Cf. Kolia-Dermitzaki, Ο στρατός και ο στρατιώτης, as above.
15 Michel Italikos, Lettres et discours, no 3, 84$_{15-17}$.
16 Michel Italikos, Lettres et discours, no 11, 130$_{19}$–131$_{6}$.
17 Michael Attaleiates, 85$_{19-22}$ "[...] εἴ τις τοῖς στρατηγοῖς ἐπιγράφει ὡς ἐπίπαν ἔχοι τὰ τῶν ἐκβάσεων, εἴτ' ἐπὶ τὸ χεῖρον εἴτ' ἐπὶ τὸ κρεῖττον συνάγοιντο, οὐ διαμάρτοι πάντως τοῦ ὀρθοῦ καὶ τῆς ἀληθοῦς διαγνώσεως." (Kaldellis / Krallis, 197, § 6). Cf. Haldon, Warfare, 229–231.
18 For the virtues, qualities and moral obligations of the ideal military leader as they are mirrored in the military treatises, the Τακτικά, see Karapli, "Περὶ τοῦ οἷον εἶναι δεῖ τὸν στρατηγόν", 297–310.
19 Cf. Lilie, Die byzantinische Gesellschaft, 962–963, 965.
20 As examples, see Michael the Rhetor, Λόγος εἰς Μανουὴλ τὸν Κομνηνόν, no VIII, 147$_{27}$–148$_{5}$, praising Manuel's army for their brave and impetuous attitude, during the siege of Zeugmin in 1161. The homily was delivered two years later, in 1163 (Introduction by A. Kazhdan, as above, X); Ioannes Skylitzes, 307$_{64-65}$ [οὓς (the Rus) εὐρώστως οἱ Ῥωμαῖοι δεξάμενοι ἐκθύμως ἐμάχοντο... Τέλος δὲ τῇ σφετέρᾳ ἀρετῇ Ῥωμαῖοι τρέπουσι τοὺς βαρβάρους (in Dorostolon)]; 296$_{60}$–297$_{73}$; 381$_{35-37}$; Michael Attaleiates, 235$_{1-3}$ (famous battles and admirable clashes of the army of the emperor Basil II); Anna Komnene, Alexias, XI, ch. 9, § 2, 349$_{50-53}$ [Alexios I Komnenos sent to Cilicia Manuel Boutoumites with the élite of the whole army, all of them

The proper organization of a campaign does not appear to be a key ingredient in the rhetoric of historiographers, although some examples do exist.[21] On the contrary, orators place sufficient emphasis on the availability of a large and well-organized expeditionary force that contributes to victory. For instance, Michael the Rhetor gives a detailed description of the armada organized and sent to Italy by Manuel I Komnenos in 1155, to take part in the operations against the Normans there. Given the fact that the homily was delivered on Christmas Day, 1155,[22] when the failure of the expedition was not yet evident, we may say that this was rhetoric of expected victory.[23]

A point of difference between historiography and works of rhetoric lies in the fact that the latter also project – apart from the immediate outcome of a victorious battle or even a series of diplomatic maneuvers – their long-term positive effects. Panegyrics of Eustathios, archbishop of Thessaloniki, along with his funeral oration for Manuel I Komnenos and the Λόγος προεισόδιος τῆς ἁγίας τεσσαρακοστῆς, and an oration by Euthymios Malakes, archbishop of Neai Patrai, for the same emperor are representative samples, and in the present paper I will use them as examples. I will confine myself to them since these rhetorical texts are full of pertinent references and my allotted space in the volume is limited. In 1173 Manuel decided to return to his offensive policy in the East, which he had abandoned in 1161, when he had concluded a treaty with the sultan of Ikonion, Kiliç Arslan II.[24] In 1175, as part of this new policy, and in response to the provocative attitude of the Seljuk leader, he proceeded to reconstruct and re-fortify Dorylaion, a city of the utmost importance for the Empire's defense and also for its commerce (due to its position on the crossroads of military and trade

---

extremely bellicose warriors and adjutant of Ares (τὸ ἐλλογιμώτατον τοῦ στρατιωτικοῦ καταλόγου, ἄνδρας μαχιμωτάτους καὶ Ἄρεως ὑπασπιστὰς ἅπαντας)], X, ch. 3, § 6, 289_{67-73}, VII, ch. 8, § 3, 223_{5-8}; Ioannes Kinnamos, Epitome, 95_{6-8}, 150_{10-12}, 198_{5-11}, 273_{20-21}; Niketas Choniates, Historia, 505_{84-93}. See also, Kolia-Dermitzaki, Ο στρατός καὶ ὁ στρατιώτης.

21 Such as the brief description of the fleet brought together in 960 for the expedition against Crete under the command of the *domestikos ton scholon* Nikephoros Phokas, Theophanes Continuatus, 474_{10-14}, 475_{18-20}.

22 Magdalino, Empire, 438–439. Though Kazhdan, Regel und seine "Quellen", X–XI, considers probable the date 1158 for the delivery of the panegyric, I shall agree with Magdalino based on the fact that at Christmas 1158 the failure of the Byzantine aggressive policy in Italy resulted in the conclusion of peace with William I of Sicily in 1158.

23 Michael the Rhetor, Εἰς τὸν αὐτὸν αὐτοκράτορα κῦρ Μανουὴλ τὸν Κομνηνόν, no IX, 156_{5-19}, description of the Byzantine naval force constructed by Manuel I in order to confront the Norman fleet in the frame of the Norman-Byzantine conflict of the year 1155–56. For the movements of the Byzantine, German, papal and Norman diplomacy before the beginning of the war and for the events during the warfare, which ended with a conclusion of peace in 1158, see Chalandon, Domination, 153–157, 185–198, 204–229, 245–254; Idem, Les Comnène, 343–381; Magdalino, Empire, 57–61.

24 On the treaty, and Manuel's political aims that led him to make peace with the Seljuk leader, see Magdalino, Empire, 76–78. Cf. Chalandon, Les Comnène, 461–467.

routes), and Soublaion / Siblia.²⁵ An additional positive result was the provision of a secure overland passage for pilgrims.²⁶ This event and further reconstruction and fortification in western Asia Minor was particularly highlighted by archbishop Eustathios of Thessaloniki on the one hand in two of his panegyrics dated at Epiphany 1176 and the beginning of Lent 1176,²⁷ as well as in the funeral oration²⁸ mentioned above, and – even more intensively – by the archbishop of Neai Patrai, Euhtymios Malakes, on the other hand. In his panegyric for the same emperor, delivered on the occasion of Manuel's return from "the victorious campaign against Persia" at the end of 1175, Euthymios refers extensively to the reconstruction and habitation or re-habitation of both the aforementioned castles;²⁹ to the contribution made by this rebuilding to the defense of Asia Minor and to raising Byzantine morale;³⁰ and to the frequent attacks by Turkish military forces that sought to impede their fortifying effort. At the same time, the rhetor highlights Manuel's bravery in confronting them and the success of the Byzantine army in preventing such attacks by the opponents. He uses rhetorical exaggeration to emphasize the importance of victory in two cases of minor conflict

---

25 Ioannes Kinnamos, Epitome, 294₈–296₂, 297₁₇₋₂₁, 298₄₋₇; Niketas Choniates, Historia, 176₄₉–177₉₀; Chalandon, Les Comnènes, 501–504; Magdalino, Empire, 95–96, 125–126 (for the Komnenian policy of building and fortifying cities and fortresses in Asia Minor, and in particular that of Manuel I, and the positive effects on the revival of provincial society and the defense of the region); Wirth, Kaiser Manuel I. Komnenos, 28. For Dorylaion and Soublaion / Siblia, see Belke / Mersich, Phrygien und Pisidien 162–163, 238–242, 382; Stone, Dorylaion Revisited.
26 Manuel's turning to an aggressive policy towards the Turkish sultan has been interpreted by certain modern scholars as the first stage of organizing a crusade, in an attempt to approach the West on the one hand (Chalandon, Les Comnène, 503–506; Lilie, Byzanz und die Kreuzfahrerstaaten, 201–203; Magdalino, Empire, 96–97; Stone, Eustathian panegyric; Idem, Dorylaion Revisited) and to demonstrate the leading position of the Byzantine emperor in the crusading states of the East (Kolia-Dermitaki, Byzantium, 59–83) while Evangelos Chrysos, in his article examining these standpoints rejected them (Chrysos, Byzantine Crusade).
27 Eustathios of Thessaloniki, Opera Minora, Λόγος Β, 17–45, here 41₇₈–42₃₈, Λόγος Μ, 202–228, here 206₃₅₋₄₄. For the dating of M, see Stone, Eustathios, 73. Cf. Wirth, in the Prolegomena of Eustathios edition, as above, 38*.
28 Eustathios of Thessaloniki, Manuelis Comneni laudatio funebris, XXIII, 208₆₉–209₁₅.
29 Euthymios Malakes, Ἐγκωμιαστικοὶ λόγοι, I, 23₂₃₋₃₂ [= Θεολογία 19 (1941/48) 527], 59–60 [= Θεολογία 20 (1949) 712–713 (editor's comments)], 42₂₃–45₂₉ [= Θεολογία 19 (1941/48) 546–549] and 77–81 [= Θεολογία 20 (1949) 152–156 (editor's comments)] and passim. In essence, the reconstruction of Dorylaion (and secondly of Soublaion) constitutes the main topic of Euthymios' speech and the means to exalt its importance and of course the main role the emperor played in this. Cf. Ioannes Kinnamos, Epitome, 294₆–295₂₀, 297₁₇₋₂₁.
30 This is what Manuel emphasizes in a hypothetical speech to his soldiers: "οὐ κτίζομεν πόλιν, ὦ ἄνδρες, ἀλλ' ἀνακαινίζομεν Ῥωμαίοις τὴν εὔκλειαν, οὐκ ἐγείρομεν τείχη, ἀλλ' ἀνυψοῦμεν ἑαυτοῖς τὰ φρονήματα, ἀποτείχισμα τοῦτο βαρβάροις, φραγμοῦ μεσότοιχον, λίθου πρόσκομμα, ἕως Πέρσης ἐλθὼν τῇ πέτρᾳ προσαράξῃ τὴν κεφαλήν, … καὶ οὐκέτι περαιτέρω προβῆναι πάντως οὐδὲ Ῥωμαίων γῆν πατῆσαι δυνήσεται. […]" Euthymios Malakes, Ἐγκωμιαστικοὶ λόγοι, I 30₁₂–₁₉ [= Θεολογία 19 (1941/48) 534]. See Stone, Dorylaion Revisited, 194, for the English translation of the passage.

with the Turks (one before Dorylaion and the other near Soublaion). A deeper reading, however, shows that behind the words the fact emerges that the outcome of these conflicts was not a significant victory. In the first case, the Turks gave up the battle after setting fire to their own houses, crops and straw, so that for one thing they could not be used by the Byzantines to feed themselves and their horses and for another, the smoke would help them to escape from the Byzantine soldiers persecuting them.[31] In the second case, the losses of the Turks were great but those of the Byzantines were equally significant.[32]

A summary of Manuel's achievements in the East is given prominent place mainly in an oration Eustathios delivered on Epiphany day: they include rolling back the Seljuks from the coastal regions to the interior (as Alexios I and John II had also managed to achieve), rebuilding cities and their walls, re-establishing the imperial power in Asia Minor, opening up the road for pilgrims, both men and women (the latter receive particular mention), transforming Turkish warriors into farmers, enforcing peace and eradicating war.[33] In his speech at Epiphany 1174, two victories are highly praised in parallel: in the West against the Germans and Venetians who besieged Ancona in 1173, and in the East the dissolution of the Turkish alliance against the empire in Philadelphia.[34] In the second case, the

---

31 Euthymios Malakes, Ἐγκωμιαστικοὶ λόγοι, I, 43$_{8-19}$ [= Θεολογία 19 (1941/48) 547]. Cf. Niketas Choniates, Historia, 176$_{60-72}$.
32 Euthymios Malakes, Ἐγκωμιαστικοὶ λόγοι, I, 45$_{3-26}$; Niketas Choniates, Historia, 177$_{72-85}$.
33 Eustathios of Thessaloniki, Opera Minora, Λόγος M, 204$_{75}$–209$_{44}$. Regarding the re-fortification of Dorylaion and Soublaion and the creation of a safe passage for the pilgrims, the orator writes: (206$_{35-44}$) "[…]τὰ νῦν δὲ ἄλλως ἐπέχεις ἐκείνην τὴν σύρροιαν καὶ παλινοστεῖν ἀναγκάζεις καὶ ἐν ἀφανεῖ καταχώννυσθαι διατειχίζων τοὺς πολεμίους καὶ τὰς ἐφόδους διείργων στερεμνίοις ἐπιτειχίσμασι καὶ ἀναχαιτίζων οὕτως αὐτοῖς τὸ ἀκάθεκτον· καὶ ἔστιν ἰδεῖν ὁδοὺς ἀβάτους τὰ πρώην Χριστιανοῖς ἄρτι λεωφόρους ἐκκειμένας καὶ ἀναπεπταμένας εἰς βάσιμον, καὶ οὐ μόνον ἀνδράσι, καὶ τούτοις ὁπλοφοροῦσιν, ἀλλὰ καὶ οἷς τὰ τῆς πορείας εὔζωνα· καὶ ὁ ἐνόδιος σίδηρος μόλις που καὶ εἰς παρηρτημένην πεπόρισται μάχαιραν· ἤδη καὶ γυναῖκες τολμῶσι τὰς ὁδοὺς ἐκείνας, […], ὅσας ὁ θεῖος πόθος ἀναθερμαίνων τόποις ἁγίοις ὅπου δή ποτε τῆς ἐκεῖ γῆς ἐπιδήμους ποιεῖ" (Stone, Eustathios, 83–84: "At present, on the contrary, you keep that confluence in check, and you force it to return and to be blocked so that it disappears, separating the enemy from us with walls, and keeping the approaches barred with firm fortifications, and thus you restrain their ungovernable nature. And it is now possible to see roads that were untrodden previously by Christians, becoming highways carrying people, extending and spreading out so that they are passable: and not only for men who are fully armed, but also for those who are lightly equipped for travel; and the iron they take on the journey is no more than a knife at their sides. Now even women venture on those roads, […] whom divinely-inspired yearning for holy places inflames, when it makes them sojourners of that land"). See also, in the funeral speech of Eustathios for Manuel (Manuelis Comneni laudatio funebris, as above, n. 28) his reference to the emperor's policy of reconstruction and / or construction of cities and fortresses with a hint to the personal participation of the βασιλεύς, mentioned by Niketas Choniates, Historia, 178$_{55-59}$ as well. Cf. Magdalino, Empire, 125–127.
34 Eustathios of Thessaloniki, Opera Minora, Λόγος O, 261–288, here 268$_{61}$–272$_{76}$.

fact that this dissolution took place without bloodshed, and peace was achieved without the loss of men, as in Ancona, was highlighted:

> "And thus the recent victories are related in nature and have the same import, and proceed in a manner worthy of equal respect; but each has a certain great and individual importance. A trophy from the land war and the naval war has been set up over there; here the land alone looks at the deed of excellence, but all that is under the sky applauds it. Oh yonder victory which was unsparing of the blood of men, one which indeed has been defined by those who are foolish in everything so as to determine its value; Oh the victory here, sparing the blood of men, of such a kind as one of the sophists chose to praise, thinking it right to raise trophies without blood having been shed!"[35]

Manuel I accomplished all of the above by fighting honorably and using stratagems, and not through dishonest means, such as poisoning a region's food and water supply, a ploy to which the Seljuks had stooped, which evidenced their cowardice.[36] I consider that the orator offers us a very interesting summary of the rhetoric of victory, from which of course all traces of failure and defeat have either been purged or presented in a vague or distorted manner.

Eustathius' speech Εἰς τὸν αὐτοκράτορα κῦρ Μανουὴλ τὸν Κομνηνόν, delivered in 1179, about three years after the catastrophic defeat at Myriokephalon is even more indicative of the way in which winners and losers are presented. The orator focuses on the Turkish invasion and aggression in Asia Minor. His oration begins with an idyllic image of the peace that prevailed there – as in the whole of the "Roman" territory – before the Seljuks appeared: there were all the signs of a prosperous country, the Turks were absent and

> "men whom the soft living of Asia possessed, each relaxed not only under his own fig tree and vine, but also wherever there was water of relaxation and a place which raises verdure which both nourishes herds and allows men to rest in it. Furthermore there began to be no need of weapons, not even for hunting exercises [...] And if a blade was carried, it not only remained alien as an uncommon use of iron, but was the subject of mockery, [...] And their course of life was one of a fortunate man, because there prevailed tranquility in affairs, a peace in which children could be reared and a life without battles, and the warlike trumpeter rendered his services to wedding processions".[37]

---

35 Ibid, 270$_{34}$–271$_{45}$, "Καὶ οὕτω μὲν ἀδελφὰ φρονοῦσιν αἱ κατὰ τὸ προσεχὲς νῖκαι καὶ πρόοδον ἔχουσι τὴν αὐτὴν καὶ τῷ πρεσβείῳ εἰς ταὐτὸν ἔρχονται· ἔχουσι δ'οὖν μέγα καὶ ἴδιόν τι ἑκατέρα σεμνόν· πεζομαχίας ἐκεῖ καὶ ναυμαχίας ἵσταται τρόπαιον, ἐνταῦθα γῇ μὲν μόνῃ βλέπει τὸ ἀρίστευμα, ἡ δὲ ὑπ' οὐρανὸν περικροτεῖ σύμπασα. Ὦ νίκης ἐκείνης μὴ φεισαμένης αἱμάτων ἀνδρῶν, ὃ δὴ τοῖς μέχρι παντὸς ἀφραίνουσιν εἰς ἐπιτιμίου δίκην ἀφώρισται· ὦ νίκης ταύτης φεισαμένης αἱμάτων ἀνδρῶν, ὁποίαν ἐν ἐπαίνῳ τίθεται καὶ τῶν τις σοφιστῶν ἀξιῶν αἱμάτων δίχα ἵστασθαι τρόπαια" (Stone, Eustathios, 33–34).
36 Eustathios of Thessaloniki, Opera Minora, Λόγος Μ, 208$_6$–209$_{29}$.
37 Ibid, Λόγος Ν, 234$_{74}$–235$_4$. Passage on 234$_{76-96}$ "[...] καὶ πάντες ἄνθρωποι, ὅσους ἡ τῆς Ἀσίας πιότης ἔνεμεν, ἀνεπαύοντο οὐ μόνον ἕκαστος ὑπὸ τὴν αὐτοῦ συκῆν καὶ τὴν ἄμπελον, ἀλλὰ καὶ ἔνθα

Eustathius continues with a vivid image of the deaths and disasters from the time of the arrival of the Seljuks until the appearance of the Komnenians:

> "There was nowhere in the land of Asia where a fountain of blood did not appear to flow. To speak of the ravages inflicted on some sanctuaries and the profaning of others, and the desecration of sacred bodies and the outraging of nature, would only ruin the festive celebration and call forth tears at an inappropriate time [...] But these things were so; and the state of order passed away, and disorder danced exultantly, and for the most part the result was to see a desert ... and it was a rare sight to see a Roman man intermingled with them, unless enslaved. So a severe storm prevailed, confusing and ruining everything, until the spring of the Komnenoi shone. And thenceforth the clouds of the enemy were scattered and the packed snow began to melt until it lost its nature, and there began then the driving back of that evil."[38]

This panegyric contains the greatest number of references to the victories of Manuel, which – according to Eustathios – were the culmination of the victories of the first two Komnenians, Alexios I and John II. Particular reference is made to the victories of the Byzantine army along the river Meander, in 1178 according to Andrew Stone,[39] where the Seljuks suffered heavy losses. Not only did a large number of their warriors die in battle and in the waters of the river, but also a large number of prisoners were captured, while many Turks were forced to surrender to the Byzantines with their families.[40] However, despite the emphasis on praising the military successes of Manuel and the first two *basileis* of the Komnenian dynasty against the Turks – expected, after all, in a panegyric – this text exudes a pessimistic mood, since Manuel appears to face the Seljuks with increasing difficulty, thus confirming the gradual increase in their power at the end of his reign.[41]

ὕδωρ ἀνέσεως καὶ τόπος χλόην ἀνίσχων βοσκήμασι μὲν τραφῆναι, ἀνθρώποις δὲ ἐπαναπαύσασθαι· ὅπλων δὲ χρεία οὐδ'ὡς εἰς γυμνάσιον κυνηγετικὸν ἤρχετο·[...]σπάθη δὲ φερομένη μὴ μόνον ξενίζειν εἶχε τῷ τοῦ σιδήρου περιττῷ, ἀλλὰ καὶ μωκίαν ἔπασχε, [...] καὶ ἦσαν τὰ πάντα μακάρων διαγωγαί, ὅτι καὶ γαλήνη πραγμάτων καὶ κουροτρόφος εἰρήνη καὶ βίος ἀπόλεμος καὶ ὁ ἐνυάλιος σαλπιγκτήριος νυμφαγωγοῖς ὑπούργει χάρισι." (Stone, Eustathios, 182–183).

38 Eustathios of Thessaloniki, Opera Minora, Λόγος N, 236$_{37-57}$ "Οὐκ ἔστι γὰρ ὅπου τῆς ἐν Ἀσίᾳ γῆς μὴ πηγὴν αἵματος ῥέειν ἐφαίνετο· θείων δὲ τεμενισμάτων τῶν μὲν ἀναστατώσεις εἰπεῖν, τῶν δὲ βεβηλώσεις, καὶ σωμάτων ἱερῶν κοίνωσιν καὶ φύσεως περιυβρισμοὺς οὐδὲν ἂν εἴη ἄλλο ποιῆσαι ἢ συγχέαι τὴν πανήγυριν καὶ δάκρυον ἐν οὐ καιρῷ προκαλέσασθαι, [...] Ἀλλ' ἦσαν μὲν οὕτω ταῦτα· καὶ ὁ κόσμος ἐκεῖνος παρῆλθεν, ἀκοσμία δὲ κατεχόρευε, καὶ τὰ πλείω μὲν ἐρημία ἦν ὁρᾶν· [...] καὶ Ῥωμαῖον παραμεμίχθαι που ἄνδρα θέα σπάνιος, εἰ μὴ ὄντι δουλεύοντα· οὕτω βαρὺς ἐκράτει χειμὼν ἀναταράττων πάντα καὶ συγχέων, ἕως τὸ Κομνηνόθεν ἔαρ ἀνέλαμψε· καὶ τὸ ἐντεῦθεν ἐσκεδάζετο μὲν τὰ νέφη τῶν πολεμίων, ἐτήκετο δὲ ἡ πηγνῦσα πρὸς ἀψυχίαν χιών, [...] καὶ τὸ μέγα κακὸν ἐκεῖνο ἀνακόπτεσθαι ἀρχὴν ἔλαβεν." (Stone, Eustathios, 186–187).

39 Ibid, 198 n. 793. Cf. Magdalino, Empire, 99 and n. 299, 300 (between 1177 and 1179).

40 Eustathios of Thessaloniki, Opera Minora, Λόγος N, 243$_{65}$–244$_{95}$, 244$_9$–245$_{32}$, 247$_{93}$–248$_{63}$. For the last reference and the relocation of Seljuks to the environs of Thessaloniki, see Stone, Eustathios, 204 n. 823, 827, 828. Cf. Lilie, Die byzantinische Gesellschaft.

41 See also Magdalino, Empire, 463–465; Stone, Eustathios, 167, 168, 186, 191 n. 772.

It should be noted that all sources pay particular attention to the use of stratagems and ruses (στρατηγήματα, μηχαναί) by the commanding general or the emperor, when the latter commands the army, and that the military manuals (known as Τακτικά) place special emphasis on the use of stratagems, since this is considered a guarantee for victory. For instance, the constitution XX of the *Taktika* of Leo VI, includes, among other material, stratagems and anecdotes from classical sources and from the sixth-century military manual known as *Mauricii Strategicon* as well.[42] The same seems to apply to the final chapters of the *Sylloge Tacticorum*, dedicated to the stratagems and ruses of classical commanders to be used as examples by the Byzantine leader of the army under the general title: Στρατηγικαὶ παραινέσεις ἐκ πράξεων καὶ στρατηγημάτων παλαιῶν ἀνδρῶν Ῥωμαίων τε καὶ Ἑλλήνων καὶ λοιπῶν ἐν κεφαλαίοις κη' (Recommendations about generalship from the deeds and stratagems of ancient men, Roman, Greek, and others, in twenty-eight chapters).[43]

Similar attention is paid by historians and orators. For instance, Ioannes Kinnamos describes how Michael Palaiologos managed to capture the fort of St Nicholas in Bari, Italy (1155), by disguising his soldiers as monks. In this way he tricked the sentries into opening the gate to allow them in, thus causing the fort to be taken by storm.[44] Eustathios of Thessaloniki also makes extensive references (among others) to strategic virtues and the use of military ruses leading to victories in many parts of his panegyrics, but mainly in the above mentioned homily for Manuel I delivered in 1179, after significant victories of the Byzantine army over the Seljuks in the valley of the river Meander in 1178.[45] In this homily the orator praises not only Manuel Komnenos, but also his grandfather, Alexios I, for their strategic virtue and their use of military trickery in order to win the battle when conditions were unfavorable.[46] Among other rhetorical forms, he

---

42 See among other, Taktika of Leo VI, constitution XV, § 8–10, XX § 15–16, 21–22, 35, 53, 99, 123, 138–139, 144, 150–151, 154,161, 168, 177, 194, 196. Cf. De velitatione, Pr. § 3–4, XIX, § 2, XXI, § 5 (how to deceive the enemy and reinforce the besieged with warriors and supplies).
43 Sylloge Tacticorum, ch. 76–77, 80, 83, 85, 87–90, 92, 94–95, 99 (Engl. transl. by Chatzelis / Harris, ch. as above, and n. 368).
44 Ioannes Kinnamos, Epitome, 140$_{7-15}$. For the Byzantine campaign of 1155–1156, see Lilie, Handel und Politik, 437–443; Magdalino, Empire, 58–61.
45 For the chronology, see above, n. 39.
46 Eustathios of Thessaloniki, Opera Minora, Λόγος N, 241$_{20}$–243$_{86}$. For instance: "'Ἔδειξας καὶ νῦν, ὦ κραταιότατε βασιλεῦ (Manuel I) οἷον ἡ στρατηγικὴ ἀρετὴ καί, ὡς ἄρα μικρὰ μὲν χάρις τῷ στρατηγοῦντι πολυδυνάμῳ τὴν στρατιὰν ὄντι νικᾶν, μεγίστη δὲ τὸ ἄλλως ἀνύειν τὰ κράτιστα· καί μοι τοῦ λόγου παράδειγμα καὶ ὁ μακαριστὸς ἐν βασιλεῦσιν Ἀλέξιος, ὃς ἐν στρατηγίαις, εἴ που μὴ ἐπιτυχῶς αὐτῷ ἡ τοῦ πολέμου σχοίη ῥοπή, [...], ἀλλὰ τὴν νίκην ἑτέρως ἐξ ὑποστροφῆς λαμπροτέραν διετίθετο μετατάττων τὸ στράτευμα" (Stone, Eustathios, 196 : "You have now also shown, O most powerful emperor, what excellence in military leadership is, and in addition, that although there is some little merit for one who as a general is victorious in an expedition on account of great strength, the greatest merit lies in the achieving of the most important

employs similes to embellish his speech: able generals are like a lion hidden in a thicket, just before it comes out to pounce on its prey, like "headlands that are firmly rooted, whenever they are shaken by the tossing of waves, do not even then collapse ignominiously afterwards, but being headlands, resist so that the waves labor in vain in their dashing against them" or like the captain of a ship who manages to steer it successfully in the storm (the ship being his army).[47] The long reference to the extraordinary strategic art of the Komnenian emperors, who developed it to cope successfully with the severe threat of a defeat, reflects, I believe, a) the great effort they made to recover the Western part of Asia Minor, and b) the significant increase in the power of the Seljuks at the time of the speech, mentioned above. At the same time the orator boasts of the empire's capability to recover, resisting the strong lurches it had suffered for more than a century. However, the art of warfare that leads to victory does not apply only to the field of battle, but to the field of diplomacy as well. This parameter is particularly prominent in rhetorical texts. Once again, Eustathios claims that Manuel's successes against the enemies of the Empire were based on his strategic skill, in other words his ability to pit enemies against each other:

"Συγκροῦσαι δὲ πολεμίους ἀλλήλοις, καὶ ἡμᾶς ἐν ἀταράχῳ καὶ οὕτω καταστῆσαι, καὶ τὸ ἐν εἰρήνῃ γαλήνιον καταπράξασθαι, τίς ἄρα κατ' ἐκεῖνον δεινότατος; Μέθοδον γὰρ καὶ ταύτην στρατηγικὴν ἐτέχνου, τὸ μὲν ὑπήκοον φυλάττειν ἀναίμακτον ἐπὶ μεγίσταις τροπαίων ἀναστάσεσι, προσαράσσειν δὲ τοὺς πολεμίους ἑαυτοῖς καὶ ἐκπολεμοῦν τοῖς ἀλλοφύλοις τὸ σφίσιν αὐτοῖς ὁμόφυλον, ὡς καὶ ἐντεῦθεν αὔξεσθαι μὲν τὰ ἡμέτερα, μειονεκτεῖσθαι δὲ τὸ πολέμιον [...] Οὕτω Πέρσαι Πέρσαις ἀντίμαχοι μεθόδοις βασιλικαῖς· καὶ ἡμεῖς εἰρηναῖον ἐπαιανίζομεν [...]"[48]

A further example are the Normans, who were defeated not only by the Byzantine army and navy, but mostly by local opponents whom "the emperor's methods" (αἱ τοῦ αὐτοκράτορος μέθοδοι) led to rebel.[49]

---

business in other ways. And for me an example to mention is the one of blessed memory among emperors, Alexios, who, when and if the scales in the conduct of war in his campaigns did not tilt effectively in his favour [...], would nevertheless achieve a more illustrious victory in another way, by wheeling around and reformulating his strategy"). Cf. Eustathios of Thessaloniki, Opera Minora, Λόγος Ο, 279_{33}–280_{57}, 281_{77-87}. See also, Alexopoulos, Ancient Military Handbooks, 47–71.

47 Eustathios of Thessaloniki, Opera Minora, Λόγος Ν, 241_{26}–243_{65}.
48 Eustathios of Thessaloniki, Manuelis Comneni laudatio funebris, 199_{73-83}. See also in Eustathios of Thessaloniki, Opera Minora, Λόγος Ο, 281_4–284_{90}, a lengthy account of Manuel's successful diplomatic moves that either overpowered or dissolved one or more Muslim coalitions. He probably means the conciliation between the sultan of Konya Kiliç Arslan and the atabeg of Aleppo Nur-ad-Din. See Magdalino, Empire, 76–78; Stone, Eustathios, n. 255 and 258.
49 Eustathios of Thessaloniki, Manuelis Comneni laudatio funebris, 199_{93}–200_3: Δράκων δὲ ὁ νησιωτικὸς, ..., πολλὰ μὲν τοῦ κατ' αὐτὸν ὁλκοῦ καὶ βασιλικοῖς ἐκολούσθη ξίφεσι, τὰ πλείω δὲ οἰκειακοῖς ἐχθροῖς συγκρουόμενος, οὓς αἱ τοῦ αὐτοκράτορος μέθοδοι ἐπανίστων, διχαστικὴν ὁποία

Another dimension of the rhetoric of victory is one of its positive outcomes: the acquisition of booty and prisoners is a source of praise and pride on the part of historiographers, sometimes expressed explicitly, other times implicitly. The issue of the status of prisoners of war (soldiers and non-combatants) and their fate after capture was the subject of my earlier article and more recently an article by Marilia Lykaki, therefore I will not dwell on it.[50] After all, it does not touch directly upon on the rhetoric of victory. It should, however, be noted that the captives played an important role – especially the eminent ones – in the exchanges of prisoners that took place mainly between Byzantines and Muslim Arabs; a fact underlined in the *Taktika* by Leo VI and other military treatises of the tenth century.[51] Clearly indicative of the fact that looting met with approval on the part of historiographers is the reference of Niketas Choniates to the victory of Alexios Branas over the Normans; after sacking Thessalonica in August 1185, the latter marched on Thrace and took Mosynopolis. According to the narrative by Niketas Choniates, after the Byzantine troops managed to break into the city, having lacked for the condiments of war for so long they reveled in slaughter, consumed the wealth of the "nations" (Isaiah 29.7 etc.), had their fill of booty and were fattened by it ("[...] ἐνειστιῶντο ταῖς σφαγαῖς ἐπὶ μακρὸν ἀπόσιτοι ὄντες καρικευμάτων ἀρεϊκῶν. Ὡς δ' ἔφαγον πλοῦτον ἐθνῶν ἐνεπλήσθησάν τε καὶ ἐλιπάνθησαν τοῖς λαφυραγωγήμασι [...]").[52] The positive outcome of the looting in question was the acquisition of weapons and horses, an event that boosted the morale of the Byzantine army and contributed to its victory (7 November 1185), which

---

τινὰ μάχαιραν τὴν ἑαυτοῦ τομώτατα σοφίαν βάλλοντος. For the policy of Manuel towards the Normans in the military and diplomatic field during his long reign, see Angold, The Byzantine Empire, 322–328; Magdalino, Empire, 43, 52–63.

50 Kolia-Dermitzaki, Remarks, 583–620; Lykaki, L'économie de pillage, 89–102; Eadem, Οι αιχμάλωτοι πολέμου στη Βυζαντινή αυτοκρατορία (6ος–11ος αι.), Athens [forthcoming]. For the issue of the prisoners of war, see also Kolias, Kriegsgefangene, 129–135; Rotman, Les esclaves et l'esclavage à Byzance; Ramaḍān, Treatment of Arab Prisoners of War, 155–194; Vučetić, Die Novelle des Kaisers Ioannes, 317–327.

51 See Taktika of Leo VI, constitution XVI, § 9: "Τοὺς δὲ αἰχμαλώτους πρὸ τοῦ τελείως καταπαῦσαι τὸν πόλεμον μὴ κτεῖνε, καὶ μάλιστα τοὺς ἐνδόξους καὶ μεγάλους παρὰ τοῖς πολεμίοις ὄντας· [...] ἵν' ἔχῃς, εἴ γε συμβῇ ἢ τῶν ὑπὸ σέ τινας κρατηθῆναι, ἢ κάστρου γενέσθαι ἰδίου σου ἅλωσιν, δι' αὐτῶν ἀντικαταλλάττειν [...], καὶ ἀντὶ τῶν πολεμίων αἰχμαλώτων ἀναλάβῃς τοὺς φίλους καὶ συμμάχους. Εἰ δὲ μὴ βούλωνται τοῦτο ποιεῖν οἱ πολέμιοι, τότε δικαίως κατὰ τὸ ἴσον ἀμύνου, διαχρώμενος ὡς βούλει ἐπὶ λύπῃ τῶν ἐναντίων" ("Do not slay the prisoners before the war has finally come to an end, in particular the important and illustrious men among them. [...] If it should happen that some of your men are taken prisoner or a walled town of yours suffers capture, then you are able to make use of those prisoners to change matters around again [...]. In exchange for the enemy captives you may receive back your friends and allies. If the enemy are not willing to do this, then, by the same token, you have the right to protect yourself, taking what action you wish to harm the enemy"); Sylloge Tacticorum, ch. 50, § 6, 8. Instructions for an alternative treatment of the captives, see in ch. 19 § 1, ch. 23 § 5. Cf. Nikephoros Ouranos, Taktika, ch. 65, 162.

52 Niketas Choniates, Historia, 358$_{82-84}$.

put an end to the Norman raid.[53] Generally speaking, the acquisition of booty and above all prisoners, and the extensive looting, are promoted as evidence of the army's success.[54]

As is well known, provisions for the participation of soldiers in the division of the spoils, including the prisoners, as a form of reward after the war and as a means of encouraging them,[55] are included in Byzantine legislation (originally in the Ecloga, later repeated in the Procheiros Nomos) and in military manuals.[56]

---

53 Niketas Choniates, Historia, 358_{87}–359_{18}. For the siege and fall of Thessaloniki by the Normans in August 1185 and the events that followed – up to their defeat in November of the same year – see Brand, Byzantium Confronts the West, 163-171. Cf. Rotolo, Οι Σικελοί στη Θεσσαλονίκη.

54 For more indicative examples, see Vita Basilii, § 37, 138_{17-30}: campaign of Basil I to Tephriki in 871: "ἐπῄει κατὰ πολλὴν τοῦ κωλύοντος ἐρημίαν λῃϊζόμενος καὶ πορθῶν καὶ κατατέμνων καὶ πυρπολῶν πάσας τὰς ὑπὸ τὸν Χρυσόχειρα χώρας καὶ κωμοπόλεις ὁ βασιλεύς, λείαν ἄπειρον καὶ αἰχμαλωσίαν περιβαλλόμενος" ("With none to hinder him, the emperor advanced, pillaging and harrying, cutting down and laying waste with fire all the countryside and the small towns subjected to Chrysocheir, and gathering countless booty and numerous captives"), § 39, 140_1–142_{13}: capture of Zapetra and Samosata in 873, § 50, 182_{42-45}: the *domestikos ton scholon* Andrew the Scythian, after his victory over the Arabs in the battle of Podandos (878/879) during his expedition against Cilicia, "returned home with rich spoils and booty and many captives". Regarding the campaign of Basil I to Tephriki, in 871, Symeon Magister, 262_{42}–263_{53}, asserts that the emperor was defeated by the Muslim Arabs repeatedly and avoided being captured only thanks to the intervention of the Armenian Theophylaktos Abastaktos, grandfather of the future emperor Romanos IV Lakapenos. The author of Vita Basilii, writes that Basil resigned from the brief siege of Tephriki due to the strong resistance of the besieged and the abundance of their supplies on the one hand, and the absence of necessities of life in his own army on the other, and that "he harried Abara and Spatha, the forts around Tephriki, as well as several other forts; evacuated his entire army intact from that region, and slowly withdrew, with, as has been said, rich booty and many captives [...]". That means that the author essentially praises Basil for his decision to end the siege of Tephriki, and to ensure the safe return of his army by projecting the capture of the fortresses around it and the acquisition of booty and prisoners from them as well. The narrative of the Vita Basilii is a typical example of historiographers's rhetoric of victory. Cf. Ioseph Genesios, Regum Libri Quattuor, 85_{52-59}; Ioannes Skylitzes,135_{1-13}. See Vasiliev (– Canard), Byzance et les Arabes, 2/1, 33–34, 82–84; Lemerle, Pauliciens, 102–103. See also Michael Attaleiates, 85_{25}–86_1.

55 Michael Attaleiates, 102_{13-18}, provides an illustrative example: the author himself, in his capacity as the κριτὴς τοῦ στρατοπέδου suggested to the emperor Romanos IV Diogenes – during the campaign of Manzikert, in 1071 – to occupy Khliat and the surrounding towns "ἵνα καὶ οἱ στρατιῶται τῆς ἐκ λαφύρων ὠφελείας πλησθῶσι καὶ προθυμότεροι γένωνται καὶ τοῖς ἐναντίοις ἐπέλθῃ δέος [...]" Kaldellis / Krallis, 239, § 11 "[...] which will also enable our soldiers to get their full share of the plunder, become more eager, and inspire fear to the enemy [...]" . See also Taktika of Leo VI, constitution XVI, § 5, ll 31-32: "Οὕτως γὰρ μάλιστα, εἰ καὶ μήπω τέλος δέξηται ὁ πόλεμος, προθυμότερος ὁ στρατὸς πρὸς τὰς μάχας γενήσεται" ("Likewise, especially if the war has not yet come to an end, the army will be more enthusiastic for combat").

56 Ecloga, title 18, Περὶ διαμερισμοῦ σκύλων, $244_{950-956}$ ("τοῦ δὲ Θεοῦ παρέχοντος νίκην τὸ ἕκτον μέρος ἀφιεροῦσθαι δεῖ τῷ δημοσίῳ καὶ τὸ λοιπὸν πᾶν μέτρον ἅπαντας τοὺς τοῦ λαοῦ ἐξ ἴσης καὶ ἐφ' ἴσης μοίρας μερίζεσθαι, τὸν μέγαν καὶ τὸν μικρόν. ἀρκεῖ γὰρ τοῖς ἄρχουσιν ἡ προσθήκη τῶν ῥογῶν αὐτῶν. εἰ δὲ εὑρεθῶσί τινες ἐκ τῶν αὐτῶν ἀρχόντων ἀνδρείως φερόμενοι, ὁ εὑρισκόμενος στρατηγὸς ἐκ τοῦ εἰρημένου ἕκτου μέρους τοῦ δημοσίου ἵνα παράσχῃ καὶ κατὰ τὸ πρέπον συγκροτήσῃ αὐτούς");

The spoils of war constituted a method of securing financial gain both for the soldiers and for the state (since, as the aforementioned legal codes decreed, the fisc received one sixth of the total booty, while the rest was distributed among the fighting men). At the same time looting, in the guise of ravaging animals and the harvest, also secured or added to army provisions while on the march or when encamped on enemy territory. Furthermore, the state received a significant influx of revenue from the ransom of prisoners, using them as soldiers, or arming and equipping its own troops with the enemy's captured weapons and horses – as we saw in the case of the Normans. This was the reason why historiographers as well as orators applauded the measure. Once more, the archbishop of Thessaloniki, Eustathios, provides a characteristic example in his oration addressed to Manuel I in 1179 referring to the victories of the year 1178 in the Meander valley, mentioned above:

> The emperor "achieved a [...] great exploit – he heaped up this pile of trophies and fashioned skillfully the greatest edifices of renown, and [...] deported a great catch of prisoners, consisting of the valorous ones who survived, along with their female cohabitants and their progeny, and all those who were not considered as commoners, who could not be described in only a few words, since they boast that they are leaders amongst their kind and deserving of fame for their bravery, and, to sum it up, they are men whom the barbarian land would purchase for a great amount".[57]

The significance of victory is reinforced by the capture of booty. For instance, in his panegyric addressed to John Komnenos praising the latter's campaign in Cilicia and Syria (1138–1139), Michael Italikos expresses his admiration for the capture of eleven cities and the rich material booty and prisoners (6.000 according to Kamāl ad-Dīn, or 5.000 according to Ibn al-Aṯīr),[58] as well as for the fact that at the same time Alexios, the emperor's son, "sacks and violently pillages" ("σκυλεύει καὶ προνομεύει ὀξέως") the city of Gastounai.[59] The passage which tells how John Komnenos (for reasons that are not exactly traceable) raised the siege of Shaizar

---

Procheiros Nomos, title 40, § 1, 227; Leges poenales militares, title 58, 1; Taktika of Leo VI, constitution XVI, § 3–5; De velitatione, X, § 17, 71$_{123-125}$ ("[...] ὁρμήσουσι καὶ αὐτοὶ θανάτου καταφρονοῦντες εἰς ἁρπαγὴν τῶν λαφύρων διὰ τὴν τοῦ κέρδους ἐλπίδα· καὶ περιγένωνται τούτων τῇ τοῦ Χριστοῦ χάριτι ῥαδίως"). Cf. Nikephoros II Phokas, Praecepta militaria, 26$_{69-79}$, 48$_{162-166}$. See also Dain, Le partage du butin de guerre, 347–352; Lykaki, L'économie de pillage, 91–93.

57 Eustathios of Thessaloniki, Opera Minora, Λόγος Ν, 246$_{84-92}$: "[...] ἐγείραντος κατόρθωμα μέγα καὶ στοιβὴν ταύτην τροπαίων ἐπισυστήσαντος καὶ εὐκλείας τεχνησαμένου μεγίστην ἐποικοδόμησιν ... καὶ τὴν ζωγρίαν πολλὴν ἀπελάσαντος ἐν τοῖς περιλοίποις τῶν ἀριστέων, ἐν τοῖς συνοίκοις, ἐν τοῖς ἐπιγεννήμασι, καὶ τούτοις ἅπασιν οὐ τοῖς λογιζομένοις εἰς χυδαῖον λαόν, καὶ ὧν οὐ βραχὺς λόγος, ἀλλὰ γένους τε αὐχοῦσι τὰ πρῶτα καὶ εἰς τὸ τῆς ἀνδρείας ἀξιουμένοις ἔνδοξον, καὶ τὸ ὅλον εἰπεῖν, οὓς ἡ βάρβαρος γῆ μεγάλων ἂν ἐπρίαιτο". (Stone, Eustathios, 204).

58 Michel Italikos, Lettres et discours, no 43, 261$_{24}$–262$_5$, with note 80.

59 Michel Italikos, Lettres et discours, no 43, 258$_{13-20}$. Gastounai or Gaston (Bağrās) was a castle near Antiocheia (ibid., 258, note 66).

during the same campaign, in exchange for a very advantageous "ransom" offer proposed by the besieged, which included a precious cross that is said to have been seized from the tent of Romanos IV Diogenes after the Battle of Manzikert (26 August 1071), is also interesting in this context. Important for the subject of the present study is the dithyrambic way of describing the "ransom", implying a victorious result of the siege and turning failure into a huge success.[60]

It is a commonplace observation that war is always followed by acts of violence against both defeated warriors and non-combatants. We are not referring solely to physical violence which leads to a decrease in the population and creates demographic problems, but also to violent acts aimed at the material possessions of the victims. Apart from looting, which we just mentioned, one of the most common outcomes of victory is the confiscation of harvest and flocks to feed the victor's army, acts that limited the victims' chances for survival, since they now lacked the means to procure their daily bread and were ruined financially.[61]

The authors of the sources that have been studied maintain an ambiguous stance on the issue of the acts of violence that follow a military victory. On the one hand, they applaud this kind of action and consider it an asset for the army and/ or its leader, especially the collection of booty and the acquisition of prisoners, for reasons that have just been mentioned. For example, the description by Michael Attaleiates of the battle fought between Byzantines and Bulgarians outside Thessaloniki in 1014 is full of admiration and pride for the bravery exhibited by Michael Botaneiates, fighting at the head of a small number of soldiers against "a countless multitude of Bulgarians":

> "He immediately joined the enemy in battle with a great charge, giving free rein, which brought him into their very midst. He filled the entire battlefield with bodies of the slain, as no one struck by his hand was able to avert death. [...] He cut through their spears and pikes with his sword, throwing his enemies to the ground. Some lost their head and arm to a single one of his blows, others he cut in half, and some cut into pieces, destroying and terrorizing them with a huge variety of woods".[62]

---

60 Michel Italikos, Lettres et discours, no 43, 263_1–265_3, with notes 91, 95. See also, Nikephoros Basilakes, In Ioannem Comnenum, § 30, 67_7–§32, 69_5, for an even more dithyrambic style; Niketas Choniates, Historia, 30_{85}–31_7; Ioannes Kinnamos, Epitome, 19_{22}–20_{16} (he mentions in addition the payment of an annual tribute to the Byzantines; Nikephoros Basilakes, § 30, 67_{13}, hints at the same subject as well). Both the above-mentioned historiographers – as did the rhetors – covered up the failure of the siege of Shaizar by presenting the exchange objects offered to the emperor as spoils of war. On the siege of Shaizar and the reasons for its raising by the Byzantine emperor, see Papageorgiou, Ιωάννης Β΄ Κομνηνός, 336–343. Cf. Runciman, A History of the Crusades, 215–217. For the importance of rhetoric as a means of propagating the deeds of the Komnenians in war, see Papageorgiou, War and Ideology.
61 On the impact of warfare on the population, see Haldon, Warfare, 239–252; Lev, The Human Cost of Warfare; Kolia-Dermitzaki, Attitude of Soldiers.
62 Michael Attaleiates, Historia, 178_{11-16}, 178_{20-23}: "πρὸς μάχην ἐκ τοῦ εὐθέος αὐτοῖς ἀντιπαρετάξατο· καὶ μετὰ πολλῆς ῥύμης καὶ ἅπαν τὸ πεδίον ἐκεῖνο σωμάτων νεκρῶν κατεσφαγμένων ἐπλήρωσε,

It should be noted that the author refers to the father of his idol, Nikephoros III Botaneiates, to whom his History is dedicated and whose ancestors take up a large part of the narrative.[63] The excessive praise of the valor of the emperor's father, however, does not diminish the value of the author's testimony with regard to the way he chooses to display it and with his perception of violent behavior towards the enemy. In a similar fashion Attaleiates describes the defeat of the Iberians at the hands of the Byzantine army during the campaign of the emperor Basil II against their ruler, George, in 1022: "On the side of the Abasgians, however, there was infinite carnage, some dying in the course of the battle and others falling in flight, for when their rout and pursuit was complete the Romans kept slaughtering them insatiably like wild sheep".[64] Even though the first two passages can be viewed as figments of the author's imagination, the historical event itself – in other words the assault in the vicinity of Thessaloniki conducted by Samuel's army – is beyond doubt, while Attaleiates' positive stance towards the necessity of violence that will lead to victory is clear. One might have said that in the third passage Attaleiates' narrative contained a small measure of sympathy for the fallen "Abasgians" (as he calls the Iberians), if it were not for the epithet "wild" attached to the term "sheep" to which he likens them. Therefore, this is once again a projection of violence as a prerequisite of victory, even if it is phrased in a milder manner.

On the other hand, Anna Komnene does not hide her revulsion at the brutal behavior of the army. It tarnished its glorious victory over Tzachas, the Seljuk emir of Smyrna who for seven years (1090–1097) had harried the coastal regions of Asia Minor and the islands of the Aegean Sea. The Byzantines became merciless when, during the peaceful surrender of Smyrna, Tzachas' seat of power, the Byzantine fleet commander and newly-appointed governor of the city, Kaspax, happened to be assassinated by one of the city's Muslim inhabitants. According to Anna Komnene's narrative "the whole fleet, including the rowers themselves, went into the city in a disorderly manner and killed everyone without mercy. And

---

μηδενὸς δυνηθέντος ἀθάνατον πληγὴν ἐκ τῆς τούτου χειρὸς ἀπενέγκασθαι [...] τοὺς πολεμήτορας ἐπὶ γῆν κατηκόντιζεν, οὗ μὲν κεφαλὴν ἐν μιᾷ πληγῇ διατέμνων, ἄλλον δὲ δεικνύων ἡμίτομον, τὸν δὲ καὶ καρατομῶν καὶ μυρίοις εἴδεσι πληγῶν καταστρέφων καὶ καταπλήττων αὐτούς." (Kaldellis-Krallis, 420, § 3). Cf. Ioannes Skylitzes, 350$_{59-66}$. See Holmes, Basil II, 412–413.

63 An explanation for Attaleiates' sympathy for Nikephoros III Botaneiates, see Kazhdan, Social Views, especially 23–32.

64 Michael Attaleiates, 181$_{16-20}$: "τῶν δ' Ἀβασγῶν φόνος ἀπείριτος γέγονε τῶν μὲν ἐν τῇ συμβολῇ τοῦ πολέμου θανατωθέντων, τῶν δὲ ἐν τῷ φεύγειν πεσόντων· παντελοῦς γὰρ γενομένης αὐτῶν τροπῆς καὶ διώξεως, ἀκορέστως οἱ Ῥωμαῖοι δίκην ἀγρίων προβάτων τούτους κατέθυον." (Kaldellis / Krallis, 429, § 7). Cf. Ioannes Skylitzes, 367$_{54-61}$; Aristakes, 23–24. On the campaign of Basil II in Iberia, see Cheynet, Basil II and Asia Minor, 98–102; Holmes, Basil II, 320–322; Whittow, Orthodox Byzantium, 384–385. On the Byzantine notion of cruelty, with special reference to the Muslims, see Ducellier, Byzance, 148–180.

it was a wretched sight to behold, as much as ten thousand killed in a short amount of time".[65] In this unadorned fashion the Byzantine author expresses her disgust at this event.

References to the army or its leaders deviating into acts of violence are rather limited in panegyrics. This is to be expected, given the fact that these orations are usually addressed to the emperor, the army's commander-in-chief according to Byzantine political theory. Their aim is to extol such qualities/virtues of his as might be included in a "mirror of princes" ("κάτοπτρον ἡγεμόνος"), among which "φιλανθρωπία" (philanthropy) and "φιλευσπλαχνία" (charity) take pride of place.[66] However, a reference to multitudes of dead enemies is both appropriate and necessary, in order to promote other imperial virtues, such as bravery, strategic skill, the ability to lead his army to victory and to force the enemy to accept peace.[67] Thus, in an oration delivered most probably in 1180 according to Peter Wirth, and harking back to the victories of Manuel Komnenos, Eustathios declares that the enemy were scattered like clouds before the wind, while their dead were piling up and both the survivors and the corpses bore witness to the emperor's valor.[68] Generally speaking, we could say that the number of descriptions of acts of violence that were penned by either historians or orators and could be included in a rhetoric of victory, is limited.

The presence of the *basileus* and his fearless attitude contribute to victory. This observation is made both by historians and by orators, especially the latter, as is to be expected. According to Leo the Deacon, when John Tzimiskes finally decided to put an end to the battle against the Rus' outside Dorostolon (April 971), which had raged for the better part of a day and had been very closely fought, he rode against the enemy, shouting to his soldiers that as Romans they had to prove their valor with deeds. The result was that their morale rose and they

---

65 Anna Komnene, Alexias, XI, ch. 5, §4, 337$_{75-78}$ "οἱ δὲ τοῦ στόλου ἅπαντες σὺν αὐτοῖς ἐρέταις εἰς τὴν πόλιν ἀτάκτως εἰσῄεσαν καὶ πάντας ἀνηλεῶς ἀπέκτενον. Καὶ ἦν εἰδεῖν θέαμα ἐλεεινὸν ὡσεὶ δέκα χιλιάδας ἀποκτανθέντας ἐν ὀξείᾳ καιροῦ ῥοπῇ." See Kolias, Η εξωτερική πολιτική Αλεξίου Α' Κομνηνού; Savvides, Ο Σελτζούκος εμίρης της Σμύρνης Τζαχάς; Ahrweiler, Byzance et la mer, 184–186.
66 Paidas, Η θεματική των βυζαντινών "κατόπτρων ηγεμόνος"; Munitiz, War and Peace; Ahrweiler, L'idéologie politique.
67 For example, Eustathios of Thessaloniki, Opera Minora, Λόγος Λ, 195$_{16}$–196$_{28}$. See also next note.
68 Eustathios of Thessaloniki, Opera Minora, Λόγος Κ, 182$_{31}$–183$_{56}$. See also Λόγος Λ', 198$_{8-11}$: "Τί δέ μοι θρόμβους μὲν ἱδρώτων λέγειν αἱματηρούς, σιγᾶν δὲ τὰ αἵματα, οἷς τὴν Λατινικὴν αὐτὸς ἐλίμνασε, πολλὴν μὲν αὐτῆς καὶ νεκροῖς καταστρώσας, οὐκ ὀλίγην δὲ καὶ καταβρέξας αἵμασιν, ἐξ ὧν ἑαυτῷ στολὴν εὐδοξίας ἔχρωζε;" (Stone, Eustathios, 140: "But why should I on the one hand mention bloody clots of sweat, but on the other remain silent about the blood with which he flooded the land of the Latins, strewing much of it with corpses, and drenching no small part of it with blood, with which he painted for himself a robe of glory?").

fought with renewed vigor, winning the battle.⁶⁹ The battle against the Cumans in 1148 was also close-fought, until Manuel charged ahead with his lance and broke their closed ranks. "When they were repulsed by the emperor's irresistible onset, the Romans thrust at them in full force and made a splendid charge", as Ioannes Kinnamos relates.⁷⁰

As far as the rhetorical texts are concerned, there are frequent references to the presence of the emperor and his bravely leading by example (after all, as I have already mentioned, valor constitutes one of the necessary elements of a *basileus*' personality). Theodore Laskaris led by example and thus emboldened his soldiers in the battle against the Latin allies of David Komnenos of Trebizond, according to an oration composed by Niketas Choniates in the summer of 1206 in honor of the emperor of Nicaea.⁷¹ Manuel Komnenos' reckless contribution to victory, during the campaign by his father, John II, against Neokaisareia (1139–1141), was of a similar nature: the enemy's surprise attack routed the troops, but Manuel rapidly intervened and his charge against the enemy saved the imperiled army.⁷²

To summarize and attempt to answer the questions posed at the beginning of this paper: historians and chroniclers, to a certain degree and keeping in mind certain exceptions that can be attributed to specific reasons (opposition to imperial policies, for instance, or disaffection towards rulers who failed to satisfy the author's private ambitions by offering him a public office, or conversely an author's sympathy for an emperor or official), draw a picture that corresponds to reality. The events they relate are not fictional ones aimed at entertaining their readers; it is simply that sometimes their narrative is influenced by personal experiences or perceptions.

---

69 Leon Diakonus, Historia, 141₅₋₁₇ (Talbot / Sullivan, History of Leo the Deakon, 186); Ioannes Skylitzes, 299₅₁–300₆₂. For the rhetoric of battle based on the comparative description of the battles in Dorostolon by Leo the Deacon and Ioannes Skylitzes, see McGrath, The Battles of Dorostolon.
70 Ioannes Kinnamos, Epitome, 95₆₋₁₃: "ὅθεν καὶ τῷ ἀνυποστάτῳ τῆς βασιλέως παρακεκινημένων ὁρμῆς Ῥωμαῖοι ὁλοσχερέστερον κατ' αὐτῶν ἐπιβρίσαντες, λαμπρὰν ἤδη τὴν ἐπαγωγὴν ἐποίουν." (Brand, Deeds, 78).
71 Niketas Choniates, Orationes et epistulae, Λόγος ΙΔ', 141₁₃₋₁₈: "Καὶ τί γὰρ οὐκ ἂν ἔδρασε στράτευμα βασιλέα βλέποντα προκινδυνεύοντα, προηγούμενον οὐ μεθεπόμενον, προασπίζοντα οὐχ ὑπασπιζόμενον, [...] καὶ τοῦ στρατηγοῦ καὶ βασιλέως τὸν συστρατιώτην ἀντιλαμβάνοντα καὶ συγκάμνοντα τοῖς ἀρχομένοις τὸν ἄρχοντα, καὶ νῦν μὲν πέλεκυν ἐγχείριον ἔχοντα δρυμοτομοῦντά τε καὶ τὰς παρόδους ἀπολειαίνοντα, νῦν δ' ἕτερον μετιόντα σωτήριον τοῖς στρατεύμασιν;". For the content of the oration and the date, see van Dieten, Erläuterungen, 146–152.
72 Michael Italikos, Lettres et discours, no. 44, 286₁₃–287₁₅. Description of the same incident, see in Niketas Choniates, Historia, 35₂₈₋₃₈. For the expedition of John Komnenos against the Dānishmendids, see Papageorgiou, Ἰωάννης Β' Κομνηνός, 322–326; Chalandon, Les Comnène, 178–183.

As has already been mentioned, orators were forced by the proximity of the events they described to the time the oration was delivered, to present actual facts. What they could do – and to a rather large extent they actually did – was to emphasize certain facets of what had happened, so that the listener would form a mental image or impression of persons and incidents that was highly positive, or on the contrary utterly negative, – all in all, a hidden truth. This is what Michael Italikos did in his oration for John Komnenos in the second half of 1138. As we saw, he managed to present John Komnenos' abandonment of the siege of Shaizar (Larissa) during his campaign in Syria in that same year as an exceptional success. He did this by concentrating on the fact that, instead of this city, John managed to sack many others, and above all on the booty, the "treasures" as the orator writes, which the emperor received in exchange for raising the blockade. Particular emphasis is placed on the fact that the booty included the extremely valuable military cross of Romanos IV Diogenes, looted from the emperor's tent after the defeat at Mantzikert in 1071. The recapture of the cross by John – an object of material and emotional but especially symbolic value – is emphasized by Niketas Choniates extensively in his Χρονική Διήγησις and more briefly in John Kinnamos' Ἐπιτομή.

This is an illuminating example that helps us answer the second question: where historians and orators describe the same event there is generally a common kernel of truth. What changes on each occasion is the prominence attributed by each author to various facets of the event, some of them mentioned in every source, others suppressed by one or the other for reasons that I have already mentioned.

As for the third question, I believe that the elements which contribute to rhetoric of victory do not change over the three centuries studied here, however significant the changes that took place during the same period on the political, economic and social level were. Historians and orators give pride of place to the capture of booty and prisoners (as a sort of particular and rather significant kind of booty), the liberation of Byzantine prisoners of war, the ability to supply the army, or sometimes (although not very often) the conversion of opponents to Christianity, such as the Pechenegs in an oration composed by John Mauropous for the victory of 1045/46 during the reign of Constantine Monomachos, or the Seljuks as a result of the re-annexation of parts of Asia Minor under Byzantine control by Manuel Komnenos.[73] Finally, atrocities committed against the defeated as a result of victory are very rarely reported in a laudatory fashion.

---

73 On this last issue, see the interesting views of Tristan Schmidt in the present volume.

Bibliography

Sources

Anna Komnene, Alexias, ed. Dieter R. Reinsch / Athanasios Kambylis (Corpus Fontium Historiae Byzantinae 40/1), Berlin / New York 2000.

Aristakes = Aristakès de Lastivert. Récit des Malheurs de la Nation Arménienne, ed. and trans. Marius Canard / Haïg Berbérian (Bibliothèque de Byzantion 5), Brussels 1973.

Ecloga, das Gesetzbuch Leons III. und Konstantinos V., ed. Ludwig Burgmann (Forschungen zur byzantinischen Rechtsgeschichte 10), Frankfurt am Main 1983.

Eustathios of Thessaloniki, Manuelis Comneni Imperatoris laudatio funebris, in: Eustathii metropolitae Thessalonicensis Opuscula, ed. Theophil L. F. Tafel, no XXIII, Frankfurt am Main 1832, 196–214 [Reprint Amsterdam 1964].

Eustathios of Thessaloniki = Eustathii Thessalonicensis Opera Minora, ed. Paul Wirth (Corpus Fontium Historiae Byzantinae 32), Berlin / New York 2000.

Euthymios Malakes = Εὐθυμίου τοῦ Μαλάκη τὰ σῳζόμενα, Β', Δύο ἐγκωμιαστικοὶ λόγοι εἰς τὸν αὐτοκράτορα Μανουὴλ Α' τὸν Κομνηνόν (1143/80), ed. Konstantinos Bonis, Athens 1949 [reprinted from Θεολογία 19 (1941/48), 20 (1949)].

Ioannes Skylitzes = Ioannis Scylitzae Synopsis historiarum, ed. Hans Thurn (Corpus Fontium Historiae Byzantinae 5), Berlin / New York 1973.

Ioannes Kinnamos = Ioannis Cinnami Epitome rerum ab Ioanne et Alexio Comnenis gestarum, ed. Augustus Meineke (Corpus Scriptorum Historiae Byzantinae 23), Bonn 1836 [Engl. transl. Charles Brand, Deeds of John and Manuel Comnenus, New York 1976].

Ioseph Genesios, Iosephi Genesii Regum Libri Quattuor, ed. Anni Lesmüller-Werner / Hans Thurn (Corpus Fontium Historiae Byzantinae 14), Berlin / New York 1978.

Leges poenales militares, in: Jus Graecoromanum, ed. Ioannes Zepos / Panayotis Zepos, vol. 2B, Athens 1931.

Le traité sur la guérilla (De velitatione) de l'empereur Nicéphore Phocas (963–969), ed. Gilbert Dagron / Haralambie Mihăescu, Paris 1986.

Leon Diakonos, Historia, ed. Karl Hase, Bonn ²1828 [Introduction, translation, and annotations by Alice-Mary Talbot / Denis F. Sullivan, The History of Leo the Deakon. Byzantine Military Expansion in the Tenth Century (Dumbarton Oaks Research Library and Collection), Washington D.C. 2005].

Michael Attaleiates = Michaelis Attaliatae Historia, ed. Eudoxos Tsolakis (Corpus Fontium Historiae Byzantinae 50), Athens 2011 [Engl. transl. Anthony Kaldellis / Dimitris Krallis, The History by Attaleiates (Dumbarton Oaks Medieval Library 16), Cambridge, MA 2012].

Michael Italikos, Lettres et Discours, ed. Paul Gautier (Archives de l'Orient Chrétien 14, Paris 1972.

Michael Psellos = Michaelis Pselli Chronographia, ed. Dieter R. Reinsch (Millennium-Studien 51), vol. 1, Berlin / Boston 2014.

Michel Psellos, Chronographie ou histoire d'un siècle de Byzance (976–1077), ed. Émile Renaud, vol. I, Paris 1926, vol. II, Paris 1928.

Michael the Rhetor = Τοῦ Θεσσαλονίκης κῦρ Μιχαὴλ τοῦ ῥήτορος λόγος ἀναγνωσθεὶς εἰς τὸν αὐτοκράτορα κῦρ Μανουὴλ τὸν Κομνηνόν, in: Fontes rerum byzantinarum, Rhetorum saeculi XII orationes politicae, ed. Wasilij Regel [Alexander Kazhdan] (Subsidia Byzantina V), Petropoli 1917, no VIII, 131–152 [Reprint Leipzig 1982].

Michael the Rhetor, Τοῦ αὐτοῦ εἰς τὸν αὐτὸν αὐτοκράτορα κῦρ Μανουὴλ τὸν Κομνηνόν, ὅτε ἦν πρωτέκδικος, as above, no IX, 152–165.

Nikephoros Basilakes, In Ioannem Comnenum imperatorem, in: Niceforí Basilacae, Orationes et epistulae, ed. Antonio Garzya, Leipzig 1984, no 3, 48–74.

Niketas Choniates, Historia = Nicetae Choniatae Historia, ed. Jan-Louis van Dieten (Corpus Fontium Historiae Byzantinae 11), Berlin / New York 1975 [Engl. transl. Harry Magoulias, O city of Byzantium. Annals of Nicetas Choniates, Detroit 1984].

Niketas Choniates, Orationes = Nicetae Choniatae Orationes et Epistulae, ed. Jan-Louis van Dieten (Corpus Fontium Historiae Byzantinae 3), Berlin / New York 1972.

Procheiros Nomos, in: Jus Graecoromanum, ed. Ioannes Zepos / Panayotis Zepos, vol. 2, Athens 1931 [Reprint Aalen 1962], 107–228.

Nikephoros Ouranos, Taktika, ed. Eric McGeer, in: idem, Sowing the Dragon's Teeth – Byzantine Warfare in the Tenth Century (Dumbarton Oaks Studies 33), Washington 1995, 88–163.

Nikephoros II Phokas, Praecepta militaria, ed. Eric McGeer, in: idem, Sowing the Dragon's Teeth – Byzantine Warfare in the Tenth Century (Dumbarton Oaks Studies 33), Washington 1995, 12–59.

Sylloge Tacticorum quae olim "Inedita Leonis tactica" dicebatur, ed. Alphonse Dain, Paris 1938 [Engl. trans. George Chatzelis / Jonathan Harris, A Tenth-Century Byzantine Military Manual: The Sylloge Tacticorum, London / New York 2017].

The Taktika of Leo VI, ed. and trans. George T. Dennis (Corpus Fontium Historiae Byzantinae 49), Dumbarton Oaks 2010.

Theophanes Continuatus, Chronographia, ed. Immanuel Bekker (Corpus scriptorum historiae Byzantinae 31), Bonn 1838.

Vita Basilii, Chronographiae quae Theophanis continuati nomine fertur liber quo Vita Basilii Imperatoris amplectitur, ed. Ihor Ševčenko (Corpus Fontium Historiae Byzantinae 42), Berlin / Boston 2011.

Literature

Ahrweiler, Hélène, Byzance et la mer (Bibliothèque Byzantine, Études 5), Paris 1966.

Ahrweiler, Hélène, L'idéologie politique de l'empire byzantin, Paris 1975.

Alexopoulos, Theocharis, Using Ancient Military Handbooks to Fight Medieval Battles: Two Stratagems of Alexios I Comnenos against the Normans and the Pechenegs, in: Ἑῷα καὶ Ἑσπέρια 8 (2008–2012), 47–71.

Angold, Michael, The Byzantine Empire, 1025–1204: A Political History, London / New York, [2]1997.

Belke, Klaus / Mersich, Norbert, Phrygien und Pisidien (Tabula Imperii Byzantini 7), Vienna 1990.

Brand, Charles, Byzantium Confronts the West, 1180–1204, Cambridge, MA 1968.

Chalandon, Ferdinand, Histoire de la domination Normande en Italie et en Sicile, Paris 1907.

Chalandon, Ferdinand, Les Comnène. Jean II Comnène (1118–1143) et Manuel I Comnène (1143–1180), Paris 1912.

Cheynet, Jean-Claude, Basil II and Asia Minor, in: Byzantium in the year 1000, ed. Paul Magdalino, Leiden / Boston 2003, 71–108.

Cheynet, Jean-Claude / Vannier, Jean-François, Les Argyroi, in: Zbornik Radova Vizantološkog Instituta 40 (2003), 57–90 [reprinted in Jean-Claude Cheynet, La société byzantine. L'apport des sceaux (Bilans de Recherche 3), Paris 2008, vol. 2, 525–561.

Chrysos, Evangelos, 1176 – A Byzantine Crusade?, in: Byzantine War Ideology between Roman Imperial Concept and Christian Religion. Akten des Internationalen Symposiums (Wien, 19.–21. Mai 2011), ed. Johannes Koder / Yannis Stouraitis, Vienna 2012, 81–86.

Cosme, Pierre / Couvenhes, Jean-Christophe / Janniard, Sylvain / Virol, Michèle, Le récit de guerre comme source d'histoire, de l'Antiquité à nos jours (Presses universitaires de Franche-Comté 1545), Besançon 2022.

Dain, Alphonse, Le partage du butin de guerre d'après les traités juridiques et militaires, in: Actes du VIe Congrès International d'Études Byzantines (Paris, 27 July – 2 August 1948), Paris 1950, 347–352.

Dennis, George, Imperial Panegyric: Rhetoric and Reality, in: Byzantine Court Culture from 829 to 1204, ed. Henry Maguire, Washington D.C. 1997, 131–140.

Ducellier, Alain, Byzance. Juge cruel dans un environnement cruel? Notes sur le "Musulman cruel" dans l'empire byzantin entre VIIème et XIIIème siècles, in: Crudelitas. The Politics of Cruelty in the Ancient and Medieval World, ed. Toivo Viljamaa / Akso Timonen / Christian Krötzk (Medium Aevum Quotidianum 2), Krems 1992, 148–180.

Haldon, John F., Warfare, State and Society in the Byzantine World, 565–1204, London 1999.

Holmes, Catherine, Basil II and the Governance of Empire (976–1025) (Oxford Studies in Byzantium), Oxford 2005.

Hunger, Herbert, Die hochsprachliche profane Literatur der Byzantiner (Handbuch der Altertumswissenschaften 5), Munich 1978.

Jeffreys, Elisabeth, Rhetoric in Byzantium. Papers from the Thirty-Fifth Spring Symposium of Byzantine Studies, Exeter College, University of Oxford, March 2001 (Society for the Promotion of Byzantine Studies. Publications 11), Aldershot 2003.

Kaldellis, Anthony, The Manufacture of History in the Later Tenth and Eleventh Centuries: Rhetorical Templates and Narrative Ontologies, in: Proceedings of the 23rd International Congress of Byzantine Studies (Belgrade, 22–27 August 2016), Plenary Papers, Belgrade 2016, 293–306.

Karapli, Katerina, "Περὶ τοῦ οἷον εἶναι δεῖ τὸν στρατηγόν": Μια ἄλλη κατηγορία "ἡγεμονικῶν κατόπτρων", in: Aureus: Volume Dedicated to Professor Evangelos K. Chrysos, ed. T. G. Kolias / K. G. Pitsakis, Athens 2014, 297–310.

Kazhdan, Alexander, The Social Views of Michael Attaleiates, in: Studies on Byzantine Literature of the Eleventh and Twelfth Centuries, ed. Alexander Kazhdan / Simon Franklin, Cambridge 1984, 23–87.

Kazhdan, Alexander, W.E. Regel und seine "Quellen zur byzantinischen Geschichte", in: Fontes rerum byzantinarum, Rhetorum saeculi XII orationes politicae, ed. Wasilij Regel (Subsidia Byzantina 5), Leipzig 1982, V–XVI [Reprint Petropoli 1917].

Koder, Johannes / Stouraitis, Yannis, Byzantine War Ideology between Roman Imperial Concept and Christian Religion, Akten des Internationalen Symposiums (Wien, 19.- 21. Mai 2011), Vienna 2012.

Kolia-Dermizaki, Athina, Byzantium and the Crusades in the Komnenian Era, in: Byzantium and the West: Perception and Reality, ed. Nikolaos Chrissis / Athina Kolia-Dermitzaki / Angeliki Papageorgio, London / New York 2019, 59–83.

Kolia-Dermizaki, Athina, Το εμπόλεμο Βυζάντιο στις ομιλίες και επιστολές του $9^{ου}$–$12^{ου}$ αι., in: Το εμπόλεμο Βυζάντιο (9ος–12ος αι.), ed. Kostas G. Tsiknakes (Ινστιτούτο Βυζαντινών Ερευνών, Διεθνή Συμπόσια 4) / Byzantium at War (9th–12th c.) (Institute for Byzantine Research, International Symposium 4), Athens 1997, 213–238.

Kolia-Dermizaki, Athina, Some Remarks on the Fate of Prisoners of War in Byzantium (9th–10th Centuries), in: La liberazione dei 'captivi' tra Cristianità e Islam. Oltre la Crociata e il Ğihād: Tolleranza e Servizio Umanitario, atti del Congresso interdisciplinare di studi storici, ed. Giulio Cipollone (Collectanea Archivi Vaticani 46), Vatican City 2000, 583–620.

Kolia-Dermizaki, Athina, War and Peace in Byzantium: Changes and Turning-Points in the Middle and Late Byzantine Period (7th–15th Centuries), in: Proceedings of the 23rd International Congress of Byzantine Studies (Belgrade, 22–27 August 2016), Thematic Sessions of Free Communications, ed. Bojanin Stanoje / Dejan Dželebdžić, Belgrade 2016, 477–485.

Kolia-Dermizaki, Athina, Ο στρατός και ο στρατιώτης: Η απεικόνισή τους στα ιστοριογραφικά και ρητορικά κείμενα (10ος–12ος αι.), in: Ιστορίες πολέμου στη νοτιοανατολική Ευρώπη: Μια προσέγγιση στη διαχρονία, ed. Athina Kolia-Dermitzaki / Vaso Seirinidou / Spyridon Ploumidis (Istoremata 6), Athens 2018, 177–206.

Kolia-Dermizaki, Athina et al. ed., Ιστορίες πολέμου στη νοτιοανατολική Ευρώπη: Μια προσέγγιση στη διαχρονία, Athens 2018.

Kolia-Dermizaki, Athina, The Attitude of the Soldiers in Warfare as Reflected in the Byzantine Sources (9th–12th centuries), in: Le récit de guerre comme source d'histoire, de l'Antiquité à nos jours, ed. Pierre Cosme / Jean-Christophe Couvenhes / Sylvain Janniard / Michèle Virol (Presses universitaires de Franche-Comté 1545), Besançon 2022, 337–353.

Kolias, Georgios T., Η εξωτερική πολιτική Αλεξίου Α΄ Κομνηνού (1081–1118), in: Αθηνά 59 (1955), 241–288.

Kolias, Taxiarchis G., Kriegsgefangene, Sklavenhandel und die Privilegien der Soldaten, in: Byzantinoslavica 54 (1995), 129–135.

Koutrakou, Nike, The Other Face of War in Byzantium: Imperial Propaganda Managing Defeat (with Particular Reference to Middle-Byzantine Times of Change), in: ΑΡΕΤΗΝ ΤΗΝ ΚΑΛΛΙΣΤΗΝ. Σύμμεικτα προς τιμήν Καλλιόπης (Κέλλυς) Α. Μπουρδάρα, Mélanges en l'honneur de Kalliope (Kelly) A. Bourdara, ed. Ioannis Tzamtzis / Panayotis Antonopoulos / Christos Stavrakos, Athens 2021, 1541–1564.

Lemerle, Paul, L'histoire des Pauliciens d'Asie Mineure d'après les sources grècques, in: Travaux et Mémoires 5 (1973), 1–144 [reprinted in idem, Essais sur le monde Byzantin (Variorum Reprints), London 1980, IV].

Lev, Yaacov, The Human Cost of Warfare: Wars in the Medieval Middle East, 9th-12th centuries, in: La liberazione dei 'captivi' tra Cristianità e Islam. Oltre la Crociata e il Ǧihād: Tolleranza e Servizio Umanitario. Atti del Congresso interdisciplinare di studi storici (Roma 16-19 settembre 1998), ed. Giulio Cipollone (Collectanea Archivi Vaticani 4), Vatican City 2000, 635-648.

Lilie, Ralph-Johannes, Byzanz und die Kreuzfahrerstaaten. Studien zur Politik des Byzantinischen Reiches gegenüber den Staaten der Kreuzfahrer in Syrien und Palästina bis zum vierten Kreuzzug (1096-1204), Munich 1981 [Engl. trans. J. C. Morris / Jean E. Ridings, Byzantium and the Crusader States 1096-1204, Oxford 1993].

Lilie, Ralph-Johannes, Die byzantinische Gesellschaft im Spiegel ihrer Quellen, in: Zbornik Radova Vizantološkog Instituta 50 (2013), 959-968.

Lilie, Ralph-Johannes, Handel und Politik zwischen dem byzantinischen Reich und den italienischen Kommunen Venedig, Pisa und Genua in der Epoche der Komnenen und der Angeloi (1081-1204), Amsterdam 1984.

Lilie, Ralph-Johannes, Reality and Invention: Reflections on Byzantine Historiography, in: Dumbarton Oaks Papers 68 (2014), 157-210.

Lyubarskij, Yakov Nikolaevich, How should a Byzantine text be read?, in: Rhetoric in Byzantium: papers from the thirty-fifth Spring Symposium of Byzantine Studies, Exeter College, University of Oxford, March 2001, ed. Elizabeth M. Jeffreys, Aldershot 2002, 117-126.

Lykaki, Marilia, L'économie de pillage et les prisonniers de guerre: Byzance, VIIe-Xe siècle, in: Pillages, tributs, captifs: Prédation et sociétés de l'Antiquité tardive au haut Moyen Âge, Colloque organisé avec le soutien de l'Institut Français d'Histoire en Allemagne, ed. Rodolphe Keller / Laury Sarti (Frankfurt, 28-29 juin 2012), Paris 2018, 89-102.

Lykaki, Marilia, Οι αιχμάλωτοι πολέμου στη Βυζαντινή αυτοκρατορία (6ος-11ος αι.), Athens [forthcoming].

Macrides, Ruth, Editor's Preface, in: History as Literature in Byzantium. Papers from the Fortieth Spring Symposium of Byzantine Studies, University of Birmingham, April 2007, ed. Ruth Macrides, Burlington 2010, IX-XII.

Macrides, Ruth, The Historian in the History, in: Φιλέλλην. Studies in Honour of Robert Browning, ed. Costas N. Constantinides / Nikolaos M. Panagiotakes / Elizabeth Jeffreys / Athanasios D. Angelou (Istituto Ellenico di Studi Bizantini e Postbizantini di Venezia - Bibliotheke 17), Venice 1996, 205-224.

Magdalino, Paul, The Empire of Manuel I Komnenos, 1143-1180, Cambridge 1993.

Maniati-Kokkini, Triantafyllitsa, Η επίδειξη ανδρείας στον πόλεμο κατά τους ιστορικούς του 11ου και 12ου αιώνα, in: Το εμπόλεμο Βυζάντιο (9ος-12ος αι) ed. Kostas G. Tsiknakes, (Ινστιτούτο Βυζαντινών Ερευνών, Διεθνή Συμπόσια 4) / Byzantium at War (9th-12th c.) (Institute for Byzantine Research, International Symposium 4), Athens 1997, 239-259.

McGrath, Stamatina, The Battles of Dorostolon (971): Rhetoric and Reality, in: Peace and War in Byzantium. Essays in Honor of George T. Dennis, S.J., ed. Timothy S. Miller / John Nesbitt, Washington D.C. 1995, 152-164.

McGrath, Stamatina, Warfare as Literary Narrative, in: A Companion to the Byzantine Culture of War, ca. 300-1204, ed. Yannis Stouraitis, Leiden / Boston 2018, 160-195.

Michaelides-Nouaros, Georgios, Ὁ βυζαντινὸς δίκαιος πόλεμος κατὰ τὰ Τακτικὰ τοῦ Λέοντος τοῦ Σοφοῦ, in: Σύμμεικτα Σεφεριάδου (offprint), Athens 1961.

Munitiz, Joseph A., S.J., War and Peace Reflected in Some Byzantine Mirrors of Princes, in: Peace and War in Byzantium. Essays in Honor of George T. Dennis S.J., ed. Timothy S. Miller / John Nesbitt, Washington D.C. 1995, 50-61.

Neville, Leonora, Why Did the Byzantines Write History?, in: Proceedings of the 23rd International Congress of Byzantine Studies (Belgrade, 22-27 August 2016), Plenary Papers, Belgrade 2016, 265-276.

Nilsson, Ingela, To Narrate the Events of the Past: On Byzantine Historians, and Historians on Byzantium, in: Byzantine Narrative. Papers in honour of Roger Scott, ed. John Burke et al., (Byzantina Australiensia 16), Melbourne 2006, 47-58.

Paidas, Konstantinos D. S., Η θεματική των βυζαντινών "κατόπτρων ηγεμόνος" της πρώιμης και μέσης περιόδου (398-1095). Συμβολή στην πολιτική θεωρία των Βυζαντινών, Athens 2005.

Papageorgiou, Angeliki, Ο Ιωάννης Β' Κομνηνός και η εποχή του (1118-1143), Athens 2017.

Papageorgiou, Angeliki, War and Ideology in the Komnenian Era. Victories on the Northern Front as Objects of Domestic Political Exploitation, in: Ιστορίες πολέμου στη Νοτιοανατολική Ευρώπη. Μια προσέγγιση στη διαχρονία. Πρακτικά Διεθνούς Επιστημονικού Συνεδρίου με αφορμή τα 100 χρόνια από τους Βαλκανικούς Πολέμους (1912/1913), ed. Athina Kolia-Dermitzaki et. al. (Αθήνα, 7-9 Νοεμβρίου 2013), Athens 2018, 249-259.

Pitsakis, Constantin, Guerre et paix en droit byzantin, in: Méditerranées 30/31 (2002), 203-231.

Polemis, Demetrios, The Doukai. A Contribution to Byzantine Prosopography, London 1968.

Abd al 'Azīz M. A. Ramaḍān, The Treatment of Arab Prisoners of War in Byzantium (9th-10th centuries), in: Annales islamologiques 43 (2009), 155-194.

Rotman, Youval, Les esclaves et l'esclavage à Byzance. De la Méditerranée antique à la Méditerranée médiévale VIe-XIe siècles, Paris 2004.

Rotolo, Vincenzo, Οι Σικελοί στη Θεσσαλονίκη το 1185, in: Η Θεσσαλονίκη μεταξύ Ανατολής και Δύσεως. Πρακτικά Συμποσίου Τεσσαρακονταετηρίδος της Εταιρείας Μακεδονικών Σπουδών, 30 Οκτωβρίου-1 Νοεμβρίου 1980, Thessaloniki 1982, 9-20.

Runciman, Steven, A History of the Crusades: The Kingdom of Jerusalem, vol. 2, Cambridge 1953, 215-217 [Reprint New York 1995].

Savvides, Alexis, Ο Σελτζούκος εμίρης της Σμύρνης Τζαχάς, in: Χιακά Χρονικά 14 (1982), 9-24 and 16 (1984) 51-66.

Skoulatos, Basile, Les personnages byzantins de l'Alexiade. Analyse prosopographique et synthèse (Université de Louvain, Receuil de Travaux d'Histoire et de Philologie, 6e série, Fasc. 20), Louvain 1980.

Stone, Andrew, Eustathian Panegyric as a Historical Source, in: Jahrbuch der Österreichischen Byzantinistik 51 (2001), 225-258.

Stone, Andrew, Dorylaion Revisited. Manuel I Komnenos and the refortification of Dorylaion and Soublaion in 1175, in: Revue des Études Byzantines 61 (2003), 183-200.

Stone, Andrew, Eustathios of Thessaloniki: Secular Orations 1167/8 to 1179 (Byzantina Australiensia 19), Brisbane 2013.

Tougher, Shawn, The Reign of Leo VI (886-912). Politics and People, Leiden / New York 1997.

Treadgold, Warren, The Early Byzantine Historians, Basingstoke 2007.

Treadgold, Warren, The Middle Byzantine Historians, Basingstoke 2013.

Treadgold, Warren, The Unwritten Rules for Writing Byzantine History, in: Proceedings of the 23rd International Congress of Byzantine Studies (Belgrade, 22-27 August 2016), Plenary Papers, Belgrade 2016, 277-292.

Tsiknakes, Kostas G. (ed.), Το εμπόλεμο Βυζάντιο (9ος-12ος αι.) (Ινστιτούτο Βυζαντινών Ερευνών, Διεθνή Συμπόσια 4) / Byzantium at War (9th-12th c.) (Institute for Byzantine Research, International Symposium 4), Athens 1997.

Van Dieten, Jan-Louis, Erläuterungen zu den Reden und Briefen nebst einer Biographie (Supplementa Byzantina 2), Berlin / New York 1971.

Vannier, Jean-François, Familles byzantines. Les Argyroi (IXe-XIIe Siecles) (Publications de la Sorbonne. Serie Byzantina 1), Paris 1975.

Varzos, Konstantinos, Η γενεαλογία των Κομνηνών, vol. I, (Βυζαντινά Κείμενα και Μελέται 20α), Κέντρον Βυζαντινών Ερευνών, Thessaloniki 1984.

Vasiliev, Alexander (M. Canard), Byzance et les Arabes, vol. 2/1, La dynastie macédonienne (867-959), Brussels 1968.

Vučetić, Martin, Die Novelle des Kaisers Ioannes I. Tzimiskes über das auf versklavte Kriegsgefangene zu entrichtende Kommerkion, in: Fontes Minores 12 (2014), 279-328.

Whittow, Mark, The Making of Orthodox Byzantium, 600-1025 (New Studies in Medieval History), London 1996.

Wirth, Peter, Kaiser Manuel I. Komnenos und die Ostgrenze. Rückeroberung und Wiederaufbau der Festung Dorylaion, in: Byzantinische Zeitschrift 55 (1962), 21-29 [reprinted in idem, Eustathiana, Gesammelte Aufsätze zu Leben und Werk des Metropoliten Eustathios von Thessalonike, Amsterdam 1980, 71-79].

Tristan Schmidt

The Merciful Emperor, the Tame Barbarian, and the Ideal of Imperial Victory in Times of Failure. Border Warfare in 11th and 12th Century Byzantium

The emperor as the ultimate military victor was a core concept of Roman and Byzantine imperial propaganda. Communicated in literature, art and performed rituals, it constituted a central aspect of the imperial ideal, and it set the discursive standards for the (self-) representation of the individual rulers.[1] Many of them made it a point to emphasize their abilities as generals and their personal bravery in battle in their propaganda.[2] Based on a general postulate of the emperor's invincibility, however, the affinity to victory did not necessarily have to be proven by concrete presence in the field.

When in 1047 a Byzantine army prevailed over invading Pechenegs, Emperor Constantine IX was "naturally" credited for the victory by his panegyrists, even though he had not even been present during the encounter.[3] In the mid-12th century, Nikephoros Kataphloron made it crystal clear that the emperor had "dressed himself" in a victory that was actually won by the encomiast's addressee, an admiral whose name is lost to us.[4] When Andronikos Kontostephanos won his famous victory over Hungary in 1167, he self-evidently shared the praise during

---

1 For the concept of imperial victory, see the article by Kolia-Dermitzaki in the present volume. For the tradition of imperial victory and its various forms of expression, see McCormick, Victory, 11–188; Angelov, Ideology, 79. For the theological aspects since Roman times, see Stephenson, Theology, 23–28; 45–50. For the concept of the emperors as "eternal victors," see Grünbart, Enemies, 140–46; Treitinger, Reichsidee, 168; 182.
2 For emperors as military victors, see, for instance, Constantine V (McCormick, Victory, 136–137), Nikephoros II (Kazhdan, Aristocracy, 47) and Alexios I (Buckley, Alexiad, 107; 141; 147–167). For the focus of Komnenian, Angeloi and Laskarid propaganda on the emperor's personal bravery, see Angelov, Ideology, 82–84; Kyriakidis, Warfare, 15–44. For earlier examples of imperial "camaraderie" with the common soldier, see an imperial acclamation from 457 (Konstantinos Porphyrogennetos, de cerimoniis I,100 (B I, 91)), presenting Leon I as his soldier's comrade, and Leon Diakonos, Historia, III, 50B–51C; IV, 74D, stylizing Nikephoros I Phokas as the teacher of his soldiers who shares their labors in the field. Kolia-Dermitzaki, ἐμπόλεμο, 231 distinguishes the "warrior-general"-type from the more passive, but godly-aided victor.
3 See below, note 17.
4 Nikolaos Kataphloron, ed. Loukaki, 34, 152–54.34.

the following triumphal procession with Emperor Manuel I.[5] The appropriation of victory indicates the imperial dominance of the public discourse and the efficiency of propaganda; it further shows that imperial victoriousness was an abstract concept, rather independent of personal involvement.[6]

For imperial panegyrics, the ever-victorious emperor constituted a conditio sine qua non in any depiction of military and political conflict. This did not leave much room for ambiguity, even when the factual outcome of a military enterprise was neither clear nor definite. In this regard, conflicts with elusive, semi-nomadic groups in the empire's border zones lead to particular predicaments, as clear victories were difficult to obtain and rarely resulted in sustainable long-term arrangements. In the 11th and 12th century, Byzantine emperors lead or ordered numerous campaigns against Turcomans, Cumans and Pechenegs who violated the border regions in Asia Minor and south of the Danube. The success of these campaigns was often limited, if they did not end in outright defeat.

Considering that since Roman Antiquity, narratives of military victory against "barbarian nomads" were central to the imperial image, the disparity and tensions between ideal and factual outcome were particularly marked.[7] It was the task of propaganda to bridge these gaps when dashing triumphs were rare and agreements overturned within weeks or months. Panegyric poetry often provided the most immediate reactions, serving as the rulers' mouthpieces during or immediately after military campaigns. The following case studies exemplify how the authors and orators adapted the traditional concept of imperial victory in order to fit the often sobering realities.[8] The investigation shows that the century-old category of the "nomadic barbarian" constituted a cornerstone in their assessments of current military and political situations, but also a basis for later revision and critique. Comparing their testimonies to historiographical comments on the same events, one witnesses a quasi-dialogue, where the evaluation of imperial border policies closely depended on the (de-) construction of imperial victory and differing concepts of the (un-) vanquished foes.

---

5 Niketas Choniates, Manuel Komnenos, E', Historia, 157:53–158:78. For Manuel's competitive propaganda regarding his generals during this campaign and the limits of imperial appropriation of victory, see Schmidt, Performing, 163–79.

6 Treitinger, Reichsidee, 168–75.

7 The concept of the *Barbaros* as opposed to the *Rhomaios* has received much attention in Byzantine studies. See Lechner, Hellenen, 73–114, at 79–81 for the emperor as the victor over barbarians; Page, Being Byzantine, 42–52; Kaldellis, Ethnography, who stresses the political agenda behind ethnographic reports (8). For the Roman tradition of imperial victory over "barbarians," see Mathisen, Behavior, 32–33.

8 For encomiastic rhetoric as the principal means to "advertise [...] military and diplomatic victories [...] in the face of the most dangerous element of opposition: the aristocracy" see Papageorgiou, War and Ideology, 249–50.

Constantine IX and the Pechenegs (1047)

The first case study is concerned with an episode from the 1040s, when groups of semi-nomadic Pechenegs who had been living between the Don and the lower Danube since the 9th century moved into the Byzantine Balkan provinces.[9] A large group crossed the frozen Danube in the winter 1046/47 under their leader Tyrach. They plundered the land, before surrendering rather unexpectedly to a Byzantine Army sent by Emperor Constantine IX. The Byzantines were reinforced by their own Pecheneg allies under a chieftain called Kegen.[10] According to the historians Ioannes Skylitzes and Michael Attaleiates, the Pecheneg capitulation was caused by a combination of the hard winter, an epidemic in their camp, and the strength of the Byzantines. The following arrangement resulted in a re-settlement of the newly arrived Pechenegs and the conversion of several of their leaders.[11]

Whereas Skylitzes and Attaleiates wrote from a chronological distance, Ioannes Mauropus, who served as an orator in the emperor's service and was later to become bishop of Euchaita, composed a laudatory speech for Emperor Constantine straight after the events. In his narrative, the invading Pechenegs widely outnumbered the Byzantines and their allies, causing despair among the latter. In this dire situation the fate of the Byzantines and their allies was turned only by a divine miracle in the form of a cross that "miraculously appeared high in the air, like [it happened] already back then, [to] the first Christian emperor" Constantine I, before his famous victory at the Milvian Bridge in 312.[12]

The difference in 1047 was that Constantine IX, in contrast to his Late Antique namesake, was not present in the field. He had entrusted command to the *dux* of Adrianople, Constantine Arianites, whose troops, encouraged by divine support, bravely engaged the disheartened Pechenegs:[13]

> "A great massacre of the barbarians occurred, and even more fear among many, fear, which brought those who had been insensible before to their senses [...]. Having thrown

---

9 For the Pechenegs and their relations to Byzantium in the second half of the 11th c., see Meško, Pecheneg Groups, 177–205.
10 For the military and political background, see Madgearu, Military Organization, 65; Lefort, Rhetorique, 273–275; Malamut, Petchénègues, 118–123.
11 Ioannes Skylitzes, IV, 458, 56–459, 64; Michael Attaleiates, 25, 10–15. Ioannes Skylitzes reports an exaggerated number of 800000 Pechenegs. Diaconu, Petchénègues, 62 estimates ca. 10000.
12 "[...] καὶ νικᾷ κατὰ κράτος ὁ σταυρὸς τοῦ Χριστοῦ, θαυμαστῶς ὑπεράνωθεν ἐντυπωθεὶς τῷ ἀέρι, ὥσπερ ἤδη καὶ πρότερον ἐπ'ἐκείνου τοῦ πρώτου χριστιανῶν βασιλέως [...]." Ioannes Mauropus, no. 182, 12, 145. For the vision in the context of Roman/Byzantine theology of victory see Stephenson, Theology, 28–30.
13 Ioannes Skylitzes, IV, 458, 48–50.

the weapons far away from their hands, they immediately stretched these [hands] out in supplication, and [...] besought the emperor's mercy. "[14]

In contrast to the historiographers, Mauropus' interpretation ascribes the success in the field to a combination of heavenly aid and imperial arms – the epidemic is not mentioned. Instead, the vision of the cross makes transcendental support for the Byzantines manifest. In addition, it is likely that the implicit parallelism to the general-emperor Constantine I served as a narrative trick to give Constantine IX a more active role as a military leader than he actually had.[15] It seems, however, that for Mauropus, the "real" victory was completed only *after* the battle, when the Pechenegs, were granted mercy and settled by the local authorities.[16] In a lengthy passage he praises Constantine for having "converted [the Pechenegs] from their previous formlessness and wickedness to their present cheerfulness and grace" and for transforming them into "a new nation of God."[17] As far as we know, the speech was intended to be held in Constantinople, on the occasion of the inauguration of the church St. Georgios in Mangana, with the captured Pecheneg leaders present.[18]

The emphasis on the events after the battle can be partly explained by Constantine's lack of personal involvement during the military encounter itself, whereas he actively participated in the subsequent negotiations. Highlighting the conversion, Mauropus re-focused the attention to the emperor's agency and further placed him in the ideal of good Christian rulership. Another, and possibly more significant reason to focus on the Pechenegs' pacification, rather than describing only their defeat, was the ongoing instability of the military and political situation. There was still a mass of Pechenegs to be dealt with by overtaxed Byzantine authorities, and everyone at court must have been con-

---

14 "γίνεται δὴ φόνος τῶν βαρβάρων πολύς, καὶ πολλῷ πλείων φόβος, φόβος, ἄγων εἰς αἴσθησιν τοὺς πρὶν ἀναισθήτους [...]. αὐτίκα γὰρ [...] τῶν χειρῶν ἀπορρίψαντες τὰ ὅπλα μακράν, εἰς ἱκεσίαν ταύτας ἐξέτεινον, καὶ τὴν εὐσπλαγχνίαν τοῦ κράτους [...] ἐξεκαλοῦντο [...]." Ioannes Mauropus, no. 182, 13, 145.
15 See Kolia-Dermitzaki, ἐμπόλεμο, 231 who already notes the need of Mauropus to enhance the military role of Constantine IX who had been absent during the campaign.
16 Ioannes Skylitzes, IV, 459, 67 confirms that "the Roman leaders" decided to spare the Pechenegs, interestingly, against the explicit advice of his allied Pecheneg leader Kegen. I follow Lefort, Rhetorique, 275 that the final decision on the settlement of the Pechenegs must have come from the emperor.
17 "[...] ἐκ τῆς πρὶν ἀμφορίας καὶ ἀτοπίας ἐκείνης εἰς τὴν νῦν ἱλαρότητα καὶ χάριν μεταβάλοντες, [...] καὶ λαὸς θεοῦ νέος ὁ παλαιὸς τὴν ἀσέβειαν[...]." Ioannes Mauropus, no. 182, 13–14, 145. This is a clear allusion to the conversions mentioned.
18 This becomes clear from Mauropus' reference to them being present in no. 183, 13, 145 (see below, note 18). Whether the Pechenegs themselves would have understood the speech may be doubted.

cerned about what would happen next. This was all the more pressing, considering how difficult it was to contain previous Pecheneg threats.[19]

In this situation, it required more than a flashy depiction of the enemy's surrender to give a convincing impression of an undisputed victory. Mauropus' aim had to be to present the Pechenegs' submission as a definite achievement, laying the basis for long lasting peace. Since the actual situation was still incalculable and there must have been serious doubts whether the agreements would last, he shifted the discussion to an ontological level, arguing with the old concept of the "barbarians'" transformation into civilized humans, culminating in their (leaders') conversion.[20] The success of this transformation was the very condition for the effusive celebration of imperial mercy:

> "[…] now they stand beside us, a miracle for those who see it, for they, who were like wild beasts, have been transformed into tame/cultivated humans, […] the brightest [thing] of all, however, […is that] out of infidels and unbelievers [have become] pious believers […]."[21]

Considering the dire situation of the Byzantines, facing an enemy that was neither completely defeated nor entirely under control, one may doubt whether the decision to avoid further fighting was the result of a deliberate integrative policy towards the Pechenegs, or rather a pragmatic attempt to contain a situation that did not leave much scope for other options. In fact, whereas Mauropus' story of success ended here, a glance at the historic aftermath indicates that the situation was anything but resolved. The newly settled Pechenegs, both those of Tyrach and of Kegen, continued to cause problems, raided Byzantine settlements, and forced Constantine to continue the war.[22]

The transformation claimed by Mauropus did not take place and it quickly became clear that the truce with the Pechenegs would not last. It takes no effort to imagine the debate at court whether the attempt to integrate the Pechenegs was really preferable to the continuation of an aggressive policy against them.[23] To

---

19 For the situation in the 1020s and 30s see Stephenson, Frontier, 81.
20 For the general motif of the "taming" emperor see Schmidt, Tierbildlichkeit, 292–294.
21 "ὥστε μεθ'ἡμῶν νῦν ἑστήκασιν εἰς θαῦμα τοῖς θεωμένοις, ἐξ ἀγρίων ὥσπερ θηρίων εἰς ἡμέρους ἀνθρώπους μεταπλασθέντες,[…] τὸ δὲ πάντων λαμπρότερον […], ἐξ ἀσεβῶν καὶ ἀπίστων εὐσεβεῖς καὶ πιστοί […]." Ioannes Mauropus, no. 183, 145.
22 Stephenson, Frontier, 91–93. Lefort, Rhetorique, 275–76, does not rule out that the imperial decision might even have been caused by a part of the army refusing to continue to fight the Pechenegs.
23 Kaldellis, Ethnography, 122–123. Indeed Lefort, Rhetorique, 302 saw the two orations in the context of a debate whether the Pechenegs should be integrated into the empire or not, which apparently took place at court and in the army. The dismissal of a part of the western army and a revolt among the soldiers after the events might have been connected to these differing positions. The latter was probably a further reason for Mauropus to omit the sections on the campaign in the winter 1046/7, in order to maintain silence on the revolt.

make things worse, a mutiny among the Byzantine troops complicated the situation further and made it even more difficult to sell the campaign and its results as a success.[24] In the end, the orator had to restructure his whole speech and decided to omit the section on the Pecheneg campaign completely; the concept of the merciful victor and the Pechenegs' transformation (=integration) had been discredited by the course of events.[25]

This is a rare case where one can actually observe how rhetorical strategies were selected and discarded according to the need of the situation. It seems, though, that the argumentative strategy Mauropus had originally aimed for was not uncommon in the courtly discourse on dealings with the Pechenegs. About 30 years later, the historian Michael Attaleiates commented on the same events.[26] Provided with better knowledge of the aftermath than Mauropus, and pleading for a vigorous, foreign policy in his own time, it is no surprise that his verdict was harsh, and that for him Constantine IX's attempts to pacify the Pechenegs had been completely in vain.[27] To prove his point, Attaleiates not only provides a report of the subsequent Pecheneg incursions and warfare,[28] but he uses exactly the opposite argument Mauropus had applied in his vision of the "barbarians'" transformation. Trying to change the Pechenegs into obedient subjects would be, so Attaleiates, as effective as if one attempted to "make an Ethiopian white";[29] they were people "[…] who did not have the habit/condition of being subjugated/civilized"[30] – in other words, not transformable.

As Anthony Kaldellis already pointed out, it is impossible to decide whether Mauropus or Attaleiates personally believed the theories of the "barbarians'" transformability.[31] That Attaleiates knew about Mauropus' discarded plans for his speech is unlikely. His treatment of the Pecheneg wars of 1047–1053 indicates

---

24 Attaleiates, Skylitzes and Mauropus report it. For the sources see Cheynet, Pouvoir, Nr. 64, 59. The campaign took place early in 1047, the revolt manifested itself in the spring 1047. The reasons for this conflict between the emperor and parts of the army are unclear, but it might be related to differing opinions about how to deal with the Pechenegs.
25 The speech Mauropus probably held at the inauguration of the St. Georgios church can be found in Ioannes Mauropus, no. 181, 137–142. It concentrates on St. George and the new church, emphasizes the emperor's philanthropy and justice, but does not mention the Pecheneg campaign. For the different versions, see Lefort, Rhétorique, 265–267.
26 In his historiographical work, written in the late 1070s. Krallis, Attaleiates, xxx–xxxi.
27 For Attaleiates'general attitude towards aggressive foreign policy, see ibid., 143.
28 Michael Attaleiates, 26–28.
29 "'Ἔγνω δὲ τότε πρῶτον ὅτι μάτην Αἰθίοπα λευκᾶναί τις ἐπιβάλλεται […]." Michael Attaleiates, 25, 27–26, 1. For a discussion of this passage see Kaldellis, Ethnography, 122.
30 "[…] τῶν Ῥωμαίων ἀρκεσθέντων τούτοις καὶ χειροήθεις οἰηθέντων ποιῆσαι τοὺς μηδέποτε γενομένους μηδ' ἕξιν ἔχοντας γίνεσθαι." Michael Attaleiates, 25, 16–18.
31 With regard to the consequences of the conversion, one might discuss whether Mauropus really believed in what he wrote (as believed by Ivanov, Mission, 256), or merely followed political goals (as stated by Kaldellis, Ethnography, 122–123).

that he blamed the later defeats mainly on Constantine IX's initial hesitation and his attempts to avoid open war.[32] The fact, however, that he explicitly took up the concept of the Pechenegs' transformation and refuted it, suggests that the image of a merciful and transforming emperor was not uncommon in the discussion on the right policy towards the Pechenegs. Knowing the historic aftermath of 1047, Attaleiates therefore might have constructed his verdict on the events in explicit reference to this optimistic idea, responding to those defending Constantine's (and, possibly, any of his successors') integrationist policy towards the "barbarians" on the grounds of their own argument and imagery.

The premise for the (de-)construction of imperial victory over the Pechenegs was, therefore, not only the military encounters, but in large part stability in the aftermath. Both Mauropus and Attaleiates bolster their verdicts on the outcome of events with underlying ontological theories regarding the "barbarian" foes. These theories preconditioned the concepts of victory, by which to measure the ruler: whereas the "transformation-thesis" went hand in hand with the ideal of the merciful victor, the "in-transformability-thesis" promoted a different ideal of force-based superiority. Both theories, therefore, acted as discursive catalysts, facilitating arguments for differing political and military approaches and immediately affected the concepts of both "victors" and "vanquished".

Alexios I and the Pechenegs (1087)

A similar narrative pattern concerning a questionable imperial victory is found ca. 40 years later, when Theophylaktos of Ochrid composed an encomiastic speech praising Emperor Alexios I's dealings with a Pecheneg invasion in the late 1080s. After the situation south of the Danube had calmed down in the third quarter of the 11th century, the Pechenegs resumed their raids in the late 1070s, often collaborating with local rebellions in Byzantine territory. In the early reign of Alexios they posed a severe threat. The defeat at Dristra in 1087 proved that a military solution was not possible. Alexios repeatedly sent embassies in 1088 and

---

32 Michael Attaleiates, 25–27. That Attaleiates, 122–23 reports that on the Mantzikert campaign of Romanos IV 1071, he himself in his capacity as a military judge demanded an oath from "Scythian" = Pecheneg auxiliaries to prevent them from defecting to the enemy, which the latter apparently respected, is not necessarily a contradiction of his verdict on their obduracy, since, as he stresses here, he let them swear their own oaths, instead of applying Roman customs. See Krallis, Attaleiates, 191. Furthermore, as Kaldellis, Ethnography, 55 assumes, he had to safeguard his own role as the one who received the oath. More indicative is his statement in the same passage that the Byzantine troops in the field camp suspected the Pechenegs of defecting to the Turkish enemy who lead a life quite similar to their own.

1089, renouncing Byzantine territories between the Danube and the Balkan mountains to restore peace.³³

Around this time, Theophylaktos held a speech after one of these truces. It is not entirely clear which event he refers to. He reports that Alexios won over Cuman troops to repel a Pecheneg invasion. Aware of the new imperial strength, the Pechenegs sent an embassy to negotiate peace, returning many places previously conquered.³⁴ From Anna Komnene we know that in 1087 a Pecheneg embassy indeed proposed a truce, which Alexios rejected.³⁵ Thereafter the Pechenegs defeated the Byzantines in battle, but could not exploit the situation, since Cumans intercepted and defeated them. The emperor then sent two more embassies and negotiated short-lived truces in 1087/1088 and early 1089.³⁶

A situation where the Pechenegs sued for peace, which was then granted by the emperor, apparently never occurred. Of the various attempts to date the speech and connect it to one of the truces, the most convincing solution has been proposed by Malamut, arguing that the encomiast wrote in 1088 and combined the news of the failed Pecheneg embassy of 1087 with the truce asked for by Alexios in the winter of 1087/8. In this way he could present this last truce as a request made by the Pechenegs, presenting an emperor in far greater control of the situation than he really was.³⁷

Theophylaktos is very concerned to present the peace as a result of Byzantine military superiority – a daring argument, considering the very recent catastrophe at Dristra:

> "If you [Alexios] had crowned the war with dangers, the army's hard work and rivers of blood, this would be a great deed [...]. But now, with this work, [it] by far surpasses the astonishment, that the enemies did not [even] wait for the experience [of military confrontation], but, condemning themselves, they took the right decision [and sued for peace]."³⁸

---

33 For the historical background see Malamut, Petchénègues, 132–138; Meško, Pecheneg Groups, 200–203; Stephenson, Frontier, 89–103.
34 Theophylaktos of Ochrid, no. 5, 219, 24–227, 15. For the term "Cuman" see Diaconu, Coumans, 9. The Cuman tribes were only loosely connected among each other. Vásáry, Cumans, 7; Malingoudis, Nachrichten, 102–103.
35 Anna Komnene, Alexias, VII.2.8.
36 Gautier in Theophylaktos of Ochrid, 93–130 and Malamut, Petchénègues, 135–141. I follow their chronology. Other chronologies set some dates slightly later, such as Vasil'evskij, Византия, 116–165; 243–332 and Diaconu, Petchénègues, 117–120; 130–133, dating Theophylaktos' speech to 1090 and connect it to a peace treaty in 1089.
37 Malamut, Petchénègues, 138–139. See also Gautier, in Theophylaktos of Ochrid, 77 and Kolia-Dermitzaki, ἐμπόλεμο, 218–219 who support the argument that Theophylaktos kept his speech deliberately unclear to disguise the fact that Alexios I requested negotiations with the Pechenegs, partly in fear of their alliance with the Cumans.
38 "καίτοι κἂν εἰ κινδύνοις καὶ στρατοῦ πόνῳ καὶ ῥείθροις αἱμάτων ἐστεφανώσω τὸν πόλεμον μέγα τε ἂν ἦν τὸ ἔργον [...]. νῦν δὲ πολλῷ πλείονι τοῦ θαύματος τῷ ἔργῳ περίεστιν ὅτι μηδὲ τὴν πεῖραν

Similar to Mauropus' speech, however, Theophylaktos' main emphasis lies on imperial mercy: while "another would have satisfied the beast of his wrath with Scythian blood"[39], Alexios granted the Pechenegs' request for peace immediately.[40] As in the case of Constantine IX, the image of Alexios as a deliberately merciful victor should evoke serious doubts. In fact, the overall historic evidence proves that the military situation was anything but favorable for the Byzantines. Not even the encomiast Theophylact can deny that the negotiations were tough and the Pechenegs obviously in a position to pose their own claims.[41] Again, the emperor's behavior seems guided by pragmatic rather than ideological motives.

To prevent the image of the merciful victor reverting into proof of imperial weakness, Theophylact therefore added another motif to his narrative: Alexios was now the brilliant mediator who "in his intercourse with the barbarians overreached everyone, both philosophers and orators," and brought them to "confess that they desired peace." In this way, the supplicant [Alexios] is transformed into the one who grants peace, and "a quarrelsome barbarian bows before the supremacy of your virtue and a savage nature is defeated by the divine character of the emperor". They are transformed from "barbarians" and "Scythians" into humans.[42]

In comparison, Theophylaktos' argumentative strategy seems very close to that Mauropus used about forty years before; as in 1047, an encomiast had to deal with a situation where the emperor was not able to achieve a definite military or political solution to the Pecheneg problem. Obligated to the *topos* of imperial victory, he applies a similar narrative pattern and integrates similar conceptual components to describe the "victor" and his "vanquished" foes:

- the emperor is presented as the active protagonist of both the victory and the ensuing negotiations;

ἀνέμειναν οἱ πολέμιοι, ἀλλ' ἑαυτῶν καταγνόντες, δικαίαν ψῆφον ἐξήνεγκαν [...]." Theophylaktos of Ochrid, 225, 18–23.
39 "[...] αἵμασι σκυθικῶν εὐωχῆσαι τοῦ θυμοῦ τὸ θηρίον·" Ibid., 27–28.
40 For Anna Komnenes emphasis of Alexios' mercy in her historiographical work see Laiou, Just War, 25. See ibid., 30 for Anna attributing the wish to convert Turks and Pechenegs to Alexios, a fact that is not explicitly mentioned by Theophylaktos here (he mentions Alexios' conversions of Turks later in the speech, though), but which fits in with the general missionary tendency propagated by the encomiasts. For this see also Ivanov, Mission, 252 who remarks that despite this image there is a lack of evidence "that Alexios actually sent missionaries to any independent barbarians."
41 Theophylaktos of Ochrid, 223, l. 21–225, l. 12.
42 "ὁ δὲ καὶ ἄλλως μὲν ἐν ταῖς πρὸς βαρβάρους ὁμιλίαις πάντας ἀποκρύπτει καὶ φιλοσόφους καὶ ῥήτορας [...] μεγαλοφροσύνης τε τὴν διάλεξιν ἐμπιπλῶν καὶ βασιλικοὺς τοὺς λόγους καὶ ἀνατεταμένους ποιούμενος. [...] ὡμολόγησαν ὡς διψῶσι τῆς εἰρήνης, [...]. οὕτως ἄρα συγχωρεῖ καὶ φιλόνεικος βάρβαρος τῷ τῆς ἀρετῆς ὑπερέχοντι καὶ νικᾷ θηριώδη φύσιν βασιλικὴ θειότης.[...] καὶ τοῦτό γε μόνον ἐκεῖνοι, οὐ βάρβαροι, οὐδὲ Σκῦθαι, [...]." Theophylaktos of Ochrid, 223, l. 20-225, l. 13; 24–25.

- the request for peace comes from the enemies, the emperor's mercy is the prerequisite for a truce;
- the emperor's negotiation position is characterized by military superiority and divine intercession (divine vision / divinely inspired charisma);
- the permanence and sustainability of the arrangement is backed by an ontological transformation of the "barbarian" nature.

As with Mauropus, it is possible to compare the argumentative strategy adopted by Theophylact with later historiography, and again, it appears that the orator's narrative pattern of peace and transformations was overturned. That Alexios I's arrangement with the Pechenegs was not sustainable becomes clear from Anna Komnene's historiographical report. She writes that soon after the truce of 1087/8, when Alexios' Cuman allies had left, the Pechenegs "became insolent [again] and, having broken the truce, they returned to their prior inhumanity, plundering the nearby towns and countryside."[43] A final victory over the Pechenegs would not be achieved before the decisive battle at Lebunion in 1091.[44]

As in the case of Mauropus and Attaleiates, historiography indirectly responded to the version presented in the propaganda and reversed the argument of the "barbarian" transformation. The Pechenegs were, as Anna argues "inconstant, like all barbarians, and [by nature] not inclined to keep treaties".[45] They resumed their aggression, so that Alexios I, who did not have enough troops at his disposal to face the threat, had to "take the lesser evil" and ask for a new truce.[46] It seems unlikely that Anna aimed for criticism of her father's policy towards the "barbarians". Writing in the 12th c., it cannot be ruled out that she implicitly criticized her brother John II who, after soundly defeating the Pechenegs in 1122, had settled them in the empire.[47] Her argument could also be understood as apologetic, demonstrating and explaining her father's limited options when facing an enemy that could not be reasoned with. In this sense her goal was similar to that of Theophylaktos: to detach the discussion concerning the failure to ensure a sustainable truce with the Pechenegs from the unfavorable military and political situation and re-connect it to the ontological nature of the "barbarians".

---

43 "τοῦτο θάρσος τοῖς Σκύθαις ἐνέλαβε, καὶ παρασπονδήσαντες τῆς προτέρας ἀπανθρωπίας εἴχοντο ληιζόμενοι τὰς παρακειμένας πόλεις καὶ χώρας." Anna Komnene, Alexias, VII.6.3, 218, 79–219, 81.
44 Stephenson, Frontier, 103.
45 "ἀστατεῖ γὰρ ὡς ἐπίπαν ἅπαν τὸ βάρβαρον καὶ σπονδὰς φυλάττειν οὐ πέφυκε." Anna Komnene, Alexias, VII.6.3, 219, 81–82.
46 Ibid., VII.5.5, 219, 97–99.
47 For John II's settlement of the Pechenegs see Ioannes Kinnamos, Epitome, I,8. I thank Roman Shliakhtin (Mainz) for pointing out this possibility.

Again, the policies recommended and the underlying concept of imperial victory depend on the chronological relation to the events. Theophylaktos wrote directly after Alexios' negotiations. His construction of imperial victory and the particular value of mercy within this concept were premised on the theory (or hope!) that the enemies could be influenced permanently by fear and argument. Anna, by contrast, knew about the unsuccessful aftermath, but also about the final victory over the Pechenegs in 1091. It was conceivably this knowledge that made her choose the contrasting theory of the unchanging Pechenegs, drop the concept of imperial mercy, and thus legitimize Alexios' continuation of warfare.[48] This latter point is of particular importance since there are indications that Alexios indeed had to convince the aristocracy who originated from Asia Minor of his military policy in the Balkans.[49] Anna's argument of the "incorrigible" Pechenegs justified his position that a military solution was the only way to end the threat – a good example of how hindsight could change argumentative patterns.[50]

Manuel I and the Turks

Under Komnenian rulers, the imperial image was dominated by the virtue of personal bravery on the battlefield. Alexios I, too, defined his position by personal leadership of the army. The encomiastic texts that are first available in large numbers from the time of John II and continue under Manuel I present countless examples of the warrior-emperor curbing his foes and "hunting" them like game. The image of the victor is very direct and active, closely tied to personal leadership and deeds in battle.[51]

Unimpressed by imperial self-representation, the political and military situation remained ambiguous as always. The eastern border in Asia Minor was particularly complicated: here the empire faced political entities such as the

---

48 This argument is very similar to that presented by Eustathios of Thessaloniki with regard to Isaakios II's Cuman policy in the 1190s. See below, 70–72.
49 See Cheynet, Pouvoir, 362; 367 who remarks that many attempted rebellions against Alexios were undertaken in the context of his Balkan campaigns by officers originating from Asia Minor.
50 It might be that Anna took up an argument found in Alexios' own era, but this cannot be proven. In this context, see Buckley, Alexiad, 152, who interprets with greater emphasis the presentation of the "barbarians'" unchangeable nature as legitimation of "the genocidal outcome" of the war against them.
51 See above, p. 55, n. 3. This goes so far that even military defeats are played down in pro-imperial historiography by focusing on heroic acts of individual protagonists, among them the emperor himself. See for example Anna Komnene, Alexias, VII. 3.8–10 about the defeat at Dristra in 1087.

Seljuk sultanate in central Anatolia, the Danishmendid emirs in the Pontos region and several principalities in Northern Syria, as well as constant border warfare with semi-nomadic Turkoman groups. These were mostly outside the control of any political authority on either side of the border zone, which made long-term agreements in that region even more difficult to maintain.[52]

The 1170s, where the next case study is set, saw intensive warfare at the border with the Seljuk sultanate. The sources report several campaigns at the beginning of the decade to repel Turkic raids into Byzantine territory.[53] In 1175 Manuel I personally lead an extensive campaign to the Anatolian plateau, rebuilding fortresses, repelling groups of semi-nomad Turks further into the hinterland and preparing a major attack on the Seljuk capital Ikonion for the following year.[54] It is probably this campaign to which the following encomium by Eustathios, the court orator and archbishop of Thessalonike, refers.

Under the impression of a successful advance towards Dorylaion, Eustathios presents Manuel as an almost eschatological savior who completes his father's and grandfather's policy of re-conquest. Through his military operations he had not only repelled aggressive and savage enemies who "had rejoiced in the blood of Christians" and were now partly "flung away" or had ceased to exist at all. "The fear of the emperor" changed the (remaining) Turks' very nature, transformed them "in a most divine manner [...] from beasts to humans," so that they would turn their swords into ploughs and switch to a sedentary and peaceful lifestyle.[55]

Byzantine-Seljuk relations were complex, as was the way Byzantines perceived and labeled their eastern neighbors. Eustathios speaks of "Persai," a label that panegyrists in particular used for the Anatolian Turks from the time of Ioannes II onwards. Although this label was often applied to "elite figures of authority" in the Seljuk state,[56] Eustathios' main focus here clearly lay on the semi-nomadic

---

52 Lilie, Turkish States, 37–39; 48–49.
53 Niketas Choniates, Historia, Manuel Komnenos, Γ', 124–125; Ioannes Kinnamos, Epitome, VI, 288–292.
54 A further principal reason for the emperor's campaign was the expansion of the Seljuk sultanate at the expense of the Danishmendid territories and thus a shift in the balance of power in Asia Minor. Korobeinikov, Raiders, 715–716.
55 "οὕτω φόβου παντὸς ἡμᾶς ἀπέλυσας, καὶ τὴν ἄλλως θηροτρόφον διὰ τοὺς θῆρας τοὺς ἐξ Ἰσμαὴλ ἀνθρώπων ἔπλησας· εἶπεν ἄν τις λύκους ἐκείνους [...] τοῖς τῶν Χριστιανῶν αἵμασι χαίροντας [...]. Νῦν δὲ οὐ μόνον ἀπεσφενδόνηνται, ἀλλὰ καὶ οἱ μὲν οὐδὲ εἰσὶν ἔτι, οἱ δὲ τοῦ εἶναι λύκοι καὶ ἐξελάθοντο, [...]. φόβος βασιλικὸς [...], οὐκ ἐξ ἀνθρώπων εἰς θῆρας, ἀλλ' ἐξ ἐκείνων εἰς τούτους μεταβιβάσας θειότατα." Eustathios of Thessaloniki, Opera minora, no. 13, 207, 73–83 (trans. Stone, Eustathios, 85–86). For the motive of the plough, see ibd., 205, 1–5. See also Ioannes Kinnamos, Epitome, I, 9 on the victory of John II over the Seljuks in 1124, which was followed by a sedentary lifestyle and conversion to Christianity.
56 Shliakhtin, Huns, 317. For the development of the term "Persai" as well as the complementary terms "Turks" and "Hagarenes" see ibid., 69–71. That in the 12th c. the term "Persai", however, also applied to the Turks of Anatolia in general (thus including the semi-nomadic elements)

groups in the border zones.[57] Their presence around Dorylaion and the frequent attacks made on the Byzantine army by their light cavalry left a deep impression on the Byzantines. It is mainly to this group that Eustathios refers when he speaks of transformation.[58]

The encomiast closely follows the model of the emperor transforming "barbarian" violence into social behavior.[59] His explicit allusions to Isaiah 2.4 and Micha 4.3 place this in the context of an eschatological state of peace in the land under the emperor's control.[60] As in the other encomiastic examples discussed here, the emperor's success is presented as a result of the fear caused by his military victories, and divine support: "These people have tested you [Manuel I], [...] a warrior, always victorious, [...], strong in everything in the God who empowers you."[61]

Unlike the previous examples, the elements of imperial mercy and direct divine intercession are not found; Eustathios displays the utmost confidence that a military solution would make it possible to "tame the bestial nature [of the Turks]," "restrain their ungovernable nature," force them into submission or drive them out – an optimism that was also reflected in the official campaign reports issued by the emperor's staff.[62] This optimism also influences how Eustathios' treats the results of Manuel's "victory," following the usual encomiastic pattern for imperial agreements with semi-nomads. He presents a seemingly defeated enemy as a permanent and sustainable solution, and resorts to the well-known argument of the "barbarians'" ontological transformation, "from beasts to humans."

---

becomes clear from the analysis by Durak, Defining, 76–77 who lists examples from historians such as Ioannes Kinnamos and Niketas Choniates. When the need occurred, "Tourkoi" and "Persai" were used to differentiate semi-nomadic groups from the regular Seljuk armies. See below, note 59.

57 Also Niketas Choniates, Historia, Manuel Komnenos, Ϛ', 177, 60 uses the term "Persai" for Nomads around Dorylaion.
58 Reported also in Ioannes Kinnamos, Epitome, VII, 295.
59 The same motif of the "Scythian" turning his sword into a plough appears in Themistios, Orationes, no. 16, 211b concerning a peace treaty between Emperor Theodosios I (or his general Saturninus) and the Goths, followed by the latter being settled on Byzantine territory. For more examples see Mathisen, Behavior, 33.
60 Eustathios of Thessaloniki, Opera minora, no. 13, 205, 95–5.
61 "τοιούτου πεπείρανταί σου μαχητοῦ νικῶντος ἀεί, [...] πάντα ἰσχύοντος ἐν τῷ ἐνδυναμοῦντί σε θεῷ." Eustathios of Thessaloniki, Opera minora., no. 13, 209, 27–29 (Translation by Stone, Eustathios, 89).
62 "[...] ἡ θηριωδία ἐτιθασσεύθη [...] καὶ ἀναχαιτίζων οὕτων αὐτοῖς τὸ ἀκάθεκτον·" Ibid., 205, 1 and 206, 36–37 (Translation by Stone, Eustathios, 81 and 83). For the bold propaganda on this campaign see Manuels's letter to king Henry I of England, preserved in Roger of Howden, Chronica, 102–104.

Supporting an ongoing campaign, Eustathios' statements are to be seen as prospective, a vision of what could, or should be.⁶³ As with Mauropus and Theophylaktos, his argument is to be understood out of a process whose final result was yet to be discovered. Later historiographical evidence, however, indicates that the military situation turned out not to be as definite as the encomiast would have made his audience believe. The war with the Sultanate and the Turkish raids continued in the same year; the major campaign in the following year (1176) ended prematurely in severe defeat at Myriokephalon. Writing with hindsight on the events, the historiographer Niketas Choniates therefore depicts the situation on the eastern front quite differently from Eustathios. In his opinion, the prime responsibility for the permanent border warfare in the 1170s lay with the Seljuk Sultan Qiliğ Arslan II, whom he describes as the typical "barbarian." He accuses him of notoriously breaking treaties, waging unjust wars and, "in a barbarian manner, changing his mind according to the situation."⁶⁴ The Byzantine reaction to these threats is depicted as a combination of military pressure and diplomatic incentive:

> "But he [Manuel I] blocked the passages for him [the Sultan] and piled up the indestructible wall of the army to make the flood flow back, or he lulled [him, a poisonous dragon] to sleep, so that he peacefully closed his eyelids, by the attractive force of seducing gold."⁶⁵

This image of the "tamed" sultan is reminiscent of Eustathios' "transformation" of the Turks. In contrast to Eustathios, however, Niketas makes it clear that these efforts were only temporary. In the end, he completely reverses the image, stating that the policy of appeasement by treaties, tributes and demonstrations of force did not produce sustainable results. Notwithstanding any agreements, the sultan continued to relapse into his usual "untrustworthy" and "malicious" behavior, and the spiral of raiding and campaigning continued.⁶⁶ Manuel even "stirred up the sleeping beast" by his own aggressive behavior. Neither "truces, nor armistices, regulating the cessation of the fighting and negotiations by embassies prevented the mutual incursions and blockades, [...]."⁶⁷

---

63 Kaldellis, Ethnography, 123 argues similarly with regard to Mauropus.
64 "[...] βαρβαρικῶς μεταλλοιούμενος τῷ καιρῷ [...]." Niketas Choniates, Historia, Manuel Komnenos, Γ', 123, 71.
65 "ὁ δὲ περιεφράγμου τούτῳ τὰς διεξόδους καὶ εἰς ἀνάρρουν τὸ ῥεῦμα ὑπανεστοίβαζε θριγγίῳ ἀρραγεῖ στρατοπέδων, ἢ ὁλκῇ χρυσίου ἐφολκοῦ κατεκοίμιζε πρὸς εἰρήνευ τὸ τούτου βλέφαρον [...]." Ibid., 83–84.
66 Niketas Choniates, Historia, Manuel Komnenos, Γ', 124, 9–13.
67 "τὰ πλεῖστα μέντοι οὐδ' αὐτὸς εἴα τὸν Περσάρχην καθεύδειν , ἀλλ' ὅσα καὶ θῆρα ὠμηστὴν ἐφυπνώττοντα ἐξηγρίαινεν ὑπονύσσων καὶ τοῦ κοίτου ἀνίστη καὶ πρὸς μάχην ἠρέθιζεν. ἀτὰρ οὐδ' ἀνακωχαὶ πολέμων, οὐδ' ἐκεχειρίαι τῶν ἀντιτάξεων σπονδαί τε καὶ ξυνθῆκαι καὶ διακηρυκεύματα πρέσβεων ἀπεῖργον τὰς κατ' ἀλλήλων ἐπελεύσεις καὶ ἀπετείχιζον, [...]." Ibid., 175, 30–35.

In contrast to Eustathios who actively supported an ongoing campaign, Choniates explained and evaluated the failure to contain Turkish incursions in Asia Minor. His blame for the unsolvable situation is much more evenly distributed. While Manuel is criticized for worsening the situation, the continuous warfare is presented as the unavoidable result of Qiliğ Arslan's unchanged nature. It is important to mention that the Seljuk sultans were not generally connected to "barbarian" nomadism, but often conceptualized as respectable figures of authority.[68] In the context of the discussion of the border warfare, however, it seems that Choniates deliberately transfers the concept of the raiding "barbarian nomad" to the Sultan who, in his very nature, embodied the unsolvable situation in Asia Minor's frontier zone.

This "ontological" cause could be read as an excuse for Manuel's failed diplomacy, or as criticism of the emperor's failure to deal with the incursions. Born in the frontier town of Chonai (mod. Honaz), Choniates must have been sensitive about the destruction in his home region.[69] His analysis of Manuel's policy in the east is complex, containing both appreciation and strong criticism of individual measures.[70] In his comments on the complicated dealings in the border zone, he seems to draw from the encomiastic repertoire. The motive of the "beastly" sultan being "lulled to sleep" by the emperor is especially prominent. Being an encomiast himself, Choniates was familiar with the strategy of praising imperial diplomacy. His reversal of the image by presenting an obdurate sultan, on the other hand, strongly resembles the skepticism of Attaleiates and Anna Komnene in their verdicts on the contractual solutions with the Pechenegs. Even though it is impossible to tell whether Choniates knew Eustathios' optimistic vision of the "taming" emperor, his reference to the obdurate "barbarian way" seems to follow a broader, ongoing discursive tradition which framed the discussions on imperial border policies in Asia Minor and in the Balkans.

---

68 Shliakhtin, Huns, 177–178.
69 For Choniates' origin from Asia Minor and his praise for Chonai see Simpson, Niketas, 11–12, for his "personal grievances" concerning the loss of territory to the Turks, and criticism of Manuel's eastern policy, culminating in the description of the battle of Myriokephalon see ibid., 324–327.
70 See also Choniates' report of a speech by Louis VII of France to his fellow crusaders in 1147, accusing Manuel of not acting properly against the Turks up to then. Niketas Choniates, Historia, Manuel Komnenos, Α', 70, 26–30 and his criticism the inactivity of former governments for having caused the loss of parts of Asia Minor. Ibid., Manuel Komnenos, Β', 72, 82–85. On the other hand, he praises Manuel for fortifying the theme of Neokastra. See Niketas Choniates, Historia, Manuel Komnenos, Δ', 150.

Isaac II and the Cumans

The last case study is a later encomium by Eustathios of Thessalonike from spring 1191, praising emperor Isaac II's dealings with Cumans.[71] The oration was delivered in the fortified town Philippopolis that lay at the center of Cuman incursions deep into Byzantine territory. The text is far less enthusiastic than the depiction of Manuel I as the victor over the Turks. In a lengthy passage, Eustathios describes the Cumans as typical barbarian nomads, "not a steadfast people, nor a stationary one, not acquainted with settling down and, therefore, also not political."[72]

The majority of the Cumans lived as semi-nomads north of the Danube, although to its south there might have been some permanent settlements as well.[73] During the whole 12th century, groups organized raids into Byzantine territory. Especially in the course of the Bulgar rebellion in 1185 they played a crucial role as the rebels' military allies, contributing to the Byzantine loss of control over large regions south of the Danube.[74] Isaac attempted several campaigns into the Bulgarian lands to suppress the rebellion, but his armies faced a number of defeats and rebellions by leading generals.[75] In 1191 Isaac went to Philippopolis, leading sorties against Cumans in the region. In this situation, Eustathios held his "improvised oration" (αὐτοσχέδιος λαλιά) in front of the emperor, his entourage, generals and aristocracy.

Despite the former setbacks, and maybe inspired by some successful campaigning in 1191, Eustathios starts with the usual presentation of the emperor as a military victor. As in the passage on Manuel as the vanquisher of the Turks, he refers to recent victories: a defeat of the Serbs and the liberation of the land from the "Alemannic plague," the crusaders under Frederick I Barbarossa.[76] In view of this superiority, what else, Eustathios asks, could the Cumans do than sue for peace, "although they are immensely savage, due to their ethnic character"?[77]

---

71 For the dating in, probably April,1191 see Schönauer in Eustathios of Thessaloniki, Quadragesima, 13*.
72 "ἔθνος αὐτοὶ οὐ στάσιμον, οὐ μόνιμον, οὐ κατοικεῖν ἐπιστάμενον, δι' αὐτὸ δὲ οὐδὲ πολιτικόν·" Eustathios of Thessaloniki, Opuscula, no. 7, col. 44a, 21–23.
73 Spinei, Migrations, vol. 2, 329–335.
74 For the incursions in the 12th c. and for Cumans that were settled in Byzantine territory see ibid., 388–395. For their role during the Vlacho-Bulgarian Rebellion and in the second Bulgarian empire see Nikolov, Cumani Bellatores, 223–229.
75 For the course of the rebellion between its outbreak and 1191 see Ritter, Rebellion, 177–202.
76 Eustathios of Thessaloniki, Opuscula, col. 43b, l. 92–44a, l. 4. It is not entirely clear if the battle at the Morava is meant here, or if the speech refers to another victory. Whereas the traditional dating of the battle is 1190 (see, for example Jireček, Serben, vol. 1, 273 and Fine, Balkans, 26), Ritter, Rebellion, 201 dates it to late 1191. In this case, Eustathios might refer to another, minor success against the Serbs. Ritter, Rebellion, 200–202.
77 "τί οὐκ ἂν ποιήσαιεν, ἢ πάντως πραγματεύσονται σώζεσθαι καὶ αὐτοί, λόγῳ μὲν τοῦ κατ' ἔθνος ἤθους δεινῶς ἐκθηριούμενοι, [...];" Eustathios of Thessaloniki, Opuscula, col. 44a, 9–12.

Apparently, this is as far as Eustathios' praise could go. Having announced an agreement between Isaac and the Cumans, with the latter being the pleading party, one would now expect the image of the "barbarian nomads'" permanent transformation. Eustathios indeed tends in that direction, although he presents a state that required constant maintenance by imperial force: the Cumans "are now forced to abate from the savageness by fear of the emperor's hand, even though they are not entirely tamed."[78] That this state is at best temporary becomes clear from his further statement that the Cumans would again slip through the emperor's hands when he tries to grasp them. Even if Isaac can bring them to reason by force and change their way of life, they would rise up again after a short time, since also "wild beasts do not abate from the utmost evil, maltreating God's flock."[79]

If Isaac really negotiated with the Cumans, as Eustathios' speech implies, these talks did not take place with an emperor in full control. His prior sorties from Philippopolis show that he was not capable of containing the incursions of the Cumans, who stood deep in Byzantine territory. Eustathios nevertheless depicts Isaac as a military victor. His application of standard imagery and references to recent successes against Serbs and Germans would not have caused too much frowning among the audience, even in an unfavorable military situation. This practice of depicting the emperor was a well-understood part of the imperial image.

The real and more delicate issue addressed here, however, was Isaac's capacity to negotiate a long-term solution with the Cumans. For Eustathios it was, even in the context of an encomium, impossible to claim that a sustainable agreement had been achieved. The audience in Philippopolis included many of Isaac's generals, who were familiar with the situation and would not be convinced. Resentment against the emperor was increasing among the aristocratic officers, many of whom had properties in the provinces threatened by ongoing warfare.[80]

As a consequence, Eustathios argues in evident contradiction to his passage on Manuel I and the Turks. Having started with the usual image of the victorious but merciful emperor who transforms the "barbarians," he then reverses the argument and presents the latter's immutable nature as the reason that excludes any permanent solution. Apart from releasing the emperor from the responsibility of negotiating a sustainable solution, the maneuver might also have aimed to support the aggressive policy towards the Vlachs, Bulgars and Cumans, a policy that after the Byzantine defeat at Berrhoia in 1190 might have lost popularity among parts of

---

78 "[…] φόβῳ δὲ τῆς βασιλικῆς χειρός, εἰ καὶ μὴ τέλεον τιθασσευόμενοι, ἀλλ' οὖν ὑφιέντες τῆς ἀγριότητος οὐ καθ' ἑκούσιον;" Eustathios of Thessaloniki, Opuscula, col. 44a, 12–14.
79 "Οὔτε γὰρ τῷ ἀρχεκάκῳ ἐπιλείψουσι θῆρες ἄγριοι τοῖς τοῦ θεοῦ λυμαινόμενοι ποιμνίοις, […]." Ibid., col. 44b, 69–70.
80 When Isaakios II. was deposed and blinded on campaign in 1195, all those military officers reported by the sources as participants of the conspiracy were aristocrats with properties in the western provinces. Cheynet, Pouvoir, 440–441.

the Byzantine elite.⁸¹ In this sense, Eustathios argues analogously to Niketas Choniates, Michael Attaleiates and Anna Komnene with the impossibility of coming to terms with the "barbarians." In order to support the emperor's ongoing military policy, he ignored the usual encomiastic pattern of victory and transformation and highlighted the threat of the enemy's unchangeable ways.

Discussion

When military operations did not lead to sustainable results and when it was uncertain whether agreements with seemingly defeated enemies would last for long, it was the task of rhetoric to harmonize the traditional ideal of imperial victory with diverging realities. When it came to the elusive, semi-nomadic groups that threatened Byzantium's border zones in the 11th and 12th centuries, the emperors often failed to achieve definite victories that would lead to stability and peace. In these contexts, the encomiasts could fall back on a standard narrative scheme that fostered the core characteristics of the traditional ideal of imperial victory and replaced ambiguity with certainty.

The examples presented show how encomiasts insistently depicted the emperor as the undisputed military victor, independent of the factual outcome of the conflict and his presence on the battlefield. Ioannes Mauropus, who focused on the Pechenegs' integration and conversion, did not fail to highlight the "great massacre" that preceded and preconditioned the peace.⁸² Theophylaktos, although praising the emperor's diplomacy, clearly emphasized his ability to end the war in "rivers of blood", bluntly disguising the fact that it was Alexios I who had requested negotiations. Eustathios set Isaac II's talks with the Cumans in the context of former imperial victories, avoiding references to the current situation and maintaining that the enemies had initiated the peace negotiations.

The emperor's military and diplomatic superiority belonged to a "political memory" that had been cultivated for centuries and gave fundamental legitimation to the sociopolitical order. The ideal was bound to the concept underlying the imperial office and had to be maintained, independent of concrete situations and individuals.⁸³ The narrative tools revolving around imperial vic-

---

81 In fact, after his success in overturning his brother, Alexios III attempted to make peace with the Bulgars. Niketas Choniates, Historia, Alexios Angelos, A', 465, 18–22. Other parts might have aimed for a continuation of the war by Alexios. Ibid., 459, 57–67.
82 When Alexander Kazhdan, Mauropous, 1319b characterizes his social attitude as "antimilitaristic," this does not mean that he could avoid the traditional registers of imperial encomia.
83 The concept of political memory is understood as a form of communicative memory which is formed and maintained in the public space (although, in the Byzantine case, we have to

tory and "barbarian" transformation were central to this end, which explains their stability in the encomiastic discourse over time. The applicability of these tools had limits, though. Both Ioannes Mauropus and Theophylaktos of Ochrid had to bolster their constructions of imperial victory and transformation with other registers of the imperial ideal: divine aid, charisma, mercy.

It would be far-fetched to assume from these testimonies alone that mercy and divine aid were more typical elements of the 11th century imperial ideal than of the 12th century.[84] Manuel I, too, was praised for his "bloodless" victories and peaceful solutions, although the heroic warrior imagery and the idealization of force clearly dominated the encomia praising him and his father John II.[85] In the texts at hand, however, the choice and application of the individual registers of the imperial image seems more closely tied to the constraints of concrete political and military situations than to general ideological preferences.

In this context, Mauropus' withdrawal of his speech on the Pechenegs indicates that the course of events made maintaining the ideal of the merciful victor entirely impossible and non-communication preferable. The limits of the encomiastic ideal also manifest themselves in Eustathios' Cuman speech, whose audience at Philippopolis was well aware of the gloomy military situation in 1191. His resort to the theory of the enemy's unchangeable nature forms a counterpart to the usual encomiastic argument of the enemies' surrender and transformation. As seen, this approach appears much more often outside encomiastic texts, in political comments by Anna Komnene, Michael Attaleiates and Niketas Choniates.

Despite the essential importance of military strength in encomiastic descriptions, it is characteristic that in the setting of border warfare, military success alone was not enough to define imperial victory. Ample attention is dedicated to the question whether the results of the campaigns and the negotiations were sustainable. In this regard, all texts apply a common strategy, connecting the ideal of victory with the ontological nature of the foes and whether these could be transformed to sedentary, peaceful and law-abiding civilized humans.

This treatment indicates that semi-nomadic groups represented a particular sub-category among the broader concept of "barbarians." There are only rare instances where the motive of transformation was applied to any other than (half-) nomadic groups. Although Germans, French and Normans were also

---

consider the elite-circles in Constantinople as the most important group). Politically guided, a common memory of the past is maintained, that represents ideals of the present and functions as a source for the legitimation of the political order. See König, Gedächtnis, 115–121.

84 Even Kazhdan, Aristocracy, 46, who emphasizes warrior heroism in the 12th c. imperial image, states that in general, Theophylact "puts military prowess at the top of his list of virtues for the rulers."

85 "Manganeios" Prodromos, ed. Rácz, 25; Michael Rhetor, 137. Magdalino, Empire, 419 emphasizes the militaristic attitude in the Komnenian imperial representation.

considered violent, greedy and untrustworthy "barbarians", military encounters with them are normally described "merely" in terms of their immediate defeat, without extensive discussions about the stability of the relations afterwards.[86]

The idea of an ontological transformation, by contrast, concentrates on Pechenegs, Cumans and Turkmen who had a mobile lifestyle, caused conflicts with the sedentary groups of the population and, in contrast to the "barbarians" from the west, were constantly present in the Byzantine border territories.[87] With regard to their capacity to strike suddenly at different places and then "slip through the emperor's hands",[88] one might speak of asymmetric warfare, even though they proved their value in open battle as well.[89] On a political and diplomatic level, too, the groups encountered by the Byzantines in the border zones proved to be challenging, and their organization in many independent groups made it difficult to find authorities to conclude truces and treaties with.

Despite the binary distinction between *Rhōmaioi* and *Barbaroi*, it thus appears that the specific situation of border warfare required sub-categories.[90] In the cases discussed here, the particular manner of moving, fighting and organization, as perceived by the Byzantine observers, made Pechenegs, Cumans and Anatolian Turks form a common group, despite their differences in other respects. Most indicative are the statements by Michael Attaleiates about the "Scythian" (=Pecheneg) auxiliaries "whose life was so similar to that of the Turks (*Turkoi*)" and of Ioannes Kinnamos, who explicitly compares the lifestyle of the Turkmen ("Persians") to the Pechenegs ("Scythians").[91] This is of particular interest with regard to the multi-faceted image of the Seljuk Turks in other

---

[86] See Page, Being Byzantine, 45; Kislinger, Drachen, 396–403, both presenting numerous examples of Franks, Latins, Venetians, and Normans characterized as violent, greedy and breaking treatises. One exemption is a speech by "Manganeios" Prodromos, ed. Miller, vol. 2, 759:254–256 talking of Prince Raymond of Antioch being "tamed" by emperor Manuel I. from a dragon to a puppy. The focus here, however, is on the derogatory aspect of Raymond's humiliation, rather than on the transformation of his "barbarism."

[87] Semi-nomadic economy heavily depended on sedentary economy, which lead both to conflict (plunder-economy) and exchange between (semi-)nomads and sedentary population. Khazanov, Nomads, 28; 31.

[88] See above, p. 71.

[89] Definitions of asymmetric warfare are built on the assumption that the party using elusive tactics is also substantially inferior in their military strength and quality of soldiers (Mack, Big Nations, 194–195; Münkler, Wandel, 154–155 and Gliwa, Tatar, 192–194 on asymmetric Tatar warfare, 16th and 17th c.) One should, however, note that semi-nomads often also proved superior in open battle against their Byzantine adversaries. For the advantages of the semi-nomadic art of war, see Khazanov, Nomads, 31–32 and Irons, Capital, 64; 70–71.

[90] For these binary categories and further subcategories, see Page, Being Byzantine, 45–51.

[91] Michael Attaleiates, 122, 7–8. For common features in lifestyle and warfare, see Shukurov, Byzantine Turks, 29. See Anna Komnene, Alexias VII.5.6 on the similar language of Pechenegs and Cumans.

contexts, where they are depicted as respected followers of a "Persian" tradition, far from any semi-nomadic connotations.[92]

The discourse on border warfare called not only for a specific categorization of the enemies, but also for particular adaptions of the concept of imperial victory. The insecurity of the empire's border regions and the inability to settle conflicts required political comments to focus on the sustainability of the results achieved, no less than on the military encounters preceding them. Here, the discussion on the "barbarians'" transformability worked as a catalyst for discussions on the right border policy, as well as for the (de-)construction of imperial victory. It also defined the concept of the border zone itself, either as a space of gradual decrease of central control, or as a sphere where the integration and control of foreign elements still functioned, as it had since Antiquity.[93]

Particularly interesting is the comparison of arguments and their dynamics between encomiastic texts and later political comments: Ioannes Mauropus on Constantine IX, Theophylaktos on Alexios I and Eustathios on Manuel I. Composing their orations during or immediately after military operations, they dedicated many lines to presenting the total and permanent transformation of the foe that would lead to a change of their habits. Instead of addressing the political and military inconclusiveness of the situation, their arguments move the discussion to the very nature of the enemies, whose ontological change perpetuates the victories and their achievements. Eustathios in his Cuman speech is the only one who openly acknowledges the limited applicability of this encomiastic argument in view of differing realities. In Mauropus' case, discussion concerning the feasibility of integrating the Pechenegs apparently took place outside the encomiastic discourse; it seems that this eventually caused him to withdraw the text that extolled their transformation.

Skepticism about the image of the victorious, merciful and transforming emperor is more evident in later historiographic comments, which seem to draw on and then refute the arguments of encomiastic discourse. The comparisons of Michael Attaleiates' with Ioannes Mauropus, Anna Komnene with Theophylaktos of Ochrid, and Niketas Choniates with Eustathios of Thessalonike present a quasi-dialogue between encomiastic praise and historiographic evaluation; the idea of transformation is the common argumentative basis for evaluation of the imperial border policy.

---

[92] Shliakhtin, Huns, 317 shows with regard to the Anatolian Turks that Byzantine authors used different terms according to their respective goal, to convey different "messages about certain aspects of the described group", be it the elite and figures of authority ("Persians"), pastoralists and raiders ("Tourkoi"), or highlighting religious aspects ("Hagarenes").

[93] For the concept of the imperial border and the "barbarian discourse" as a semantic means to foster a clear border between the empire and the (inferior) world around it see Münkler, Imperien, 151–152.

Author/Orator	Ioannes Mauropus	Michael Attaleiates	Theophylaktos of Ochrid	Anna Komnene	Eustathios of Thessalonike	Niketas Choniates	Eustathios of Thessalonike
Emperor	Constantine IX	Constantine IX	Alexios I	Alexios I	Manuel I	Manuel I	Isaac II
events referred to	Campaign and subsequent truce/treaty with Pechenegs	Campaign and subsequent truce/treaty with Pechenegs	truces with Pechenegs	truces with Pechenegs	Manuel repels Seljuks/ Turkomans	Attempts to contain the Seljuk Sultan's aggression and Turkoman raids	Isaac II tries to repel Cuman raids
chronological distance to events	directly after the events	later	directly after the events	later	directly after the events	later	directly after the events
prerequisites for peace/ submission of the enemy	military victory + divine miracle + emperor's mercy	military victory + epidemic	military superiority + diplomacy + emperor's mercy	threat by Cumans and Pechenegs + diplomacy	military victory	military victories + diplomacy	military superiority
transformation of the "barbarians"	complete	impossible	complete	impossible	complete	temporary	impossible

It would be too simple to claim direct references between the various texts and authors. Mauropus' speech, for instance, was never publicly presented; it is highly unlikely that Attaleiates, who wrote much later, knew about it. Neither did Anna and Niketas necessarily know about the speeches by Theophylact and Eustathios. What awards the discussion a dialogue-like character is their general inclination to meet at the same argumentative level, when commenting on imperial border policies. Independent of their particular goals, authors and orators connected the discussion on its efficacy not (only) with the political and military ability of the protagonists, but also to the very nature of those they dealt with. As a consequence, postulates on the (im-)possibility of altering the enemies' "barbarism" were closely related to the question whether agreements concluded with such groups could be successful or were bound to fail.

Regardless of the question whether individual authors and orators personally believed in the theories of barbarian transformation,[94] the common basis proved to be a useful argument for all disputants, enabling them to safeguard questionable political agreements, or excuse, criticize and explain their failure. It seems reasonable to argue that the encomiasts who commented during or immediately after the events set the standards for the following discussion. That the historiographers discussed here refuted the argument of the "barbarian transformation" does not imply that they rejected the underlying theory in general. On the contrary, they frequently write about members of the Byzantine elite, such as Tatikios, Alexios I's half-Turk general, and Monastras who was half-Cuman (?), neither concealing their origins nor seeing these as hindrances for their integration.[95] Nor do we have to assume that the encomiasts believed in the one or the other theory, judging by their rhetoric arguments. The dynamic of the arguments is rather the result of anthropological knowledge and theory applied in a political discourse, which does not necessarily reveal the personal beliefs and concepts of those participating.

---

94 See Kaldellis, Ethnography, 9: "Ethnographic accounts [...] are too political, for they were designed to score points in internal Roman debates and not primarily to present objective information about foreigners." I also support his skepticism (ibid., 123) that the situative ideology presented in the encomia says little about the authors' personal beliefs and ideals and rather followed "what was demanded by the occasion."
95 For Tatikios, see Anna Komnene, Alexias, IV.4.3; Brand, Turkish Element, S. 3. For Monastras as a "*Mixobarbaros*" see Anna Komnene, Alexias, XI.2.9. Moravcsik, Byzantinoturcica, vol. 2, 192 and Brand, Turkish Element, 19 assume that Monastras was of (half-)Cuman descent, although other populations that also spoke or understood Turkic languages cannot be excluded. See also Michael Attaleiates on the Pecheneg auxiliaries in the camp of Romanos IV keeping their oaths. For this see above note 34.

Bibliography

Sources

Anna Komnene, Alexias = Anna Comnenae, Alexias, ed. Diether R. Reinsch / Athanasios Kambylis, 2 vols. (Corpus Fontium Historiae Byzantinae 40, 1-2), Berlin / New York 2001.

Konstantinos Porphyrogennetos, de cerimoniis = Constantine VII Porphyrogennetos, Le livre des cérémonies, ed. and trans. Gilbert Dagron / Bernard Flusin / Denis Feissel (Corpus Fontium Historiae Byzantinae 52).

Eustathios of Thessaloniki, Opera minora = Eustathii Thessalonicensis Opera Minora, ed. Paul Wirth (Corpus Fontium Historiae Byzantinae 32), Berlin / New York 2000 [Engl. transl. Andrew F. Stone, Eustathios of Thessaloniki. Secular Orations 1167/8 to 1179, with an introduction and commentary (Byzantina Australiensia 14), Brisbane 2013].

Eustathios of Thessaloniki, Opuscula = Eustathii metropolitae Thessalonicensis opuscula accedunt Trapezuntinae historiae scriptores Panaretus et Eugenicus, ed. Gottlieb L. F. Tafel, Amsterdam 1964 [repr. of Frankfurt am Main 1832].

Eustathios of Thessaloniki, Quadragesima = Eustathios von Thessalonike, Reden auf die große Quadragesima. Prolegomena, Text, Übersetzung, Kommentar, Indices, ed. Sonja Schönauer (Meletemata. Beiträge zur Byzantinistik und Neugriechischen Philologie 10), Frankfurt 2006.

Ioannes Kinnamos, Epitome = Ioannis Cinnami Epitomē rerum ab Ioanne et Alexio Comnenis gestarum, ed. August Meinecke (Corpus Scriptorum Historiae Byzantinae), Bonn 1836.

Ioannes Mauropus = Iohannis Euchaitorum Metropolitae quae in Codice Vaticano Graeco 676 supersunt, ed. Paul de Lagarde, Amsterdam 1979.

Ioannes Skylitzes = Ioannis Scylitzae Synopsis Historiarum, ed. Hans Thurn (Corpus Fontium Historiae Byzantinae 5), Berlin / New York 1973.

Leon Diakonos, Historia = Leonis Diaconi Caloënsis Historiae libri decem et liber de velitatione bellica Nicephori Augusti e recensione Caroli Benedicti Hasii [=Karl Benedikt Hase] (Corpus Scriptorum Historiae Byzantinae 3), Bonn 1828.

Loukaki, Marina, Les Grâces à Athènes. Éloge d'un gouverneur Byzantin par Nikolaos Kataphlôron (Byzantinisches Archiv 36), Berlin / Boston 2019.

"Manganeios" Prodromos, ed. Emmanuel Miller, Recueil des historiens des croisades. Historiens grecs, vol. 2, Paris 1881 [repr. Farnborough 1967].

"Manganeios" Prodromos, ed. István Rácz, Bizánci Költemények Mánuel Császár Magyar Hadjáratairól, Budapest 1941 (Magyar-Görög Tanulmányok 16).

Michael Attaleiates = Michaelis Attaliatae Historia, recensuit Eudoxos Th. Tsolakes (Corpus Fontium Historiae Byzantinae 50), Athen 2011.

Michael the Rhetor = Τοῦ Θεσσαλονίκης κῦρ Μιχαὴλ τοῦ ῥήτορος λόγος ἀναγνωσθεὶς εἰς τὸν αὐτοκράτορα κῦρ Μανουὴλ τὸν Κομνηνόν, in: Fontes rerum byzantinarum, Rhetorum saeculi XII orationes politicae ed. Wasilij Regel [Alexander Kazhdan], (Subsidia Byzantina V), Petropoli 1917, no VIII, 131-152 [Reprint Leipzig 1982].

Niketas Choniates, Histoira = Nicetae Choniatae Historia, ed. Jan-Louis van Dieten (Corpus Fontium Historiae Byzantinae 11,1), Berlin / New York 1975.

Roger of Howden = Chronica Magistri Rogeri de Houedene, ed. William Stubbs, vol. 2, London 1869.
Themistios orationes = Themistii orationes, recensuit Heinrich Schenkl, ed. Glanville Downey, vol. 1, Leipzig 1965.
Theophylaktos of Ochrid =Théophylacte d'Achrida. Discours, traités, poésies, ed. Paul Gautier (Corpus Fontium Historiae Byzantinae 16,1), Thessaloniki 1980.

Literature

Angelov, Dimiter, Imperial Ideology and Political Thought in Byzantium, 1204–1330, Cambridge et. al. 2007.
Brand, Charles M., The Turkish Element in Byzantium, Eleventh-Twelfth Centuries, in: Dumbarton Oaks Papers 43 (1989), 1–25.
Buckley, Penelope, The Alexiad of Anna Komnene: Artistic strategy in the making of a myth, Cambridge 2014.
Cheynet, Jean-Claude, Pouvoir et contestations à Byzance (936–1210) (Byzantina Sorbonensia 9), Paris 1990.
Diaconu, Petre, Les Coumans au Bas-Danube aux XIe et XIIe siècles (Bibliotheca Historica Romaniae. Études 56), Bukarest 1978.
Diaconu, Petre, Les Petchénègues au Bas-Danube (Bibliotheca Historica Romaniae 27), Bukarest 1970.
Durak, Koray, Defining the 'Turk': Mechanisms of Establishing Contemporary Meaning in the Archaizing Language of the Byzantines, in: Jahrbuch der Österreichischen Byzantinistik 59 (2009), 65–78.
Fine Jr., John V. A., The Late Medieval Balkans: A Critical Survey from the Late Twelfth Century to the Ottoman Conquest, Ann Arbor, MI 1987.
Gliwa, Andrzej, The Tatar Military Art of War in the Early Modern Period: An Example of Asymmetric Warfare, in: Acta Poloniae Historica 114 (2016), 191–229.
Grünbart, Michael, The Enemies of the Empire: Portrayed Images, in: A Companion to the Byzantine Culture of War, ca. 300–1204, ed. Yannis Stouraitis (Brill's Companions to the Byzantine World 3), Leiden / Boston 2018, 124–159.
Holmes, Catherine, Basil II and the Governance of Empire (976–1025), Oxford 2005.
Irons, William, Cultural Capital, Livestock Raiding, and the Military Advantage of Traditional Pastoralists, in: Nomadic Pathways in Social Evolution, ed. Nikolay N. Kradin / Dimitri M. Bondarenko / Thomas J. Barfield (The Civilization Dimension Series 5), Moscow 2003, 63–72.
Ivanov, Sergey A., Mission Impossible: Ups and Downs in Byzantine Missionary Activity from the Eleventh to the Fifteenth Century, in: The Expansion of Orthodox Europe. Byzantium, the Balkans and Russia, ed. Jonathan Shepard, Aldershot 2007, 251–266.
Jireček, Constantin, Geschichte der Serben, vol. 1 (bis 1371), (Allgemeine Staatengeschichte. Abt. 1. Geschichte der Europäischen Staaten 1), Gotha 1911.
Kaldellis, Anthony, Ethnography after Antiquity: Foreign Lands and Peoples in Byzantine Literature, Philadelphia, PA 2013.

Kazhdan, Alexander P., The Byzantine Aristocracy and the Imperial Ideal, in: The Byzantine Aristocracy IX to XIII Centuries (BAR International Series 221), ed. Michael Angold, Oxford 1984, 43-57.

Kazhdan, Alexander P., Mauropous, John, in: Oxford Dictionary of Byzantium, London 1991, 1319.

Khazanov, Anatoly, Nomads of the Eurasian Steppes in Historical Retrospective, in: Nomadic Pathways in Social, ed. Nikolay N. Kradin / Dimitri M. Bondarenko / Thomas J. Barfield Evolution (The Civilization Dimension Series 5), Moscow 2003, 25-49.

Kislinger, Ewald, Von Drachen und anderem wilden Getier. Fremdenfeindlichkeit in Byzanz? in: Laetae segetes iterum, ed. Irena Radová, Brünn 2008, 389-404.

König, Helmut, Das Politische des Gedächtnisses, in: Gedächtnis und Erinnerung. Ein interdisziplinäres Handbuch, ed. Christian Gudehus / Ariane Eichenberg / Harald Welzer, Stuttgart / Weimar 2010, 115-126.

Kolia-Dermitzaki, Athina, Το εμπόλεμο Βυζάντιο στις ομιλίες και τις επιστολές του 10ου και 11ου αι. Μία ιδεολογική προσέγγιση, in: Το εμπόλεμο Βυζάντιο (9ος-12ος αι.), (Ινστιτούτο Βυζαντινών Ερευνών, Διεθνή Συμπόσια 4), Athens 1997, 213-238.

Korobeinikov, Dimitri A., Raiders and Neigbours: The Turks (1040-1304), in: The Cambridge History of the Byzantine Empire, c. 500-1492, ed. Jonathan Shepard, Cambridge et. al. 2008, 692-727.

Krallis, Dimitris, Michael Attaleiates and the Politics of Imperial Decline in Eleventh-Century Byzantium (Medieval and Renaissance Texts and Studies 422), Tempe, AR 2012.

Kyriakidis, Savvas, Warfare in Late Byzantium, 1204-1453 (History of Warfare 67), Leiden / Boston 2011.

Laiou, Angeliki E., On Just War in Byzantium., in: Byzantine Warfare, ed. John Haldon, Aldershot 2007, 17-41.

Lechner, Kilian, Hellenen und Barbaren im Weltbild der Byzantiner: Die alten Bezeichnungen als Ausdruck eines neuen Kulturbewußtseins, Munich 1955.

Lefort, Jacques, Rhétorique et politique: trois discours de Jean Mauropous en 1047, in: Travaux et Mémoires 6 (1976), 265-303.

Lilie, Ralph-Johannes, Twelfth-Century Byzantium and the Turkish States, in: Byzantinische Forschungen 16 (1991), 35-51.

Mack, Andrew, Why Big Nations Lose Small Wars: The Politics of Asymmetric Conflict, in: World Politics 27.2 (1975), 175-200.

Madgearu, Alexandru, Byzantine Military Organization on the Danube, 10th-12th Centuries (East Central and Eastern Europe in the Middle Ages 22), Leiden / Boston 2013.

Magdalino, Paul, The Empire of Manuel I Komnenos 1143-1180, Cambridge 1993.

Malamut, Elisabeth, L'image Byzantine des Petchénègues, in: Byzantinische Zeitschrift 88 (1995), 105-147.

Malingoudis, Phaidon, Die Nachrichten des Niketas Choniates über die Entstehung des Zweiten Bulgarischen Reiches, in: Byzantina 10 (1979), 51-147.

Mathisen, Ralph W., Violent Behavior and the Construction of Barbarian Identity in Late Antiquity, in: Violence in Late Antiquity. Perceptions and Practices, ed. Harold A. Drake et. al., Aldershot 2006, 27-35.

McCormick, Michael, Eternal Victory: Triumphal Rulership in Late Antiquity, Byzantium, and the Early Medieval West, Cambridge / Paris 1986.

Meško, Marek, Pecheneg Groups in the Balkans (ca. 1053–1091) according to the Byzantine sources, in: The Steppe Lands and the World Beyond them: Studies in Honor of Victor Spinei on his 70th Birthday, ed. Florin Curta / Bogdan-Petru Maleon, Iași 2013, 179–205.

Moravcsik, Gyula, Byzantinoturcica, vol. 1: Die byzantinischen Quellen der Geschichte der Türkvölker, vol. 2: Sprachreste der Türkvölker in den byzantinischen Quellen, Berlin ²1958.

Münkler, Herfried, Der Wandel des Krieges: Von der Symmetrie zur Asymmetrie, Weilerswist ³2014.

Münkler, Herfried, Imperien. Die Logik der Weltherrschaft – vom Alten Rom bis zu den Vereinigten Staaten, Reinbek ²2008.

Nikolov, Alexandar, Cumani bellatores in the Second Bulgarian State (1186–1396), in: Annual of Medieval Studies at Central European University Budapest 11 (2005), 223–229.

Page, Gill, Being Byzantine: Greek Identity before the Ottomans, Cambridge et. al. 2008.

Papageorgiou, Angeliki, War and Ideology in the Komnenian era: Victories on the northern front as objects of domestic political exploitation, in: Ιστορίες πολέμου στη Νοτιοανατολική Εθρώπη. Μια προσέγγιση στη διαχρονία. Πρακτικά Διεθνούς Επιστημονικού Συνεδρίου με αφορμή τα 100 χρόνια από τους Βαλκανικούς Πολέμος (1912/1913) (Αθήνα, 7–9 Νοεμνρίου 2013), ed. Athena Kolia-Dermitzaki et. al., Athens 2018, 249–259.

Ritter, Max, Die vlacho-bulgarische Rebellion und die Versuche ihrer Niederschlagung durch Kaiser Isaac II. (1185–1195), in: Byzantinoslavica 71 (2013), 162–210.

Schmidt, Tristan, Politische Tierbildlichkeit in Byzanz, spätes 11. bis frühes 13. Jahrhundert (Mainzer Veröffentlichungen zur Byzantinistik 16), Wiesbaden 2020.

Schmidt, Tristan, Performing Military Leadership in Komnenian Byzantium: Emperor Manuel I, His Generals, and the Hungarian Campaign of 1167, in: Dumbarton Oaks Papers 76 (2022), 163–179.

Shliakhtin, Roman, From Huns into Persians: The Projected Identity of the Turks in the Byzantine Rhetoric of Eleventh and Twelfth Centuries, unpublished Dissertation Budapest 2016.

Shukurov, Rustam, The Byzantine Turks 1204–1461 (The Medieval Mediterranean 105), Leiden / Boston 2016.

Simpson, Alicia J., Niketas Choniates: A historiographical study, Oxford 2014.

Spinei, Victor, The Great Migrations in the East and South East of Europe from the Ninth to the Thirteenth Century. 2 Bde., Amsterdam 2006.

Stephenson, Paul, The Imperial Theology of Victory, in: A Companion to the Byzantine Culture of War, ca. 300–1204, ed. Yannis Stouraitis (Brill's Companions to the Byzantine World 3), Leiden / Boston 2018, 23–58.

Stephenson, Paul, Byzantium's Balkan Frontier: A Political Study of the Northern Balkans, 900–1204, Cambridge et al. 2000.

Treitinger, Otto, Die oströmische Kaiser- und Reichsidee nach ihrer Gestaltung im höfischen Zeremoniell: Vom oströmischen Staats- und Reichsgedanken, Darmstadt ²1956.

Vásáry, István, Cumans and Tatars: Oriental Military in the Pre-Ottoman Balkans, 1185–1365, Cambridge 2005.

Vasil'evskij, V. G., Византия и печенеги (1048–1094). Приложения, in: Журнал Министерства Народного Просвещения 164, 11 (1872), 116–165 and 164, 12 (1872), 243–332.

Alexandra Vukovich

Victory and Defeat Liturgified. The Symbolic World of Martial Ritual in Early Rus

> *postera die...rex, solum se pre caeteris culpabilem deo professus atque prostratus, hoc fecit lacrimis votum profusis... Nec mora, erectus a terra, post missae celebrationem sacramque communionem... sumpsit rex clipeum lancea cum sacra.*[1]

The Lenten homily composed by Nikifor I, the Byzantine metropolitan of Kiev (1104–1121) and addressed to Vladimir (Monomakh) Vsevolodich (Prince of Kiev, d. 1125)[2] is a document that details both both Byzantine political theory and unintentionally demonstrates the different approaches to rulership in Rus and Byzantium.[3] Both documents are functionally 'mirrors of princes', but the relationship between ruler and state (or states) reflects two different political systems and methods rulership. When the Byzantine prelate addresses Vladimir as the "valiant head, and head of all the Christian land", he is writing from within a Byzantine political sphere that presumes the assimilation between ruler and state. By Nikifor's reckoning, the ruler commands from a fixed seat of power, thus power is centralised around the ruler and carried out throughout his land by his subordinates, his military commanders and other servants.[4]

The foreigness of the system outlined by Nikifor is obvious in Vladimir Monomakh's own treatise on rulership, his *Pouchenie* (Lesson), which reflects an entirely different understanding of effective princely rule, based on the mechanics of rulership in Rus where the princes of Rus ruled from multiple fortified towns, each with its own dependencies.[5] The *Pouchenie* contradicts Nikifor's letter, outlining an ideology of rulership based on the practicalities of being a prince in Rus. Mobility, personal leadership, face-to-face interactions and exchanges, as well as Christian virtues are both the ideal and the exigencies of ruling

---

1 Thietmar, Chronicon 2.10, 48: 24–33.
2 See genealogical tables reproduced at the end.
3 Dölker, Der Fastenbrief, 38–40; Franklin / Shepard, Emergence of Rus, 313–15; Chichurov, Politicheskaia ideologiia srednevekov'ia, 19–32, 140–146; Dvornik, Byzantine Political Ideas in Kievan Russia, 73–121, 112–114.
4 See Chichurov, Politicheskaia ideologiia srednevekov'ia, 140–146.
5 Vukovich, Enthronement in Early Rus, 211–239, esp. 215–217.

within Rus. Rather than ruling from a fixed seat and drawing from a varied staff to aid in administration and expansion, a prince of Rus must personally involve himself in all matters of rule, especially those related to war and warfare.[6] Thus, the focus of the *Pouchenie* is on personal rule and personal involvement in war and matters of state (described principally as running the household). Vladimir Monomkah warns that a prince of Rus should neither rely on his steward and entourage, nor indeed on his military commanders, but should endeavour to involve himself in all matters. This vision of rulership in Rus is substantiated by the numerous chronicle accounts that depict the prince in perpetual motion, whether in times of war or in times of peace. The antinomy between Byzantine precepts of the ideal ruler and rulership and the local culture of Rus articulated in the *Pouchenie* reflects a gap both in style and substance.

In the *Pouchenie*, this type of princely movement (itinerancy) in Rus is linked to warfare, both because it was essential to extracting payment and labour in exchange for princely protection within the existing territory of the Rus principalities, but also because it shaped the physical space of Rus.[7] It was through constant movement and associated warfare that the territory of Rus (controlled by fortified towns and their dependencies) expanded in the pre-Mongol period. Descriptions of this expansion are communicated within the framework of Christian providence. Here, the chronicles of Rus offer a proleptic argument, describing the outcomes of battles and the capture of territory as providential events. In this sense, princely victory and the attendant territorial control or expansion are liturgified, placed within a formally Christian narrative. The Byzantine style of these accounts is reflected in the use of divine intercession, that of the Mother of God, Eastern Christian military saints, and other holy figures, and functions to narratively elevate winners over losers and frame their victory as providential. Given that power in Rus functioned laterally amongst a non-centralized princely clan, chronicle accounts narratively structure the myriad power plays and power players vying for the fortified towns and settled dependencies of the principalities of Rus.

Similarly, in the passage that introduces this study, Thietmar, the Prince-Bishop of Merseburg (d. 1018), illustrates through the episode of 'The Holy Lance' (a relic of Constantinian origin) that God is a highly selective patron. Otto's prayer before the Holy Lance is a narrative moment demonstrating the role of divine will and providence in victory. It is a "consensual ritual against fractious rebels" who make war, wherein a certain faction is appointed as righteous and providentially victorious.[8] In this episode, prayers and invocations of the divine

---

6 Povest' vremennykh let, 157.
7 See Vukovich, The Gift Economy, 74–91.
8 Buc, Dangers of Ritual, 47. Based on Moses's prayer against the Amalekites in Exodus 17.12.

resulting in divine designations of victors and liturgified military undertakings, express the worthiness and righteousness of victors over those whom they had defeated.[9]

Military Rituals in Rus

The wider military rituals of the princes of Rus as described by the chronicles of Rus include princely triumph and entry (or *adventus*)[10] following military success, the ritual of oath-taking by "kissing the Cross" (крестоцелование)[11] to establish or maintain peace during or between periods of internecine conflict, and to a lesser extent commensality (dining rituals and celebrations), which usually took place once peace had already been established. During periods of active conflict, whether against fellow princes or regional enemies and allies such as the Hungarians or Poles, military rituals depicted in the chronicles of Rus serve to enhance camaraderie between allies, or to enhance the optics of battle and martial prowess. The rhetoric of intercession in the chronicles of Rus invokes the role of Providence in aiding military success and promoting certain princes over others, depicting princely victory as being divinely ordained.[12]

Vladimir Monomakh warns in his *Pouchenie* that princes should not be hasty in drawing their weapons and engaging in violence.[13] And yet, war against the pagan groups bordering Rus, internecine conflict, and minor conflagrations are a staple of chronicle accounts about the princes of Rus and their activities throughout the medival period. Ritualised attitudes and gestures are attributed to princes in battle, acclamations and liturgical invocations, and expressions of divine intercession are provided so that the outcomes of conflicts are shaped into providential events. Ritual acts – invocations and supplication – give meaning, drama, and density to the providentially-inspired victories. The active and decisive role of divine forces is visually translated into princely associations with warrior saints and other martial figures. Official iconographies on coins and on churches promote the image of the prince as warrior and give further substance

---

9 Buc, Dangers of Ritual, 47–51; McCormick, Eternal Victory, 342–362.
10 Ceremonial entry or adventus is broadly represented throughout the medieval and early modern periods and has been treated by historians as well as cultural anthropologists, see Geertz, Centers, Kings, and Charisma, 150–171; Dotzauer, Ankunft des Herrschers, 245–288.
11 On oath-taking in Rus, see Stefanovich, Eid des Adels; idem., Drevnerusskaia kliatva, 383–403; idem., Expressing Loyalty in Medieval Russia: Oath vs. Oral Formulas, 127–136. See also Filiushkin, Institut krestotselovaniia, 42–48; Mikhailova / Prestel, Cross Kissing, 1–22.
12 Compare with the religiously-inflected triumph of John II Komnenos, see Magdalino, The Triumph of 1133, esp. 59–60.
13 PVL 1, 157.

to the prescriptions of the *Pouchenie* and chronicle accounts.[14] The ritualized evocation and invocation of warrior saints – along with the usual holy intercessors – ritualized the outcomes of battles in order to make manifest the invisible justice of God and to promote victors.

The chronicles of Rus provide more information on the military campaigns of princes than on any other type of event. These campaigns follow oath-breakings, perceived violations of succession principles, attempts to seize territory from other princes, and to honour alliances. Divine intercession is manifested both as a habitual ritual act undertaken before the commencement of a campaign and as a rhetorical device relating the role of divine providence in victory and designating the victor as the most righteous party to hostilities. The tropes employed in the chronicles of Rus are common to medieval literature and are part of the stock of medieval devices to shape narratives and to designate events as providential, whether they resulted in victory or defeat. In certain accounts, battle and prayer are conflated and victory is ritualized on the battlefield through prayers for intercession. The princes of Rus also integrated the symbols of victorious rulership and divine intercession in their personal iconographies – on seals and coins – and the ideal of the ruler as intercessor is depicted on the facades of the churches of Vladimir-Suzdal.[15] Accordingly, the prince was not simply victorious because he ruled, he ruled because he was victorious, and military victory evoked a prince's legitimacy and authority.

The practice of power in the annalistic descriptions of princely rule in Rus emphasizes war as an instrument of establishing and maintaining rule, as well as obtaining wealth in the form of new towns and dependencies. The material aspect of this war economy is subsumed by the rhetoric of providential victory. Whether chronicle bias (for one region or prince over another) or the articulation of a literary leitmotif common to the medieval period, the deployment of divine intercessors, both figures and symbols, draws an ideal. Princes are exonerated for engaging in war through divine approbation, even if they previously transgressed the precepts of peace and consensus.

Divine intercession

Intercession for victory in the chronicles of early Rus does not follow a prescribed context and evocations of intercession occur in accounts of divinely inspired war against pagans, against polities, and between princes. Military victory for the

---

14 The northern principalities, beginning with Novgorod, were the initial site of princely association with warrior saints, see Androshchuk, Images of Power, 117–120.
15 White, Byzantine Military Saints, 94–201.

advancement of Christianisation represents an actuation of the deeds of Vladimir Sviatoslavich in the tenth century. The nomadic peoples depicted in the chronicles of Rus – although allies and marriage partners at times – provided an ideal group for ritualised military action. In the following example from the Kievan Chronicle, the exemplarity of victory against the Polovtsi (the western branch of the Cuman-Kipchak Turkic peoples) recalls past princely victories and makes manifest their righteousness as Christian rulers and defenders of the Christian faith:

> "And they met another group of them [Polovtsi] and they [the princes] clashed with them and God the prayers of their fathers and grandfathers helped Mikhailko and Vsevolod against the pagans, and they killed some of the pagans and captured others that week. They captured four hundred young male prisoners, but they let them go back to their own lands. They returned to Kiev praising God and the Holy Mother of God, and the power of the True Cross an the holy martyrs."[16]

The narrative structure of the account for the year 1174 emphasizes the intercession of the ancestors who helped to spread Christianity throughout Rus; magnanimity in victory (they release their prisoners);[17] and prayers through the evocation of the Lord, the Holy Mother of God, the life-giving Cross, and the holy martyrs. These evocations point to Riurikid supremacy over the pagans and manifest the dynasty's sanctity through divinely inspired actions. The spiritual nexus combines both the brother-martyrs Boris and Gleb, as well as the early Christian princes of Rus, all of whom represent the triumph of Eastern Christianity as the religion of the Rus state (or states). It is notable that the principal giving of praise and offering of prayers occurs at Kiev, a primary dynastic centre of the earliest period of Rus.

Similarly in the account for the year 1151 wherein Iziaslav Mstislavich (Prince of Kiev, d. 1154) retakes Kiev from Iurii Vladimirich (Prince of Vladimir-Suzdal and Kiev, d. 1157) with the assistance of his brother, Rostislav Mstislavich (Prince of Smolensk, Novgord, then Kiev, d. 1167) and his co-ruler Viacheslav Vladimirich (Prince of Kiev, d. 1154) whose presence legitimates Iziaslav's ascension to the throne of Kiev.[18] The princes enter Kiev and pay homage (поклонившеся) to the Mother of God at the Tithe Church and at St. Sophia where they are met by

---

16 PSRL 2, col. 563: "[…] и срѣтоша ѣ изнова друзиѣ [Polovtsi] и ступишасѧ [the princes] с ними и бишасѧ крѣпко и поможе Бъ̃ Михалкови и Всеволоду на поганѣи дѣднѧ и wтьнѧ млтва и сбысться в недѣлю самы поганые избиша а другые изыимаша. И полонъ w̃еша д̃ ста чади и пустиша е во своеси а сами възворотишасѧ Кыеву славѧще Ба̃ и сту̃ю Бц̃ю и силу ч̃ьтьнаго кр̃с̃та и св̃тае мчн̃ка помогающа на бранѣхъ на поганые."
17 It is possible that this constitutes a rhetorical trope. Similarly, in 1161, Iaroslav Andreevich releases the people of Kiev whom he had imprisoned following the siege of Kiev, see PSRL 2, col. 516.
18 PSRL 2, col. 433.

the people of Kiev. Churches that had been founded by the major figures of the tenth and eleventh centuries, Vladimir Sviatoslavich and Iaroslav Vladimirich respectively, very likely bore a historical and dynastic prestige and it is unsurprising that they are mentioned as the main centres for the offering of prayers to the Mother of God, who was one of a restricted, and yet, varied group of holy figures interceding on behalf of favoured princes during battle.[19]

However, it was not only the Kievan princes who focussed devotion on the Mother of God, Andrei Iurevich (Prince of Vladimir-Suzdal, d. 1174) offers prayers to the Mother of God on, at least, four occasions in the Laurentian Chronicle.[20] The Mother of God was a common figure of intercession – as the protectress of Constantinople and Kiev – and the princely clan of Rus founded many centres of worship in honour of the *Bogoroditsa*.[21] The tale of the victory over the Volga Bulgars includes a detailed account of the intercession of Christ and the Mother of God on behalf of Andrei Iurevich who is joined by the Byzantine emperor Manuel Komnenos during several battles in 1164.[22] During the 1149 battle against the Polovtsi, the Laurentian and Hypatian Chronicles both include an account of Andrei Iurevich praying to God before drawing his sword and invoking the assistance of St. Theodore, whereupon he is delivered by the saint's intercession.[23] It is notable that although chronicles often mention the intercession of holy figures on behalf of princes – usually figures of universal or local devotion such as Christ, the Mother of God, the Holy Cross or the dynastic saints of the princes of Rus, SS Boris and Gleb – the appearance of patron saints is rare.[24] The account relating the victory of Andrei Iurevich and that of Manuel Komnenos exists in several versions, the fullest being the twelfth-century 'Tale of the Miracles of the Icon of Our Lady of Vladimir' (incorporated into the sixteenth-century *Prologue*). The version preserved in the *Nikon Chronicle* interpolates the medieval narrative, but includes additional information, padding out the account.[25] The parallel acts of the Rus prince and Byzantine emperor, con-

---

19 White, Byzantine Military Saints, 94–132.
20 Between 1149 and the prince's death in 1175, see PSRL 1, cols. 367–374; PSRL 2, cols. 580–595.
21 For a list, see White, Byzantine Military Saints, 217–219.
22 Hurwitz, Prince Andrej Bogoljubskij, 90–91.
23 See: PSRL 1, col. 325; PSRL 2, col. 390. St Theodore was not Prince Andrei's personal saint, but the battle did occur on the saint's feast day, thus the invocation would have been appropriate, see: White, Byzantine Military Saints, 179–181. As has been discussed above, the festal calendar provided an ample stock of holy intercessors to be called upon in times of need.
24 White, Byzantine Military Saints, 113–119. Whereas the Mother of God, Christ, and the Holy Cross are standard tropes in the shaping of events as providential, see: PSRL 2, cols. 362–363.
25 For the published account, see Zabelin, Sledy literaturnogo, 46–47; for an English translation and commentary, see Pelenskyj, Russia and Kazan, 145–49. The Nikon Chronicle account and the chronicle itself are very complex, as are most interpolations that refract back onto early Rus a post-Mongol, Muscovite consciousness. The shaping of information in later texts needs

sistent across all accounts, relate the overall message; namely, that Eastern Christian princes acted in concert, directed and protected by holy intercessors, in order to expand Christianity by battling non-believers.

In another account of military struggles against the Polovtsi in the year 1174, Igor Riurikovich, Prince of Pereiaslavl, defeats the pagans and is honoured by the senior princes of the dynasty. The chronicle narrative creates a nexus for divine action: the pagans are defeated on the day of the feast of the prophet Elijah (who opposed the worship of the idol Baal), Igor attends church on the feast day of SS Boris and Gleb, then he attends a service at St. Michael's church at Pereiaslavl[26] on the day of the feast of the Elevation of the Cross.[27] The evocation of dynastic saints, the symbol of Christianity, along with a veterotestamentary figure who promoted monotheistic worship endows Igor's campaign with divine approval and the dynastic mandate to defend the Christian faith. The polyvalence of the cult of SS Boris and Gleb is evident here, since the brother-martyrs not only create consensus in times of internecine conflict, but also display cohesion amongst princes of the Riurikid dynasty and emphasise their Christian duty as martyrs for the Christian faith.

It is possible that the churches of Rus – largely princely foundations – would have organised prayers for the princes and their victory against pagans and, possibly, each other, a practice that is attested to in the Byzantine Empire.[28] In the Byzantine tradition, monastic prayers – although their origins and contents are unknown – were offered for the health of the emperor (as their patron) and, more generally, for the salvation of the state.[29] Prayers for intercession and for salvation were also offered during special services organized by the patriarchs of Constantinople for the protection and preservation of the city and its inhabitants during the great sieges of the seventh and eighth centuries.[30] To my knowledge, specific prayers or litanies are not recorded for the salvation of early Rus during periods of war. However, the chronicles of Rus describe princes attending liturgies before and after battle and interacting with the clergy. The account of the commencement of hostilities between Iziaslav Mstislavich and his partisans, and Iurii Vladimirich allied with the Olgovichi and Davidovichi princes (of southern principalities); Iurii – invoking the principle of seniority and patrimonial – at-

---

to be read through the ideological position of Muscovy in the early post-Mongol period, see the classical and complete work on this topic: Miller, Legends of the Icon, 657–670.

26 This church is mentioned several times when princes worship at Pereiaslavl and offer prayers for divine assistance, see PSRL 2, cols. 383 and 404.
27 PSRL 2, col. 569.
28 McCormick, Eternal Victory, 241.
29 The emperors Anastasius and Justinian receive prayers from the monks of Palestine, see: Cyril of Scythopolis, Vita Sabae, 143.6–9, 174.24–175.4.
30 See Photius, Homilies, 31.31–32.4, 37.21–3, 48.20–5.

tempts to reclaim Pereiaslavl from Iziaslav. Iziaslav attends matins at the church of St. Michael at Pereiaslavl and is beseeched by the bishop Efimii not to make war against his uncle:

> "Iziaslav heard matins at St. Michael's church and the bishop Iefimian came out of the church shedding tears and beseeching him: 'O Prince! Make peace with your uncle and you will receive the grace [salvation] of God and you will save your land from great ill.' And he [Iziaslav] did not want to consider that this could lead to a great many battles, saying: 'I took Kiev and Pereiaslavl by risking my own neck.'"[31]

The account demonstrates a clear bias against Iziaslav who, although he attends a church service, rejects the Christian exhortation of the bishop and asserts, hubristically, that he has thus far made his own fortune. The refusal to recognise dynastic seniority and the rejection of the bishop's admonishment foreshadow the military disaster that soon follows. In effect, following his victory against Iziaslav, Iurii Vladimirich enters Pereiaslavl and praises God and St. Michael for granting him victory, which he ascribes to providence rather than his own military prowess.[32] This episode depicts one of the few times that a member of the clergy of Rus intervenes directly in the internecine wars of the princely clan. Most often, churches provide the settings for the *profectio bellica*[33] of the Rus princes, adding a ritual element to the commencement of hostilities, and only passing mentions are provided of church services before battle. For example, in the ninth century, special litanies for the eve of battle are attested to the in the *Tactica* of Leo VI.[34] The *Primary Chronicle* account for the year 1107 refers to deliverance from the Polovtsi and their "mangy, godless, predatory" leader Boniak who had reached the outskirts of Kiev and had pillaged the Klov, Vydubichi, and Caves monasteries and burned the princely *dvor* (palace or hall) at Berestovo.[35] Following these events, Sviatopolk Iaroslavich (Prince of Kiev, d. 1113) and Vladimir Monomakh (Prince of Pereiaslavl, then Kiev, d. 1125) designed a more aggressive strategy against the Po-

---

31 PSRL 2, col. 380: "Изѧславъ ѿслоуша wбѣднюю оу с҃томъ Михаилѣ и поиде изъ ц҃ркве Иефимьяноу же еп҇поу слезы проливаючю и молѧщюсѧ емоу: 'кн҃же оумирисѧ съ стрьемъ своиⷨ много спсⷱ҇ние примеши ѿ Б҃а и землю свою избавиши ѿ великие бѣды.' wнъ же не восхотѣ надѣесѧ на множество вои река: 'добылъ есми головою своею Киева и Переиславлѧ.'"
32 It is the reverse in the Kievan Chronicle, see PSRL 2, col. 383. Rostislav, Iziaslav, and Viacheslav again call upon the Mother of God during battle against Iurii Vladimirich after which Viacheslav praises the Mother of God over the Golden Gates of Kiev. The topographic mention evokes the Byzantine profectio bellica in which the emperor prays for divine favour at the Chalke and continues to the Hagia Sophia followed by a liturgical procession to the Blachernae church for a final service, see: Leo the Deacon, Histories, 8.1, 128.1–129.8.
33 Kantorowicz, The King's Advent, 37–75, 55–56.
34 Leo VI, Tactica, 14–I, 126–127.
35 PVL 1, 151.

lovtsi,³⁶ which led to a series of campaigns that penetrated into the steppe frontier of Rus.³⁷ Sviatopolk Iaroslavich had a prominent role in organising his fellow princes, participated in the campaign, and was also a founder and patron of churches and monasteries.³⁸ It is entirely unsurprising that the Caves Monastery would receive Sviatopolk and offer prayers to his health and military success:

> "Sviatopolk arrived at the Caves Monastery for matins on the day of the feast of the Assumption of the Holy Mother of God (Aug. 15) with great rejoicing because our enemies had been vanquished through the prayers to the Holy Mother of God and our holy father, the great Theodosius. It was thus Sviatopolk's custom that before he went to war or on some other mission, he would kneel beside the tomb of Theodosius and, having received the blessing of the abbot, he would then go on his way."³⁹

The main difference between the descriptions of prayers and litanies for victory in Byzantine and early Rus texts is that the depiction of ritualised victory is highly personalised in the accounts from Rus. A prince, personally, pays homage, offers prayers, and receives blessing before departing on a military campaign. The prince's army, allies, and other princes are very rarely mentioned and there is no display of collective blessing for the military campaign. In this instance, the preparation for battle involves prayers before the relics of Theodosius, the former abbot of the Caves Monastery, and personal prayers and blessings from the current abbot.

Collective prayers for intercession are not depicted as part of a campaigning army's activities in Rus. However, an instance of collective effervescence is related for the year 1146 when Vsevolod Olgovich (Prince of Chernigov, d. 1146) – who had wrested Kiev from the descendants of Vladimir Monomakh – attempts to take Zvenigorod from Vladimirko of Galich (d. 1153). Vsevolod's troops set fire to the city, but the city is delivered through divine intervention:

> "And God and the Holy Mother of God delivered the city from the heat of battle and they [the people] raised a *Kyrie eleison* with great joy, thanking God and his immaculate mother [...] and from there, they all returned from whence they came. Vsevolod returned to Kiev where he fell ill and he called for his brother, Igor, and for Sviatoslav."⁴⁰

---

36 PVL 1, 183.
37 See Franklin / Shepard, Emergence of Rus, 272–277.
38 See PVL 1, 190–192. Sviatopolk founded the sumptuous golden-domed church of St. Michael in Kiev and may have overseen the first compilation of the PVL, see Franklin / Shepard, Emergence of Rus, 279–282.
39 PVL 1, 258: "Святополкъ же прииде заутреню в Печерьскыи манастырь на оуспенье с͠тыя Б͠ца и братья цѣловаша и радостью великою яко врази наши побѣжены быша м͠лтвами с͠тыя Б͠ца и великого Федосья ѡц͠а нашего. И тако бо ѡбычаи имаше С͠тополкъ коли идаше на воину или инамо оли поклонивсѧ въ гроба Федосьева и м͠лтву вземъ оу игумена сущаго тоже идаше на путь свои."
40 PSRL 2, col. 320: "Б͠ъ же и с͠тая Б͠ца избави городъ ѿ лютыя рати и възваша *коури иелисонъ* с радостью великою хвалѧще Б͠а͠и прч͠стоую его м͠трь [...] и ѿтоудоу възвратишасѧ кождо въ

The chant is not raised in favour of any specific prince and implores divine intercession against the bellicose actions of Vsevolod Olgovich. The litanic character of the phrase – the direct transcription of the Greek phrase into Slavonic script – accentuates the liturgified nature of the invocation. The use of the phrase clearly emulates traditional Byzantine chants of *Kyrie eleison* before and during combat.[41] The chanting of *Kyrie eleison* accentuates the ritual character of the moment of deliverance by making evident God's plan for both princes and their subjects. The account of the 1151 battle at the Rut (or Rutets) River includes a series of ritualised acts on both sides of the battlefield. Iurii Vladimirich arrives with his allies attended by drums and trumpets, Andrei Iurevich is saved from death – through the intercession of God and the Mother of God – when his helmet falls off during battle, and Iziaslav Mstislavich is saved – having been struck on the head – by the intervention of a sign (a *panteleimon*)[42] by which he is recognised as a prince:

> "'I am Iziaslav, I am your prince,' and he removed his helmet from his head. And many heard this, and beheld, themselves, with great joy their emperor and prince. And all of his retainers raised a *Kyrie eleison*, the soldiers having won [the battle], they rejoiced as their prince also lived."[43]

Following this episode, the people cry *Kyrie eleison* and rejoice in their salvation and to the health of Iziaslav Mstislavich who was struck on the forehead and is wounded. The extended narrative of the Kievan Chronicle provides a providential reading for several key stages of the battle and promotes the divinely inspired salvation of certain princes. The duplicitous Vladimir Davidovich (Prince of Chernigov, d. 1151) is killed – an event that is described as traumatic for the dynasty – in battle, while Iziaslav Mstislavich and Andrei Iurevich are delivered by divine intervention. The chanting of *Kyrie eleison* further amplifies the rhetoric of divine intervention and follows a common medieval trope in both the Byzantine cultural sphere and the kingdoms of the post-Roman world where

---

свояси. Всеволодъ же пришедъ в Киевъ разболисѧ и посла по брата своего по Игорѧ и по Стославa."

41 For example, the citizens of Thessalonica turned to St. Demetrios during the sieges of the 6th and 7th centuries and were instructed to shout Kyrie eleison: in the Miracula Demetrii (BHG, 516z–523), 187, 204–206, 256. In the 10th century, nightly hymns, litanies, and the chanting of Kyrie eleison are prescribed before battle, see Nicephoros Phocas, Praecepta militaria, 20.22–21.3.

42 Perhaps a reference to the intervention of St. Panteleimon, the 4th century Byzantine healer saint.

43 PSRL 2, cols. 439: "'Азъ Изѧславъ есмь кнѧзь вашь.' И снѧ съ себе шеломъ и позна и. И то слышавше мнози и въсхытиша и руками своими с радостью яко цр҃ѧ и кнѧза свое͡г. И тако възваша *кирелѣиса*[н] вси полци радующесѧ полкъ ратны[х] побѣдивше а кнѧза свое͡г живого."

the phrase was also directly translitterated from the Greek phrase into local languages.[44]

Prayers for the princes of Rus during times of hostilities and war are often partisan in the chronicles of Rus and identify the victor even before hostilities have commenced. Two types of examples were discussed above, those depicting divinely inspired princes doing battle against pagans and those depicting princes fighting each other during the internecine conflict of the mid-twelfth century. Chronicle narratives contradict moral injunctions against violence,[45] such as monastic exhortations for princes and their subordinates to live in peace; instead violence is ritualised and liturgified and military victory – both over pagans and over other princes – is celebrated.

The iconography of intercession

In her study of Byzantine military saints in early Rus, Monica White determined that the application of saintly images on the seals of the princes of Rus reveals the emergence of new forms of veneration focused on personal and family patrons instead of a defined group of holy warriors.[46] White examined the iconographies of military saints on the seals of the princes of Rus. The iconographies of princely seals reflect both divine intercession on a military model and promote the martial values of the Rus princely clanin a ritualised form. The influence of Byzantine iconography is both undeniable and non-negligible; however, there are salient differences between the representation of military saints on Byzantine imperial seals and those of Rus.[47]

Much like the coins of the early princes of Rus, princely seals include personal saints and local trappings of power. This was particularly evident for the coins of Iaroslav Vladimirich (Prince of Kiev, d. 1054), which bear the princely emblem on the obverse and associated the prince with the representation of St. George in Byzantine military attire and bearing a spear (figure 1).[48] Byzantine emperors did not normally associate themselves with military saints on their coins; however,

---

44 For example, in the Old High German Ludwigslied composed after Louis III's (881) defeat of the Vikings at Saucourt describing how the Franks prepared for battle against the Northman: "Ioh alle saman sungen *Kyrrieleison.*" Von Steinmeyer, Sprachdenkmäler, 86.47–8.
45 For example, the Pchela in its chapter on princely rule gives a long definition, ascribed to Chrysostom, of the good ruler who is a moral arbiter and a philosopher-king, see Pickhadze / Makeeva, Pchela, 143.
46 White, Byzantine Military Saints, 111–121, esp. 112.
47 The presence of Byzantine seals and their influence on their Rus counterparts is discussed in: Ivakin / Khrapunov / Seibt, Byzantine and Rus Seals, 221–223, 245–263.
48 Sotnikova / Spasskii, Tysiacheletie drevneishikh monet Rossii, figs. 222–227.

they often did on their seals.[49] One known seal attributed to Iaroslav Vladimirich features on the obverse a bust of St. George clad in armour, holding a spear in his right hand and a shield in his left hand, which follows the depiction of the saint on his coins.

Figure 1: Iaroslav I (1019–1054), Silver Coin, find location: unknown, Staatliche Museen zu Berlin, no. 18216120

Princely association with military saints – probably bearing the baptismal name of the princes who issued them – is extremely common on seals. Valentin Lavrentievich Ianin identified three categories of princely seals – all bearing images of saints – and determined the periods during which they circulated. The three types of seals were those of the archaic tradition (tenth to the final quarter of the eleventh centuries), those with Greek inscriptions (mid-eleventh to the early twelfth century), and those with images of two saintly figures (eleventh to thirteenth centuries).[50] Furthermore, there was probably no precise time when a given type of seal came into or went out of use, and it is very likely that a range of types was in circulation in any one period. There are also other types of seals that may have belonged to princes, but remain uncategorized since it is impossible to determine the identity of the depicted figure, and the inscription is illegible.

The portraits of the Byzantine military saints on Rus seals are nearly identical to those featured on a number of contemporary seals produced in the Byzantine Empire, such as those of John Komnenos (father of Alexios I), which features a figure identified as St. George and a portrait of the emperor.[51] On seals from Rus, it appears that princes were identified by the military saint depicted. In the Byzantine context, emperors were depicted alongside or on the reverse of saintly warriors (figure 2). Association between emperors and military saints is particularly evident in the Middle Byzantine period when Komnenian emperors begin

---

49 Cheynet, Par Saint Georges, Par Saint Michel, 115–134.
50 Ianin, Aktovye pechati drevnei rusi, 33, 41, 87.
51 Zacos, Byzantine Lead Seals, vol. 1, 70–73, figs. 77–80; Ianin / Gaidukov, Aktovye pechati, vol. 3, 259, no. 2a.

to appear on coins dressed in military attire and brandishing weapons.[52] The emperor in military attire with his sword drawn appears on Byzantine coins from the reign of Isaac I Komnenos (1057–59) (figure 3).[53] Michael Psellos in his *Chronographia* described Isaac Komnenos as a shrewd military leader desirous of revolutionising the Byzantine empire;[54] he was the first Komnenian emperor and the first emperor to issue coins with legends entirely in Greek with his family name as part of the imperial titulature. Since Isaac Komnenos attained the imperial rank through a military coup, it is possible that he wanted to insist on the martial aspect of his rule and the emperor's role as military leader and protector of the empire, and he issued coins promoting this rhetoric.[55] The representation of the emperor in military attire and with his sword drawn associated with a military saint in armour and bearing arms, articulates divinely-inspired rulership while legitimating martial authority.[56]

Figure 2: Nomisma histamenon of Isaac I Komnenos (1057–1069), Dumbarton Oaks, Byzantine Collection, Washington, DC (BZC.1955.1.4319)

---

52 Grotowski, Arms and Armour of the Warrior Saints, 104–117. For a chronology of warrior saints as imperial patrons.
53 The seal of Isaac Komnenos; gold histamenon of Isaac Komnenos, see Grierson, Byzantine Coins, pl. 52.918, 919.
54 Michael Psellos, Chronographia, 51.
55 Tiberius III had been the last emperor to issue coins featuring the sword and Constantine IX Monomachos' class 4 histamenon (1054/55) and his miliaresion (1042–55) featured the imperial sword, see Grierson, Byzantine Coins, 200.
56 This iconography is found both on seals and coins, see Grierson, Byzantine Coins, pl. 52 featuring the emperor with his sword drawn. This representation is similar to some Rus seals, see: Ianin, Aktovye pechati, 236, even though the variety of martial representations on Rus seals exceeds that of Byzantine imperial seals and coins.

Figure 3: Seal of Isaac I Komnenos (1057–1059), find location: Istanbul, Dumbarton Oaks, (BZC.1948.17.2961)

Warrior figures articulate intercession while ritualising the military actions and martial legitimacy of the emperor as a leader of armies, and as a warrior himself. The iconography of a seal belonging to Alexios III Angelos (1195–1203) – grandson of Alexios I Komnenos – encompasses this ideology by depicting SS George and Demetrios stretching out their hands toward the Mother of God who holds a shield bearing an image of Christ Emmanuel.[57] The visual rhetoric of the military saints accompanied by the emperor in military attire on seals (and coins), reflects a ritual pattern of iconic warfare in the form of the emperor, represented as a warrior, assisted by a holy army that includes not only military saints, but also Christ and the Mother of God.[58]

The iconographic patterns for Rus seals differ from the Byzantine practice in their consistent association of princes with their own patron saints and those of their forefathers.[59] Byzantine imperial seals with depictions of the emperor and military saints did not reflect association through patronage or a system of baptismal names, rather the visual rhetoric of martial figures was demonstrative of an ideological shift towards rule based on military prowess in the Middle Byzantine period.[60] Similarities exist in the function of the visual rhetoric of association between temporal rulers and saintly figures on Byzantine and Rus seals, particularly in the conveyance of military might as a principal source for political authority. Saintly figures could act as intercessors, and military saints associated with those who ruled by military might demonstrated the icono-

---

57 Stepanenko, Bogomater' Nikopeia i sviatye voiny', 44.
58 Between the mid-ninth to late twelfth centuries, the iconographic seals of reigning emperors used a restricted array of images of Christ, the Mother of God, or the Mother of God with the infant Christ, the most popular being the Mother of God, see Zacos, Byzantine Lead Seals, vol. 1, 50–99, nos. 57–109.
59 White, Byzantine Military Saints, 117.
60 Magdalino, The Empire of Manuel I Komnenos, 418–420.

graphic and, by extension, political emphasis on victory as legitimising political authority.

As in Rus, the built landscape of Constantinople reflected a predilection for the cult of the Mother of God;[61] however, by the end of the twelfth century – besides the Mangana – there were at least nine churches in Constantinople dedicated to St. George, several sanctuaries dedicated to St. Theodore, and two churches dedicated to St. Demetrios founded in the twelfth century.[62] The cult of the military saints in Constantinople appears to have continued from the Late Antique tradition, but increased in prominence in the Middle Byzantine period under the Komnenian Dynasty.[63] Churches dedicated to military saints are known from Kiev, but it is after the political changes of the mid-twelfth to early thirteenth centuries and the emergence of Vladimir-Suzdal as a principality rivalling Kiev, that the divine intercession of military saints becomes a primary referent for depictions of ritualised rulership.

It is possible that the military might of Iurii Vladimirich as well as his close connection with the Byzantine Empire in the 1140s – Iurii was allied with Vladimirko of Galich and Manuel I Komenos against Géza II of Hungary and Iziaslav Mstislavich – initiated the process of cultural production with an emphasis on ritualised warfare.[64] Andrei Iurevich continued his father's cultural oeuvre and adopted and developed Kievan traditions, which included the veneration of SS Boris and Gleb and the military saints; the introduction of the feast day honouring the Intercession (Pokrov) – Andrei brought the Byzantine icon of the Mother of God from Vyshgorod to Vladimir – to expand the cult of the Mother of God in Vladimir-Suzdal, and promoted the cult of the Saviour through the establishment of another feast day and the building of at least two churches.[65]

It is believed that Vsevolod Iurevich was exiled at the Byzantine court in Thessaloniki with his mother and siblings on the orders of Andrei Iurevich after Iurii Vladimirich's death in 1157.[66] The Tipografskaia Chronicle (based on the older recension of the Synodal manuscript that contains some additional information to the oldest extant manuscripts of the early chronicles of Rus) recounts that the princes of Rus and their mother were received by Manuel I Komnenos in 1162:

In that same year, Mstislav and Vasilko and the Iurevichi left for Constantinople with their mother. They brought with them a third brother, the young

---

61 See remarks of: Pentcheva, Icons and Power, 82–93.
62 Ianin, Aktovye pechati, 69–70, 76–78, 150–154, 89–94.
63 Grotowski, Arms and Armour of the Warrior Saints, 121–123.
64 Pashuto, Vneshniaia politika drevnei Rusi, 186–201.
65 White, Byzantine Military Saints, 177–179; Krivosheev, Gibel' Andreia Bogoliubskogo.
66 Kazhdan, Rus-Byzantine Princely Marriages, 414–429.

Vsevolod. The Emperor presented Vasilko with four towns on the Danube and he presented the region of Otskalan to Mstislav.[67]

John Kinnamos, the Byzantine historian covering the period of 1118–1176 (the reigns of John II and Manuel I), corroborates the account provided by the Slavonic narrative. Kinnamos' history mentions the arrival, three years later (1165), of an unknown prince from Rus who receives the territory that had previously been gifted to the "son of George (Iurii)":

> "In that time, Vladislav, one of the princes from Tauroscythia sought refuge amongst the Romans. He brought with him his children and wife and all of his power and authority. A region on the Danube was presented to him, the one which the emperor had previously presented to Vasilko, the son of George who had seniority amongst the leaders of Tauroscythia when he had come."[68]

Vsevolod's return to Rus either took place in 1170 according to the Kievan Chronicle, or after 1174 according to the younger recension of the Novgorod First Chronicle (based on the Commission manuscript of the mid-fifteenth century). The Kievan Chronicle states that in the third year following the death of Andrei Iurevich (1177), Andrei's half-brother, Vsevolod, "called Dmitrii Iurevich in baptism", arrived from Thessaloniki.[69] It is possible that Vsevolod assimilated Byzantine ideas and cultural norms during his Byzantine exile and that the culture of late twelfth and early thirteenth century Vladimir-Suzdal was largely influenced by Vsevolod's experience of Middle Byzantine culture.

There are several historical artefacts that reflect a Byzantine cultural influence in Vladimir-Suzdal during Vsevolod's reign. Monica White has examined the introduction of the name Konstantin (Constantine) into the Rus naming system.[70] It may be notable that Vsevolod named his son Konstantin (b. 1186) since that name had only appeared once before, as the baptismal name of Mstislav Vladimirich (Prince of Chernigov, d. 1035), and had never appeared in the general Riurikid naming system. The name again appeared in 1130s when Iurii Vladimirich founded a town named Ksniatin in his patrimony of Vladimir-

---

67 PSRL 24, col. 80: "Мстислав же и Василко съ матерію и Всеволода молодово брата своего пояша съ собою третиято и идоша къ Царюграду. И дасть царь Василкови с братомъ в Доунаи 4 городы, а Мстиславу дасть волость отъ Скалана."

68 "Κατὰ τὸν αὐτὸν χρόνον καὶ Βλαδίσθλαβος, εἷς ὢν τῶν ἐν Ταυροσκυθικῇ δυναστῶν, σὺν παισί τε καὶ γυναικὶ τῇ αὐτοῦ δυνάμει τε τῇ πάσῃ αὐτόμολος ἐς Ῥωμαίους ἦλθε, χώρα τε αὐτῷ παρὰ τὸν Ἴστρον δεδώρηται, ἣν δὴ καὶ Βασιλίκᾳ πρότερον τῷ Γεωργίου παιδί, ὃς τὰ πρεσβεῖα τῶν ἐν Ταυροσκυθικῇ φυλάρχων εἶχε, προσελθόντι βασιλεὺς ἔδωκε." Ioannes Kinnamos, Epitome Historiarum, 236–237. This "Vladislav" is not known from Russian chronicles and it is possible that the name is a combination of common Slavonic names, see Freidenberg, Trud Ioanna Kinnama kak istoricheskii istochnik, esp. 42.

69 PSRL 2, col. 543 / NPL, col. 468.

70 White, Veneration of St Constantine in pre-Mongol Rus, 351–362.

Suzdal.⁷¹ White agrees with Fyodor Uspenskii and Anna Litvina that Vsevolod's introduction of the name Constantine was most likely a general reference to his Byzantine culture rather than a specific reference to a Byzantine emperor, in this case, either Constantine I (a reference to the Christianisation) or Constantine IX Monomachos (a reference to the connection between the Riurikids and Byzantium).⁷² White also discusses the possibility that Vsevolod brought the *ciborium* or grave covering of St. Demetrios from Thessaloniki to Rus, an event which is recorded in the Laurentian Chronicle.⁷³

Vsevolod's patron saint, St. Demetrios of Thessaloniki, a Byzantine military saint, is portrayed as a warrior unsheathing his sword on Vsevolod's seals.⁷⁴ Vsevolod dedicated his grand cathedral church to St. Demetrios. Founded between 1193 and 1197, the iconography of the church of St. Demetrios may have reflected the personal taste of Vsevolod reflected in the coherent theme exploring different facets of rulership incarnated by the biblical, martial, mythological, and historical rulers represented on the church's facade (figure 4).⁷⁵ William Brumfield writes: "In view of the austerity of sculpted ornament on Vsevolod's earlier churches...the profusion of stone sculpture for his palace church, dedicated to St. Demetrios of Thessaloniki, must be attributed to its role as a statement of princely authority."⁷⁶ The church of St. Demetrios features a series of sculptural icons that suggest a melange of Romanesque, Middle Byzantine, and Northern European⁷⁷ influences with highly stylised sculptural elements, featuring martial themes that promote Vsevolod's military prowess and divinely-ordained authority.⁷⁸

The church of St. Demetrios offers several examples of martial authority: a row of twelve haloed riders, some brandishing swords, decorates the south and west facades.⁷⁹ It has been noted, albeit not entirely convincingly, that SS Boris and

---

71 White, Veneration of St Constantine in pre-Mongol Rus, 354.
72 White, Veneration of St Constantine in pre-Mongol Rus, 355; Litvina / Uspenskii, Vybor imeni u russkikh kniazei, 149.
73 The Laurentian Chronicle recounts: "[...] принесена [быс] дска ис Селуна гробнᵃя ста Дмитрия (... the grave covering of St Demetrios was brought from Salonica.)" PSRL 1, col. 414; "И принесъ доску гробную изъ Селуна стаᵍ мᶜнка Дмитрия мюро непрестанно точащю на здравьє немощны́ᵐ в тои црькви постави. И сорочку того^ж мчн҃ка ту же положи (The grave covering of St. Demetrios was brought from Salonica, an endless myrrh flowed for the health of the enfeebled in that church [where the covering] had been placed. And they placed the remains of the martyr there.)" PSRL 1, col. 437; see White, The 'Grave Covering' of St Demetrios, 95–114.
74 Ianin, Aktovye pechati, vol. 1, 208, nos. 211–212.
75 Vagner, Skul'ptura Vladimiro-suzdal'skoi Rusi, 44–45.
76 Brumfield, History of Russian Architecture, 52.
77 The teratological decoration (interlaced pattern featuring fantastic animal heads) is a Northern European design-motif. See Obolensky, Byzantine Commonwealth Eastern Europe, 458.
78 See Skvortsov, Khudozhestvennaia kul'tura, 307–329, 316–323.
79 Gladkaia, Rel'efy dmitrievskogo sobora vo Vladimire, 144–159; and White, Byzantine Military Saints, 187–189.

Figure 4: Cathedral of Saint Demetrios, Façade

Gleb join the ranks of the warrior-saints. According to Kämpfer, they are portrayed holding crosses on the north facade, and riding horses into battle along with other saints on the south and west facades.[80] The possible inclusion of SS Boris and Gleb riding into battle on Vsevolod's frieze further illuminates the emphasis on SS Boris and Gleb in Suzdal in the thirteenth century, and the elaboration of their cult as uniting feature for the Rus princely clan.[81] A unique feature of the iconography of the facade is the inclusion of a representation of Vsevolod enthroned on a cushioned settle with his sons (north facade, left bay), one of whom he holds in his lap.[82] The sculpture depicting the founder has been

---

80 Kämpfer, Herrscherbild, 130–133. The identities of the military saints in the freize are derived from their number, leading to the conclusion that the two remaining figures represented the dynastic saints Boris and Gleb.
81 White, Byzantine Military Saints, 192. The cult of SS Boris and Gleb was promoted from the time of Iurii Vladimirich who founded a new Vyshgorod at Kideshka (178, n. 36), and continued into the thirteenth century at Iurev-Polskoi, see: Vagner, Skul'ptura Vladimiro-suzdal'skoi Rusi, 76–77.
82 The five sons have been identified as: Konstantin, Georgii, Iaroslav, Vladimir, and Sviatoslav. Vagner suggests that the son on Vsevolod's knee would be the youngest (Sviatoslav), born during the construction of the cathedral. Voronin disagreed, stating that the figure was

interpreted as a veterotestamentary evocation of the ruler styled as the founder of a new dynasty.[83] The western facade of the church features veterotestamentary kings: King David with his harp (the warrior, musician, poet, and ancestor of Jesus) and King Solomon (the law-giver, poet, and builder of the Temple).[84] The depiction of King David is a dominant element of the church. King David is represented enthroned with his right hand raised in blessing and his left holding his harp. The aspect of King David as the divinely appointed king of Judah who defeated his enemies and thus united the various factions within his kingdom is perhaps a corollary to the oeuvre of Andrei Iurevich and to the struggle for power over Suzdal that marked the period following his assassination in 1174.[85]

The Ascension of Alexander (south facade, right bay) and the deeds of Hercules embody Vsevolod's political and military ambitions.[86] Both iconographies communicate sacred rulership and symbolise the apotheosis of royal and imperial power through its proximity to and association with the supreme authority of Christ (western facade). The sculptural icon depicting the Ascent of Alexander shown frontally in a two-wheeled chariot, holding meat in each hand for the griffons drawing the chariot is a representation of the martial ruler's apotheosis. As André Grabar has noted, this scene is similar to the thirteenth century carvings on the western facade of St. Mark's cathedral in Venice,[87] and was a well-known scene in Byzantine art[88] and letters.[89]

Vladimir because his baptismal name was Dimitrii (as was Vsevolod's), see Voronin, Zodchestvo severno-vostochnoi Rusi, vol. 1, 436.

83 Kämpfer, Herrscherbild, 128, 130–132, fig. 69; Brumfield, History of Russian Architecture, 52–56.
84 Discussion of iconographic significance of image of King David, see Vagner, Skul'ptura drevnei Rusi, 130–134.
85 For example, Bogoliubskii's church of the Divine Intercession. See Brumfield, History of Russian Architecture, 45–51.
86 Wörn, Studien zur Herrschaftsideologie des Großfürsten Vsevolod III., esp. 39.
87 Demus, San Marco in Venice, 111. The narthex and new façade were constructed during the thirteenth century, which was a period of renovatio when the ideal of the Imperium Romanum was promoted. The sculptural decoration of the façades appears to have been imported from elsewhere, perhaps spolia imported from Byzantium after the Iconoclast period, see the reliefs of the Palaia or Little Metropolis of Athens, Ebersolt, Monuments d'architecture byzantine, 59, 168, pl. 20.
88 All of the examples of this scene date from the Middle Byzantine period, see Étienne Coche de la Ferté on the background of the iconography of the scene, Sur quelques bagues byzantines de la Collection Stathatos, esp. 76; Grabar, Le succès des arts orientaux, 32–60, figs. 10b-c; Supka, Luftfahrt Alexanders des Grossen, 307–314, fig. 1.
89 The Alexander Romance was probably known in Rus by the mid-twelfth century through what Istrin referred to as the Iudeiskii Khronograf, which included certain books from John Malalas (up to the beginnings of Roman History, excluding Book 3), the Alexander Romance, the treatise on the Brahmans by Palladius, and Josephus' Jewish War. The earliest compendium extant dates to the mid-thirteenth century, but is thought to have been compiled earlier from sources that had already been translated to Slavonic. See Istrin, Aleksandriia russkikh

The Byzantine iconographic tradition reflected the rhetorical commonplaces of ritualised rulership with depictions of religious, legendary, and historical figures such as King David, Alexander the Great, and Constantine I. The resemblance of the Byzantine emperor to these figures was a basic theme in Byzantine panegyric and political thought, wherein the emperor was eulogised as an ideal Christian ruler and God's representative on earth.[90] The comparison of the emperor with veterotestamentary kings, legendary heroes, and quasi-legendary emperors reflects both a moral and a political legitimacy, such as piety to avert divine anger, zeal for orthodoxy, philanthropy, and military success. George Dennis has noted that Late Antique praise rhetoric focussed on peace, justice, and love of orthodoxy; but that towards the tenth century, military exploits and the emperor, both as warrior and supplicant, became increasingly common *topoi*.[91] Theological orthodoxy found its expression largely in the divine liturgy and was thus made known to the faithful. Political orthodoxy – articulated by a literary elite – incorporated theological motifs along with imperial, consular, and civic ideals and communicated them through rhetoric, both through textual and iconographic representation.[92]

Both the chronicles of Rus and the edifactory literature of Rus (compilatory texts such as the *Izbornik of 1073*, the *Izbornik of 1076*, the *Pouchenie Vladimira Monomakha*, the *Pchela*,[93] the *Slovo* of Daniel the Prisoner,[94]) contain discourses on rulership based on a Byzantine ideal. However, without the inheritance of Late Antique ideological artefacts, the Rus inherited pre-Christian ideals of rulership through references in translated Christian literature.[95] As discussed in the introduction, an antinomy becomes apparent between Byzantine ideal rulership and local practices. The portrayal of the acts and deeds of princes – the discourse of the *Pouchenie Vladimir Monomakha* (Lesson of Vladimir Monomakh) along with the ritual enthronement and depiction of the succession configurations of Rus – provides an alternate image of princely rule, one based on the practicalities of rulership, on personal interactions and on the non-centralised functioning

---

khronografov, 351–353; Tvorogov, Drevnerusskie Khronografy, 16–17; Franklin, Malalas, esp. 278.
90 Dennis, Imperial Panegyric, 131–141.
91 For example, Arethas the Deacon for Leo VI in the tenth century, Theophylaktos for Alexios I in the 11th century, and Manuel Holobolos for Michael VIII Palaiologos in the thirteenth century all promote the image of the emperor as military leader. Dennis, Imperial Panegyric, 139–140.
92 Cameron, Christianity and the Rhetoric of Empire, 1–15.
93 On the pedagogical role of texts such as the *Pchela*, see Maksimovich, Obraz ideal'nogo pravitelia, 28–42, 39–41.
94 On didactic literature, see: Budovnits, Pamiatnik rannei dvorianskoi publitsistiki, 138–157; in its Byzantine context, see Franklin, Echoes, 507–535.
95 For example, Agapetus' treatise on ideal rulership in the Pchela, see Ševčenko, Neglected Byzantine Source, 142–143.

dynastic culture of early Rus. Edificatory literature focusses on iconic rulership based on Byzantine ideals,[96] charity, piety, and the submission of the prince to divine will. War and military are rarely evoked as the signifiers of legitimacy and authority;[97] however, these are represented as practical modes of rulership. The chronicles of Rus offer many examples attesting to the military prowess and might of princes as the principal means of imposing their rule, in enforcing succession principles or contravening them, and in creating consensus around their rule.

Within this paradigm, the evocation of divine intercession juxtaposes heavenly occurrences onto the earthly court.[98] The protocol of the heavenly court created an eternal archetype, placing earthly events into a providential framework. Chroniclers in Rus provided narrative strategies in order to convey divine intercession as a means of describing princely actions as righteous, while ritualising behaviours ideologically opposed to the depictions of hieratic rulership that dominate edificatory literature and occasionally appear in the chronicles. However, princes were also implicated in articulating iconic rulership with a military ideal. Princely patronage in Rus made visible divine protection and intercession. Depictions of military saints on Rus seals and coins gave symbolic expression to intercession along with the military ideal of rulership, and the iconographies of the churches of Vladimir-Suzdal – founded after Vsevolod Iurevich's Byzantine exile – offer a definite commentary on the political order and give visual definition to the multiple sources of iconic rulership with emphasis on the prince as defender of orthodoxy (both spiritual and political) through his military might.[99] Such foundations also conveyed the real authority and power of princes by offering a tangible reminder of social and economic stimui.[100]

The narrative sources of Rus fix warfare and conflict in the rhetoric of divine providence. The maintenance of political order through superior military might is ritualised, expressing both the fact of Christian soteriology that rulers were subject to God and that rulers were elevated to a place of greater proximity to intercessors. Intercession implying the existence of a unified moral community whose ideals were defined by its rituals, projected the image of immutable princely authority when it was called into question.

---

96 Cyril of Turov made use of Barlaam and Joasaph in his address to Basil Abbot of the Caves Monastery, which contained a short 6th century treatise on ideal kingship presented to Justinian I by Agapetus. The reference describes the ideal prince as adorned with a "wreath of wisdom" and with the "purple robe of justice". See Ševčenko, Neglected Byzantine Source, 148–150. The same reference to the "wreath" and the "purple robes" is ascribed to Rostislav Mstislavich in his epitaph in the Kievan Chronicle, see PSRL 2, col. 530–531.
97 Haldon, Warfare, State and Society, 15–17.
98 Maguire, The Heavenly Court, 258–259.
99 Noble, Topography, Celebration, and Power, 45–91.
100 Brown, Power and Persuasion in Late Antiquity, 82–84.

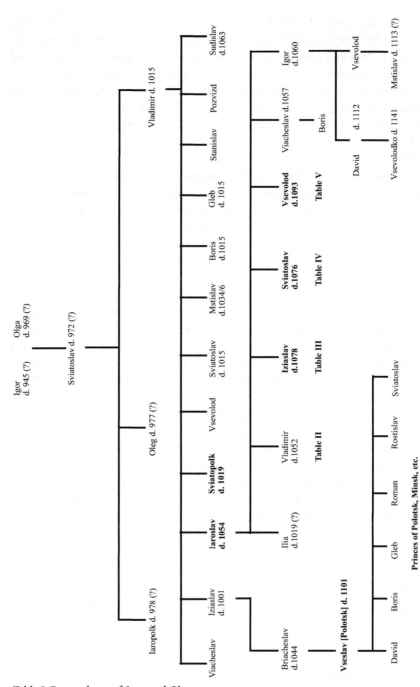

Table I: Descendants of Igor and Olga

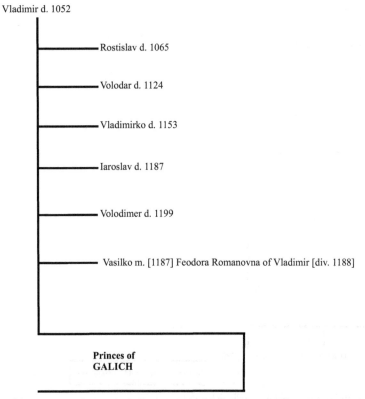

Table II: Descendants of Vladimir Iaroslavich [of Novgorod]

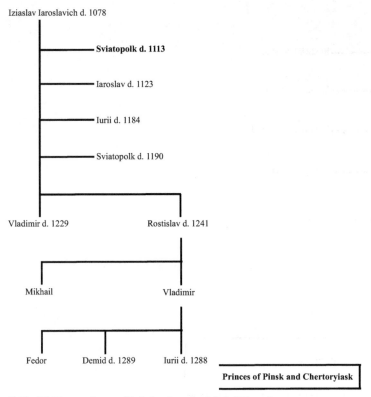

Table III: Descendants of Iziaslav Iaroslavich [of Turov]

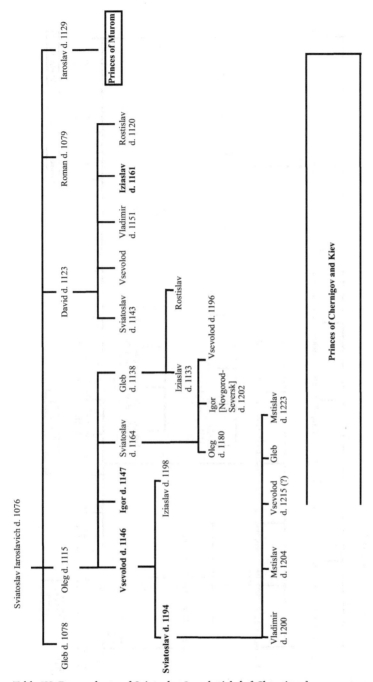

Table IV: Descendants of Sviatoslav Iaroslavich [of Chernigov]

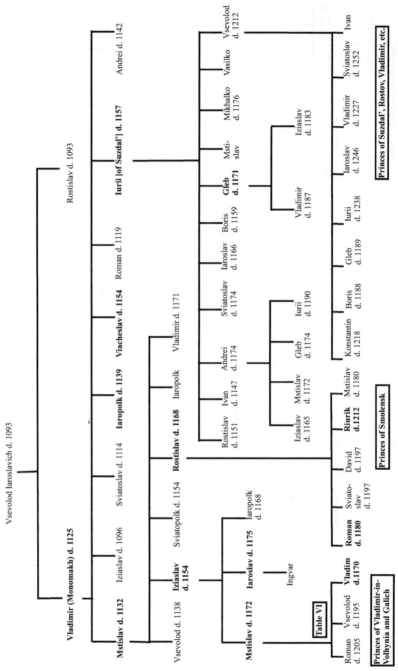

Table V: Descendants of Vsevolod Iaroslavich [of Pereiaslavl']

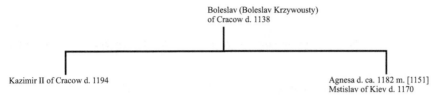

Table VI: Descendants of Mstislav Iziaslavich [Romanovich Princes]

Bibliography

Sources

Cyril of Scythopolis, Vita Sabae, ed. Eduard Schwartz, Kyrillos von Skythopolis (Texte und Untersuchungen 49), Leipzig 1939.
Ianin, Valentin Lavrentievich, Aktovye pechati drevnei rusi X–XV vv., 2 vols., Moscow 1970.
Ioannes Kinnamos = Epitome rerum ab Ioanne et Alexio Comnenis gestarum, ed. August Meineke (Corpus Scriptorum Historiae Byzantinae 23), Bonn 1836.
Leo VI, Tactica = Leonis imperatoris Tactica, ed. Rezsö Vári, Budapest 1922.
Leo the Deacon, Histories = Leonis diaconi Caloensis historiae libri decem et Liber de velitatione bellica Nicephori Augusti, ed. Karl B. Hase (Corpus Scriptorum Historiae Byzantinae 30), Bonn 1828.
Michael Psellos, Chronographia = Histoire d'un siècle de Byzance (976–1057), ed. and trans. Émile Renault, Paris 1932.
Miracula Demetrii (BHG, 516z–523) = ed. Paul Lemerle, Le plus anciens recueils des miracles de saint Démétrius et la pénétration des Slaves dans les Balkans, vol. 1, Paris 1979.
Nicephorus Phocas, Praecepta militaria, ed. Iurii Alexandrovich Kulakovsky, Strategika imperatora Nikifora (Zapiski imperatorskoi akademii nauk 8), St. Petersburg 1908.
Photios, Homilies, Φωτίου Ὁμιλίαι, ed. Basileios Laourdas (Ἑλληνικά, Παράρτημα 12), Thessaloniki 1959.
PSRL 1 = Polnoe sobranie russkikh letopisei, vol. 1, Moscow1928/1962.
PSRL 2 = Polnoe sobranie russkikh letopisei, vol. 1, Moscow 1908/1962.
PVL = Povest' vremennykh let, vol. 1, ed. Dmitrij S. Likhachev and Varvara P. Adrianova-Peretts, Moscow 1950.
Thietmar, Chronicon = Thietmari Merseburgensis episcopi Chronicon, ed. Robert Holtzmann (Monumenta Germaniae Historica; Scriptores rerum Germanicarum in usum scholarum, Nova Series 9), Berlin 1935.

Literature

Androshchuk, Fedir, Images of Power: Byzantium and Nordic Coinage, c. 995-1035, Kyiv 2016.
Brown, Peter, Power and Persuasion in Late Antiquity, Madison 1992.
Brumfield, William, A History of Russian Architecture, Cambridge 1993.
Buc, Philippe, The Dangers of Ritual: Between Early Medieval Texts and Social Scientific Theory, Princeton 2001.
Budovnits, Isaak U., Pamiatnik rannei dvorianskoi publitsistiki (Molenie Daniila Zatochnika), in: Trudy otdela revnerusskoi literatury 8 (1951), 138-157.
Cameron, Averil, Christianity and the Rhetoric of Empire: The Development of Christian Discourse, Berkeley CA 1991.
Cheynet, Jean-Claude, Par Saint Georges, Par Saint Michel, in: Travaux et Mémoires 14 (2002), 115-134.
Chichurov, Igor S., Politicheskaia ideologiia srednevekov'ia: Vizantiia i Rus': k XVIII Mezhdunarodnomu kongressu vizantinistov, Moscow 1990.
Coche de la Ferté, Étienne, Sur quelques bagues byzantines de la Collection Stathatos, in: Comptes rendus des séances de l'Académie des Inscriptions et Belles-Lettres 1956 (100.1), 72-81.
Demus, Otto, The Church of San Marco in Venice (Dumbarton Oaks Studies 6), Washington DC 1960.
Dennis, George, Imperial Panegyric: Rhetoric and Reality, in: Byzantine Court Culture from 829 to 1204, ed. Henry Maguire, Washington DC 1997, 131-141.
Dölker, Albrecht, Der Fastenbrief des Metropoliten Nikifor an den Fürsten Vladimir Monomakh (Skripte des slavischen Seminars der Universität Tübingen 25), Tübingen 1985.
Dotzauer, Winfried, Die Ankunft des Herrschers: Der fürstliche 'Einzug' in die Stadt (bis zum Ende des Alten Reichs), in: Archiv für Kulturgeschichte 55 (1973), 245-288.
Dvornik, Francis, Byzantine Political Ideas in Kievan Russia, in: Dumbarton Oaks Papers 9 (1956), 73-121.
Ebersolt, Jean, Monuments d'architecture byzantine, Paris 1934.
Filiushkin, Aleksandr I., Institut krestotselovaniia v Srednevekovoi Rusi, in: Klio. Zhurnal dlia uchenykh (2004), 42-48.
Franklin, Simon / Shepard, Jonathan, The Emergence of Rus, c. 950-1300, London / New York 1996.
Franklin, Simon, Echoes of Byzantine Elite Culture in Twelfth-Century Russia?, in: Byzantium-Rus-Russia: Studies in the Translation of Christian Culture (Variorum Collected Studies), Aldershot 2002, 507-535.
Franklin, Simon, Malalas, in: Slavonic, Byantium-Rus-Russia: Studies in the translation of Christian Culture (Variorum Collected Studies Series 754), Aldershot 2002, 276-287.
Freidenberg, Maren M., Trud Ioanna Kinnama kak istoricheskii istochnik, in: Vizantijskij Vremennik 16 (1959), 29-51.
Geertz, Cifford, Centers, Kings, and Charisma: Reflections on the Symbolics of Power, in: Culture and its Creators, ed. Joseph Ben-David / Terry Nichols Clark, Chicago 1977, 150-171.

Gladkaia, Magdalina, Rel'efy dmitrievskogo sobora vo Vladimire. Opyt kompleksnogo issledovaniia, Moscow 2009.
Grabar, André, Le succès des arts orientaux à la cour byzantine sous les Macédoniens, in: Münchner Jahrbuch der bildenden Kunst 3.2 (1951), 32–60.
Grierson, Philip, Byzantine Coins, London / Berkeley / Los Angeles 1982.
Grotowski, Piotr, Arms and Armour of the Warrior Saints. Tradition and Innovation in Byzantine Iconography (843–1261) (The Medieval Mediterranean 87), Leiden 2014.
Haldon, John F., Warfare, State and Society in the Byzantine World 565–1204, New York 1999.
Hurwitz, Ellen, Prince Andrej Bogoljubskij: The man and the myth (Studia historica et philologica 12.4), Florence 1980.
Istrin, Vasilii M., Aleksandriia russkikh khronografov, Leipzig 1893.
Ivakin, Hlib / Khrapunov, Nikita / Seibt, Werner, Byzantine and Rus Seals. Proceedings of the International Colloquium on Rus-Byzantine Sigillography (Kyiv, 13.–16. September 2013), Kyiv 2015.
Kämpfer, Frank, Das russische Herrscherbild: von den Anfängen bis zu Peter dem Großen. Studien zur Entwicklung der Ikonographie im byzantinischen Kulturkreis (Beiträge zur Kunst des christlichen Orients 8), Recklinghausen 1978.
Kantorowicz, Ernst, The King's Advent and the Enigmatic Panels in the Doors of Santa Sabina, in: Selected Studies, ed. Ernst Kantorowicz, Locust Valley NY 1965, 37–75.
Kazhdan, Alexander, Rus-Byzantine Princely Marriages in the Eleventh and Twelfth Centuries, in: Harvard Ukrainian Studies 12/13 (1988–1989), 414–429.
Krivosheev, Yurij V., Gibel' Andreia Bogoliubskogo: Istoricheskoe rassledovanie, St. Petersburg 2003.
Litvina, Anna F. / Uspenskii, Fyodor B., Vybor imeni u russkikh kniazei v X–XVI vv., Moscow 2006.
Magdalino, Paul, The Empire of Manuel I Komnenos, 1143–1180, Cambridge 1993.
Magdalino, Paul, The Triumph of 1133, in: John II Komnenos. Emperor of of Byzantium: In the shadow of father and son, ed. Alessandra Bucossi / Alex Suarez, Milton Park 2016, 53–70.
Maguire, Henry, The Heavenly Court, in: Byzantine Court Culture from 829 to 1204, ed. Henry Maguire, Washington DC 1997, 247–258.
Maksimovich, Kiril. A., Obraz ideal'nogo pravitelia v drevnerusskoi "Pchele" i politicheskaia mysl' Vizantii, in: Drevniaia Rus 7 (2002), 28–42.
McCormick, Michael, Eternal Victory. Triumphal Rulership in Late Antiquity, Byzantium and the Early Medieval West, Cambridge 1986.
Mikhailova, Yulia / Prestel, David, Cross Kissing: Keeping One's Word in Twelfth-Century Rus', in: Slavic Review 70 (2011), 1–22.
Miller, David, Legends of the Icon of Our of Vladimir: A Study of the Development of Muscovite National Consciusness, in: Speculum 43 (1968), 657–670.
Noble, Thomas F. X., Topography, Celebration, and Power: The Making of a Papal Rome in the Eighth and Ninth Centuries, in: Topographies of Power in the Early Middle Ages, ed. Mayke de Jong / Frans Theuws, Leiden 2001, 45–91.
Obolensky, Dimitri, The Byzantine Commonwealth Eastern Europe 500–1453, London 1971.
Pashuto, Vladimir T., Vneshniaia politika drevnei Rusi, Moscow 1968.

Pelenskyj, Jaroslav, Russia and Kazan: Conquest and Imperial Ideology (1438-1560s), Berlin 1974.
Pentcheva, Bissera, Icons and Power: The Mother of God in Byzantium, Pennsylvania PA 2006.
Pichkhadze, Anna A. / Makeeva, Irina I., "Pchela": drevnerusskii perevod, Moscow 2008.
Ševčenko, Ihor, A Neglected Byzantine Source of Muscovite Political Ideology, in: Harvard Slavic Studies 2 (1954), 141-179.
Skvortsov, A. I., Khudozhestvennaia kul'tura X-pervoi poloviny XIII v., Moscow 1988.
Sotnikova, Marina P. / Spasskii, Ivan G., Tysiacheletie drevneishikh monet Rossii. Svodnyi katalog russkikh monet X-XI vekov, Leningrad 1983.
Stefanovich, Petr S., Der Eid des Adels gegenüber dem Herrscher im mittelalterlichen Russland, in: Jahrbücher für Geschichte Osteuropas 53 (2005), 497-505.
Stefanovich, Petr, Expressing Loyalty in Medieval Russia: Oath vs. Oral Formulas, in: Oralité et lien social au Moyen Âge (Occident, Byzance, Islam): parole donnée, foi jurée, serment, ed. Marie-France Auzépy / Guillain Saint-Guillain, Paris 2008, 147-156.
Stefanovich, Petr, Krestotselovanie i otnoshenie k nemu tserkvi v Drevnei Rusi, in: Srednevekovaia Rus' 9 (2004), 86-113.
Stepanenko, Valerii Pavlovich, Bogomater' Nikopeia i sviatye voiny', in: Preslavka knizhovna shola, Sofia 1995.
Supka, Géza, Beiträge zur Darstellung der Luftfahrt Alexanders des Grossen, in: Zeitschrift für christliche Kunst 24 (1911), 307-314.
Tvorogov, Oleg V. Drevnerusskie Khronografy, Leningrad 1975.
Vagner, Georgii K., Skul'ptura Vladimiro-suzdal'skoi Rusi: g. Iur'ev-Pol'skoi, Moscow 1964.
Von Steinmeyer, Ernst, Die kleineren althochdeutschen Sprachdenkmäler, Berlin 1916.
Voronin, Nikolai N., Zodchestvo severno-vostochnoi Rusi XII-XV vekov, Moscow 1961-62.
Vukovich, Alexandra, Enthronement in Early Rus: Between Byzantium and Scandinavia, in: Viking and Medieval Scandinavia 14 (2018), 211-239.
Vukovich, Alexandra, The Gift Economy of the Princes of Rus, in: Ruthenica 15 (2019), 74-91.
White, Monica, Military Saints in Byzantium and Rus', 900-1200, Cambridge 2013.
White, Monica, The 'Grave Covering' of St Demetrios between Byzantine and Rus, in: Saints and Their Lives on the Periphery: Veneration of Saints in Scandinavia and Eastern Europe, ed. Haki Antonsson / Ildar Garipzanov, Turnhout 2010, 95-114.
White, Monica, Veneration of St Constantine in pre-Mongol Rus, in: D. Sveti car Konstantin i hrišćanstvo, vol. 2: Međunarodni naučni skup povodom 1700. godišnjice Milanskog edikta, 31. maj-2. jun 2013 (Niš: Centar za crkvene studije, 2013), ed. X. Bojović, 351-362.
Wörn, Dietrich, Studien zur Herrschaftsideologie des Großfürsten Vsevolod III. "Bolshoe gnezdo" von Vladimir (1176-1212): Ein Beitrag zur Erforschung der historiographischen und künstlerischen Formen der Herrscherverherrlichung im russischen Hochmittelalter, in: Jahrbücher für Geschichte Osteuropas 27.1 (1979), 1-40.
Zabelin, Ivan E., Sledy literaturnogo truda Andreiia Bogoliubskogo, in: Arkheologicheskie izvestiia i zametki 2-3 (1895), 37-49.
Zacos, George, Byzantine Lead Seals, vol. 1, Basel 1972.

II Practices of Celebrating Victory and Triumphs

Jörg Rogge

After the Battle. Triumphs and Victory Celebrations in Late Medieval England

'Triumph' is not the best term to describe the actions and festivities that took place after a military leader had won a battle in the Middle Ages. However, the term 'triumph' is and was widely spread and was used to describe different kinds of rituals and ceremonies in various contexts. Kings and princes in Europe staged some kind of triumph as a part of court festivities, coronation processions or triumphal entries in cities. In 1512, the emperor Maximilian I. designed a triumph that did not portray any real occurrence (military activity) but was a product of the emperor's imagination.[1]

It might occur to you that the medieval triumphs were modelled on Roman triumphs. However, my examples, which I discuss in this paper, show no signs of direct influence from an antique model.[2] I deal with a specific form and aspect of triumph, which is closely connected to the victory on the battlefield. I use the term 'victory celebration' to indicate how military leaders have celebrated their victories and how they have organized their public self-portrayal. In this sketch, I will try to give a few answers to the following questions: who staged the victory celebrations? Where were they staged? Which message were they supposed to convey? The examples to answer some of the questions are mainly from the British Isles.

However, the first example is from the realm of the German Kings. In July 1044 the German King Henry III celebrated his victory over a Hungarian army under the command of Samuel Abba near Menfö by the river Raab[3]. The chronicles report that the king wanted to celebrate a divine service on the battlefield. King Henry III appeared barefoot and dressed in woolen cloth. In front of a particle of

---

1 Eichberger, Illustrierte Festzüge, 73–98; Helas, Lebende Bilder.
2 Pogorzelski, Triumph, 22–24 sums up the requirements for a triumph in Rom: just war, victory over foreign enemies, at least 5000 killed enemies. During the early republic the triumphs were also a religious ceremony. During the Roman Imperial Period (26–27) victories were always attributed to the prince; the commanders could not perform their own triumphs any longer.
3 Boshof, Salier, 121.

the holy cross he bent his knees and prayed. He forgave his enemies, and the other combatants held hands as a sign of remission and peace.[4]

In 1070, William the Conqueror founded Battle Abbey (St. Martin's Abbey of the Place of Battle) at the location where the Battle of Hastings had taken place in 1066 and where King Harold had allegedly been slain. It was the duty of the monks to pray for the souls of the warriors. In addition, William wanted to mark the spot where God had bestowed him with the crown.[5] God was responsible for the victory and – in the words of William of Malmesbury – "it was God's hand that protected him [so that] not a drop of his blood was spilt".[6]

These two examples give an impression of the chroniclers' general perspective on and their interpretation of victory celebrations: first, thanksgiving to God for his support, which indicated the legitimacy of the action against the enemies. Second, the moral justification of the war, which was presented as a duel between good and evil (Henry III against the rebellious Hungarians under Samuel Abba; William against the usurper Harold). In the end the victory was an *iudiucum dei*.[7]

The next example of a triumph was intended to indicate the definitive end of the political independence of Wales. During the winter of 1282/83, King Edward I of England and his army leaders and troops were able to defeat the princes Llywelyn and David of Wales. Llywelyn was slain in an ambush in December 1282 and his brother David was captured in June 1283. In October 1283, he was executed for being a traitor and a rebel.[8] After his victory over the Welsh troops and the death of their leaders, King Edward wanted to savor and celebrate his great victory, without disregarding his duties concerning the consolidation of the conquest. He set up a castle-building program and in March 1284 he announced the Statute of Wales, with which the Welsh principality Gwynedd was subjected to the rule of the English crown. Three newly created counties and Flint formed the Principality of Wales. Edward I converted the other principalities in Wales into a so-called *terra*; a land that was united with the English crown. The newly created Principality of Wales was incorporated into the English realm. For the exercise of authority, important offices and administrative practices were implemented in Wales: Sheriffs, Coroners, the Exchequer, counties, Hundreds, and the grant of law per writs.[9]

Nevertheless, Edward I wanted to show his success and the victory over the Welsh with symbolic and solemn public demonstrations of the new status of the defeated enemies. It started in July 1284 with a tournament held in Nefyn (on the

---

4 Annales Altahenses maiores, 35; Die größeren Jahrbücher von Altaich, 39.
5 Peltzer, 1066, 245.
6 William of Malmesbury, Gesta Regum Angleorum, 457.
7 Cram, Iudicium Belli, 90–92.
8 Prestwich, The three Edwards, 12–15.
9 Davis, Colonial Wales, 16–17.

north-west coast), one of the favorite residences of the vanquished princes of Wales. To celebrate the victory properly, knights from England as well as Europe were invited.[10] Then the king led a great triumphal progress through Wales from September to November 1284.

The festivities were the joyous part of his actions. The other side of the coin was his treatment of the symbols and signs of the political independence of Wales. Here he showed his determination to eradicate Welsh independence forever. Additionally, he demonstrated his piety. He ordered the transfer of the Abbey of Aberconwy, the favored Cistercian House of the Gwynedd dynasty, to a location seven miles distant from the original site to make room for his new castle at Conway. In this case he was not considerate towards the monks and their abbey, although in general he was eager to express his devotion and thanks to God and the saints for supporting his political and military efforts. Solemnly Edward I donated Llywelyn's golden crown to the shrine of Edward the Confessor in Westminster Abbey. The crown was considered to have been King Arthur's crown and contemporary chroniclers stressed the transfer of rule that was symbolized by the donation of the crown ("Wallensium gloria ad Anglos, licet invite, est translate").[11] The seal plates of the Welsh princes were melted down, transformed into a chalice and donated to Edward's new monastic foundation (1277) Vale Royal.

The most important sign of the independence of Wales was the sacred relic of the True Cross, also known as the cross of Neith (*Y Groes Naid*), with a particle of the cross of Christ. It was handed over to Edward I in June 1283. It was an acknowledgement "that the dynasty which had cared for it, and gained its protection, through the ages had been irretrievably destroyed".[12] In May 1285, the cross was shown in a solemn procession in London led by the king and the queen, attended by 14 bishops and many magnates of the realm. In the later years of his reign the king regularly took the cross with him on his travels for private worship.[13] The victory celebrations had a secular component that aimed to secure military success for a long time by annexing parts of Wales to the crown. However, the donation of the Welsh crown and chalice to abbeys indicate that King Edward saw himself in the old tradition of thanksgiving to God for his support in the war against the Welsh.

When Henry V followed his father on the English throne in 1413, one of his political objectives was to revive the struggle for the French crown. His first military expedition to the continent in 1415 reached its peak in the victory over a

---

10 Davis, Conquest, 355–356.
11 Vale, Edward III, 17–18.
12 Smith, Llywelyn ap Gruffudd, 581.
13 Prestwich, Edward I, 203–204; Prestwich, The piety of Edward I, 126.

superior French army (according to the number of warriors) near Agincourt on 25 October.[14] Although this victory was not decisive and the struggle and fighting continued in the years to come, this victory was nevertheless considered to be a sign that King Henry V was waging a just war and that his claim for the French crown was legitimate. In a parliament at the beginning of November 1415, while the king was still in France, the chancellor praised God for his help. With his support, the small English army had achieved a great victory over the superior French troops.

The Londoners, the members of parliament and the king agreed that this unexpected victory should be celebrated properly. While the king travelled home from France, preparations for welcoming him and celebrating his entry into the city were made.[15] On Saturday, 23 November, the mayor of London with his councilors and other citizens greeted the king outside the city. Then they all returned, and the king followed with his own, "though only quite modest, retinue." This indicates that Henry's entry into the city and his passage through London to St Paul's cathedral was not staged like a Roman triumph. Henry was not accompanied by his whole army, and he presented only six important prisoners (the dukes of Orleans and of Bourbon, the counts of Eu, of Vendome, of Richemont, and Marshal Boucicaut) to the public.[16] The Londoners had decorated the path of the king through the city with seven pageant stations with figures and heraldic displays.[17] They were intended to demonstrate the status of the city and its prestige, as well as veneration for the victorious king. The city had also invested money and ships in Henry's campaign.

At the end of London Bridge, two giant warders (one with the keys to the city) guarded the entry to the *Civitas Regis Iustitiae* (London).[18] The king could read this inscription on a wall as he passed by. Some towers and houses had been covered with cloth decorated with the royal arms and those of St George and of St Edward the Confessor. On his way the king was honored by choirs of young girls and young men.[19] At the same time, they stressed the intervention of God by singing the Agincourt Carol: God fought for the king and therefore all English

---

14 Curry, Agincourt, 270: At night after the battle in the English camp a feast was held and the noble French prisoners had to serve the English king and his officers.
15 An in-depth-description is found in the Gesta Henrici Quinti, 101–113. Relatively detailed also The chronicle of Adam Usk, 259–263. Further source extracts regarding the return of the king in: Curry, The Battle of Agincourt, 265–271. See also Curry, Henry V, 72–75 and the account of the events on 23. November by Mortimer, 1415, 479–484.
16 Curry, Henry V, 73.
17 Coldstream, 'Pavilion'd in Splendour', 153–171.
18 Barron, Pageantry on London Bridge, 91–104 describes and analyses six royal entries between 1413 and 1432. The Pageants on London Bridge on the account of the entry of Henry V cost ca. 19 pounds, twice as much as those for his coronation (94).
19 Barron, Henry V and London, 232.

were obliged to thank him for the victory.[20] At the Cheapside Cross, young maidens sang: "Welcome Henry ye fifte, King of Englond and of Fraunce". It was as if another David was coming who had slain a Goliath (the French army). A choir of boys, who represented the hierarchy of angels and stood on London Bridge, sang *"benedictus qui venit in nomine Domini"* as the king approached.[21] London was entirely decorated like a New Jerusalem and the pageants – as Gordon Kipling has observed – "welcomed the King to heaven by virtue of his faithful service to the Lord rather than by right of his earthly glory".[22] Of course, the onlookers did not disregard the secular aspects of the entrance of the king: wine ran through the conduits at Cheapside and elsewhere in the city. Free wine was intended to strengthen the adoration of the lowborn people for the king and might have helped to increase the joyful atmosphere of that day.

However, at the core of all the festivities was thanksgiving. King Henry V showed that he ascribed the victory at Agincourt to God rather than to himself. In his biography of Henry V the Italian Tito Livio Frulovisi wrote that "the king did not suffer this honor to be ascribed to him but put all praise and glory to God".[23] The author of the *Gesta Henrici* informed his readers in a similar manner: "Indeed, from his quiet demeanor, gentle pace, and sober progress, it might have been gathered that the king, silently pondering the matter in his heart, was rendering thanks and glory to God alone, not to man".[24] This observation corresponds with the statements of the king. Henry repeated more than once that he considered himself to be an instrument of God's will and that the killing of the French nobles and their defeat had been a divine intervention to punish the French for their sins.[25] One of their sins was of course the rejection of his claim to the French throne.

The last two stations of the king's procession through London affirmed this impression. At the High Altar of St Paul's, the king gave thanks and made an offering; having done this, he rode to Westminster Abbey to make an offering at the shrine of St Edward the Confessor.[26] Then he left the church and went to the Palace of Westminster. Henry's own conduct in the procession demonstrated that he had not won the battle with courage and brute force but because "his

---

20 Jones, 24 Hours at Agincourt, 273 has the refrain: "Our king went forth to Normandy, With grace and might of chivalry, There God for him wrought marvellously, Wherefore England might call and cry, To God give thanks for victory".
21 Gesta Henrici Quinti, 111.
22 Kipling, Enter the King, 207.
23 Curry, The Battle of Agincourt, 268.
24 Gesta Henrici Quinti, 113.
25 Curry, Agincourt, 295–96.
26 Allmand, Henry V, 98–99.

cause was just and because he was devout and temperate, not bloodthirsty, arrogant or self-satisfied".[27]

The last example are the actions that took place after the battle of Bosworth, 22 August 1485. After about two hours of heavy fighting, King Richard III was killed and his adversary, Henry Tudor, won the day.[28] This was the first time since the death of King Harold in the Battle of Hastings in 1066, that an English ruler had lost his life and his reign in battle.

According to Polydore Vergil in his *Anglica Historia*, Henry immediately thanked God with many prayers for the victory he had gained. Then, overwhelmed by incredible happiness, he climbed a nearby hill. After he had praised his soldiers and ordered the wounded to be tended, and the dead to be buried, he gave his undying thanks to all his nobles and promised he would remember their support.[29] Henry, like his contemporaries, knew that, apart from all battle tactics and the reluctance of Richards's troops to engage properly in the fight (some had even deserted), the outcome of the battle had revealed the will of God. The Crowland Chronicle stressed that "Henry VII submit himself again to trail of battle" and that in "the end a glorious victory was granted by heaven to the earl of Richmond (Henry VII)".[30] Here, as in the case of King Henry III's victory over the Hungarian army in 1044 mentioned above, the contemporaries again argued with the *iudicum dei* topos.[31]

Meanwhile, the crown of Richard III had been found in the spoils. Sir Thomas Stanley took it and placed it on Henry's head. This was obviously an unofficial coronation; in the accounts of the events, it is described however because of the victory and as a manifestation of the soldiers' will to make him king.[32] At Henry's command, the body of Richard III was publicly displayed in Leicester for two days, in order to show his wounds and confirm that he had died on the battlefield.[33] All these actions were intended to indicate that Henry had defeated Richard, the usurper of the English crown, and was the legitimate claimant to the throne. During his first parliament in November, he declared again that he was the rightful king because of inheritance and the judgment of God.

---

27 Lewis, Kingship and masculinity, 112.
28 Skidmore, Bosworth; a compilation of extracts from written sources in: Dockray, Richard III, 120–133.
29 Polydore Vergil. An edition of the manuscript in the Vatican (Codices Urbinates Latini 497 und 498) in: Hay, The Anglica Historia, 2: "Interea Henricus more triumphantis imperatoris Londinum profectus est", S 3: "Henry meanwhile made his way to London like a triumphing general". – Hay has collated also the printed editions from 1543, 1546 and 1555.
30 The Crowland chronicle continuations, 183 and 181.
31 Clauss, Der Krieg als Mittel, 128–141.
32 Skidmore, Bosworth, 311. Henry VII was anointed and crowned on Sunday, 30 October.
33 Skidmore, Bosworth, 318.

On 3 September 1485 Henry entered London.[34] Like the fifth Henry he was received by the Mayor and Aldermen of London together with other citizens outside the city. Together they made a procession (with carts laden with spoils) through parts of the city to St Paul's. He and his victory were praised with paeans of victory throughout the streets.

At the rood by the north door Henry offered three standards from the battle (St George, a dragon on a white and green silk drapery, and a banner of Tarteron with the Image of the Dun Cow[35]). This was a statement of his divine right to rule and kingship, proven by his victory. Then, after prayers and singing the *Te Deum*, Henry moved to the palace of the bishop of London. For several days' plays, pastimes and pleasures of various kinds took place in the city. The Londoners not only celebrated the victor of Bosworth but also showed their relief that a civil war appeared to have been avoided.

There is no evidence of a purely secular triumph or celebration of a victory in battle up to 1500. The celebration always had a strong liturgical connotation. The winners, and even the so-called battle heroes or soldier kings like Edward III and Henry V, saw the necessity of thanking God for his help in the first place. These examples underline the assumption that the personal piety of the kings was a part of their exercise of rule and authority. They tried to show to the audiences the connection of their personal piety and the celebration of English superiority in the wars against their enemies. The superiority was based on the idea that the English had legitimate reasons for war. These were rebellion and treason in the case of Wales, a claim to the throne and inheritance in the case of France. God, who helped the kings to fulfill their duties, had also confirmed the legitimate reason. They therefore made offerings to monasteries, churches, and shrines. Henry V's entrance to London in 1415 was the best public display of this connection. The king as the proud sovereign and commander enters his earthly city

---

34 Skidmore, Bosworth, 334–335; Polydore Vergil, Cap. 26 Henry VII, paragraph 1: "Meanwhile Henry began to make his way towards London, with the country folk everywhere rejoicing, congratulating, and hailing him as king. And when he drew close to the city, Lord Mayor Thomas Hill, Sheriffs Thomas Bretain and Richard Chester, together with all the aldermen and the entire city most dutifully came to greet him, and not only did each and every man offer his greetings, but everybody desired to clasp the victorious hands of the approaching men who had killed the tyrant, as one man offered his congratulations, another gave his thanks that by their doing the republic was safe, the authors of those evils having been done away with. And so, rejoicing was celebrated by all orders of society, and in all the saints' churches throughout the city God was honored with thanksgiving for several days. But Edward's friends were particularly happy because in their minds they perceived that the opposite faction was doomed to destruction" [http://www.philological.bham.ac.uk/polverg].
35 The Dun cow of Dunsmore Heath (an area west of Dunchurch near Rugby in Warwickshire, England) was a savage beast slain by Guy of Warwick (legendary in 10th Century). A large narwhal tusk is still shown at Warwick Castle as one of the ribs of the Dun Cow.

and, at the same time, he enters a spiritual city, which presents itself as a New Jerusalem, as a humble subject of God, the King of Heaven.[36]

The victory celebrations were in most cases a sequence of actions and performances, which comprised the immediate actions after the victory on the battlefield, the public demonstration and communication of the victory, liturgical thanksgiving for the help of God and secular festivities with wine, beer, singing and tournaments. If the victory was decisive not only for the battle but for the war or conflict in total (Wales 1283), the celebration of the victory also included the symbolic and political demonstration that political independence had come to an end. The last aspect of the victory celebrations I like to stress concerns the provisions the kings took to honor their dead comrades and fighters. William the Conqueror, Henry V and Henry VII commanded their troops on the battlefields to take care of the dead knights (at least) of their party. In addition, they made offerings to saints' shrines and altars or even ordered a new monastery (Battle Abbey) to be built to take care of the souls of the dead warriors.

Bibliography

Sources

Annales Altahenses maiores, ed. Edmund von Oefele (Monumenta Germaniae Historica, Scriptores rerum Germanicarum in usum scholarum 4), Hannover 1891.

Die großen Jahrbücher von Altaich, ed. and trans. Ludwig Weiland (Die Geschichtsschreiber der deutschen Vorzeit 46), Leipzig 1940.

Gesta Henrici Quinti, ed. Vivian H. Galbraith / Roger Mynors, Oxford 1975.

Polydore Vergil, Anglica Historia (1555 version), ed. Dana F. Sutton, online edition [http://www.philological.bham.ac.uk/polverg/].

The Chronicle of Adam Usk, 1377–1421, ed. Chris Given-Wilson, Oxford 1997.

The Crowland Chronicle Continuations: 1459–1486, ed. Nicholas Pronay / John Cox, London 1986.

William of Malmesbury, Gesta Regum Angleorum / The History of the English Kings, vol. 1, ed. Roger A. B. Mynors / Rodney M. Thomson / Michael Winterbotton, Oxford 1998.

Literature

Allmand, Christopher, Henry V, New Haven / London 1997.

Barron, Caroline M., Henry V and London, in: The Battle of Agincourt, ed. Anne Curry / Malcom Mercer, New Haven / London 2015, 226–234.

---

36 Kipling, Enter the king, 208.

Barron, Caroline M., Pageantry on London Bridge in the Early Fifteenth Century, in: 'Bring futh the pagants': Essays in early English drama presented to Alexandra F. Johnstone, ed. David N. Klausner / Karen Sawyer Marsalek, Toronto / London 2007.

Boshof, Egon, Die Salier, Stuttgart ³1995.

Clauss, Martin, Der Krieg als Mittel und Thema der Kommunikation: Die narrative Funktion des Gottesurteils, in: Gottes Werk und Adams Beitrag. Formen der Interaktion zwischen Mensch und Gotte im Mittelalter, ed. Thomas Honegger et al. (Das Mittelalter; Beihefte 1), Berlin 2014, 128-141.

Coldstream, Nicola, 'Pavilion'd in Splendour': Henry's Agincourt Pageants, in: Journal of the British Archaeological Association 165 (2012), 153-171.

Cram, Kurt-Georg, Iudicium Belli: Zum Rechtscharakter des Krieges im deutschen Mittelalter, Munster / Cologne 1955.

Curry, Anne, Agincourt: A new history, Strout 2010.

Curry, Anne, Henry V: Playboy Prince to Warrior King, London 2015.

Curry, Anne, The Battle of Agincourt: Sources and interpretations, Woodbridge 2000.

Davis, Robert Rees, Colonial Wales, in: Past and Present 65 (1974), 3-23.

Davis, Robert Rees, Conquest, Coexistence, and Change: Wales 1063-1415, Oxford 1987.

Dockray, Keith, Richard III: A reader in history, Gloucester 1988.

Eichberger, Dagmar, Illustrierte Festzüge für das Haus Habsburg-Burgund: Idee und Wirklichkeit, in: Hofkultur in Frankreich und Europa im Spätmittelalter, ed. Christian Freigang / Jean-Claude Schmitt (Passagen 11), Berlin 2005, 73-98.

Hay, Denys, The Anglica Historia of Polydore Vergil, 1485-1537, London 1950.

Helas, Philine, Lebende Bilder in der italienischen Festkultur des 15. Jahrhunderts, Berlin 1999.

Jones, Michael, 24 Hours at Agincourt, London 2016.

Kipling, Gordon, Enter the King: Theatre, Liturgy, and ritual in the medieval civic triumph, Oxford 1998.

Lewis, Katherine J., Kingship and masculinity in late medieval England, London / New York, 2013.

Mortimer, Ian, 1415: Henry V's year of glory, London 2009.

Peltzer, Jörg, 1066: Der Kampf um Englands Krone, Munich 2016.

Pogorzelski, Richie, Der Triumph: Siegesfeiern in antiken Rom, Mainz 2015.

Prestwich, Michael, Edward I, New Haven / London 1997.

Prestwich, Michael, The piety of Edward I, in: England in the thirteenth century, ed. W. Marc Ormrod, Woodbridge 1986, 120-128.

Prestwich, Michael, The three Edwards, War and state in England, 1272-1377, London / New York 2003.

Skidmore, Chris, Bosworth: The birth of the Tudors, London 2014.

Smith, J. Beverley, Llywelyn ap Gruffudd: Prince of Wales, Cardiff 2014.

Vale, Juliet, Edward III and Chivalry: Chivalric society and its context, 1270-1350, Woodbridge 1982.

Klaus Pietschmann

Musical Echoes of Victory and Defeat in Fifteenth-Century Court Culture[*]

Military victories and defeats are usually associated with music. Acoustic signals such as drums and brass fanfares were of central importance in warfare. They were regarded as visible and audible regalia which constituted central elements of a representational court culture. These signals unequivocally refer to their original context like auditory markers in diverse contexts. In the liturgy, for example, timpani and trumpets evoke the notion of celebrating the emperor's God-given battle fortunes, e.g. in Te Deum compositions. Funeral marches, however, confer their specific character during military parades in honor of fallen soldiers through their tonal encoding which clearly distinguishes them from other parade events. These codes, a standard of early modern music culture and often documented in musical tradition, are in contrast extremely uncommon in late medieval music which is the topic of this talk. A rare exception is Guillaume Dufay's *Gloria ad modum tubae* – this piece, albeit isolated, confirms that sound codes with military connotations in the broadest sense did already exist in the first half of the 15th century (example 1). The ostinato in the bass voice, resembling an almost obtrusive repetition of the fanfare motif, appears peculiar within the tradition of 15th century mass settings. This poses a riddle for research as there is no information on the function and circumstance of its origin.

But if cases like this were so rare – what then comprises the musical echoes of Victory and Defeat in 15th-Century Court Culture? This will be clarified by means of two examples which give insight into the role and the potential meanings of music composed in courtly contexts: on the one hand Guillaume Dufay's *Lamentatio Sanctae Matris Ecclesiae Constantinopolitanae* on the occasion of conquering Constantinople, on the other hand the so-called *L'homme armé* masses, totaling about 40 mass compositions of the 15th and 16th centuries using the melody of a military connoted French chanson. I will show that music always had

---

[*] English translation: Stephan Summers. Some parts of this article are revised passages of Pietschmann, L'homme armé.

the function here of subjecting military victories and defeats to liturgical analogies and channeling them to serve the Christian message of salvation.

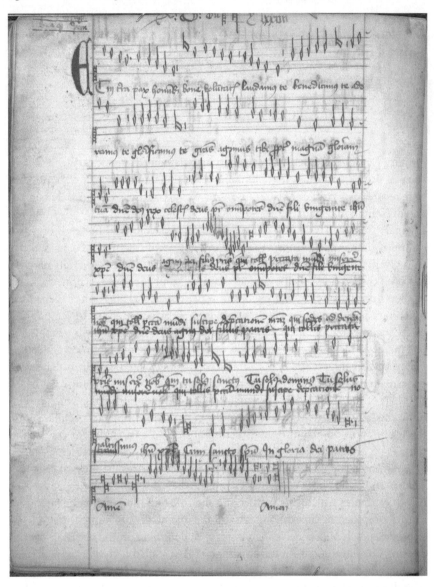

Example 1: Guillaume Dufay, "Gloria ad modum tubae" (Aosta, Seminario Maggiore, Codex 15, fol. 95v–96r)

The first example, Dufay's *Lamentatio*, belongs to a smaller group of compositions from the 15th and 16th centuries, musically and textually following the *Lamentationes Hieremiae prophetae* from the Old Testament on the destruction of Jerusalem and of the Temple. As liturgical chants, these lamentations were an integral part of the Triduum sacrum, the highlight of the Holy Week.[1] In February of 1456, Dufay writes in a letter to Piero and Giovanni de' Medici: "In the past year I composed four lamentations for Constantinople, which are quite good, three of them for four voices; the lyrics had been sent to me from Naples."[2] At this time, Dufay was employed by the Dukes of Savoy, and after having worked in the Papal Chapel for several years he was in direct contact with the political elite of his time as documented by this letter. Not much is known about his contact to Naples mentioned here and only one of the lamentations has been preserved. It was assumed sometimes that they were composed for the Feast of the Pheasant on February 17, 1454, in Lille. According to a report by Olivier de la Marche, at a certain point of the lavish spectacle a representative of the church began to sing a lamentation. However, the text quoted by de la Marche does not correspond with Dufay's preserved lamentation which is why this event is no longer considered as the original purpose for this composition. In it, the mother of the Church of Constantinople, i. e. the Mother of God, expresses her sorrow to God the Father. This French text is combined with the biblical-liturgical chant in the tenor voice:

O très piteux de tout espoir, fontaine,
Père du fils dont suis mère éplorée,
Plaindre me viens à ta cour souveraine
De ta puissance et de nature humaine
Qui ont souffert, telle dure vilaine,
Faire à mon fils qui tant m'a honorée,
Dont suis de bien et de joie séparée,
Sans qui vivant veuille entendre mes plaintes.
À toi, seul dieu, du forfait me complains
Du gref tourment et douloureux outrage
Que voit souffrir plus bel des humains
Sans nul confort de tout humain lignage.

Tenor:
Omnes amici ejus spreverunt eam
Non est qui consoletur eam
Ex omnibus caris ejus.

Most merciful source of all hope,
Father of the son whose weeping mother I am,
I come to complain at your sovereign court
Of your authority and of human nature,
Which have allowed such harsh cruelty
To be inflicted on my son, who has so honored me;
Whereby I have been parted from happiness and joy,

---

1 Marx-Weber, Lamentatio.
2 Gülke, Guillaume Du Fay, XXIII–XXIV.

Without any living being who will hear my complaints.
To you, only God, I appeal from the sentence,
From the grievous torment and painful injury
That I watch the fairest of men suffer,
With no consolation from your human speech.

Tenor:
All her friends have betrayed her:
Among all her lovers there is none to comfort her.[3]

Dufay creates the lamenting tone of this composition almost automatically by setting the voices in French similar to the tenor voice, which itself sings the Gregorian reciting tone of the lamentation in elongated note values.[4] Although the composition makes use of the customary change of two-, three- and four-part settings and organizes these according to contemporary techniques, an impression of artless simplicity mirroring the sorrowful substance of the text is conveyed. By employing the liturgical lamentation and musically approximating the other voices simultaneously, Dufay not only draws an analogy of the fall of Constantinople and the biblical destruction of Jerusalem. He also achieves a 'liturgification' of his composition, placing it on the same level as the lamentation on Christ's death on the cross during the Holy Week. This musical range of associations is equivalent to the French main text which addresses the deity directly. The verse "I come to complain at your sovereign court" is particularly emphasized through its full-part setting which also builds a bridge to the courtly sphere: this lamentation addresses the sovereign of every court at which it is performed. A call for a crusade is undoubtedly implied here, similar to the Feast of the Pheasant where this had been stated explicitly before.

An intertwining of eschatological and worldly levels of meaning of this kind can also be found in the second field, which will be addressed in this paper. As mentioned earlier, the chanson "L'homme armé" served as the basis for approximately 40 mass compositions of the 15th and 16th centuries; using simple words and a catchy melody this chanson sings of the armed warrior, his fearsome appearance, and military mobilization in general (example 2). By employing this melody in a mass composition, the military sphere is implicitly evoked and transferred into the rite of the mass. Therefore, a mass liturgy in which such a composition is performed overall adopts the semantic field of the military in the invariable parts – Kyrie, Gloria, Credo, Sanctus and Agnus Dei.

---

3 Guillaume du Fay, Lamentatio, 5.
4 Ibid., 1–4.

Example 2: The melody of the chanson "L'homme armé"

In the 15th and 16th centuries, including secular melodies in mass compositions was far from unusual;[5] however, this group of works is extraordinary in so far as songs as simple and catchy as this were hardly ever drawn upon – in addition to the circumstance that no other melodic model was used more often than this song. One assumes that the origins of this compositional tradition go back to the crusade propaganda after 1453 and to the newly founded chivalric orders such as the Order of the Golden Fleece.[6] These were headed by the rulers of Burgundy, the Aragonese court and the popes, thereby forming a context in which many of these masses can be placed. However, the main indicator for making this connection stems from a secular composition. The combinative chanson *Il sera par vous combatté | L'homme armé* was presumably written at the Burgundian court and combines the *L'homme-armé* song with a second singing voice with its own lyrics alluding to the imminent fight against the Turks (example 3).

---

5 For general overviews over the history of mass settings in the given period and the conflicting views in former and recent research see Finscher, Messe and Wiesenfeldt, Messe.
6 Aside from Laubenthal, L'homme armé see especially Planchart, Origins as well as van der Heide, New Claims.

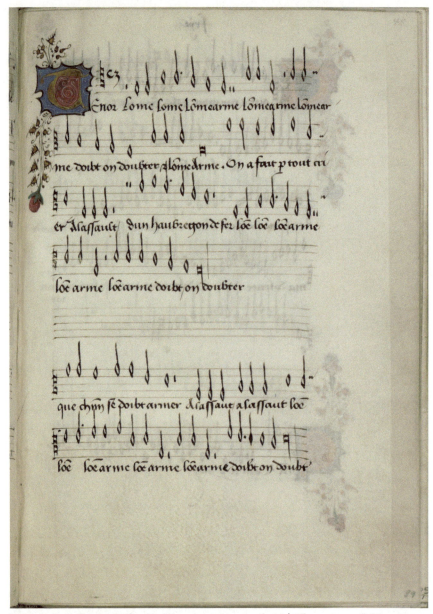

Example 3: Guillaume Dufay (?): "*Il sera par vous combatté | L'homme armé*" (New Haven, Beinecke Library, MS 91 "Mellon Chansonnier", fol. 44v–44r)

The assumption expressed by Alejandro Planchart that the Chanson was composed directly before the Burgundian crusade initiative seems very plausible.[7] Accordingly, possible performance contexts of the *L'homme armé* masses are the chapters of the Order of the Golden Fleece and of other chivalric orders.[8]

In this context, another tradition going back to the 13th century, which provided votive masses addressing the liberation of the Holy Land with certain mass forms, proves significant.[9] Especially after the fall of Byzantium and the growing Ottoman threat after 1453 various *Missae contra Turcos* were published, confirmed by the pope and equipped with indulgences. While individual mass propers indeed focused on peace prayers, the call for divine support for the passage of arms predominates, legitimized especially by biblical references to the Maccabees. In the context of liturgical sources the musical sphere in general or even specific compositions are never mentioned which is why corresponding references to possible musical ordinary settings are missing in these forms. Hence, *L'homme armé* masses can also be interpreted as counterparts to the *Missae contra Turcos*. A connection with crusade propaganda can be established in so far as that they offered the possibility of correspondingly reattributing meaning even to the *ordinarium missae* and therefore facilitate propaganda in all parts of the rite of the mass.

This process, however, is embedded in an older tradition of associating the liturgy of the mass with an overarching sacralization of military fitness. As early as the 12th century, French interpretations of masses show an equation of the rite of the mass with armed engagement in the name of Christ against Satan. Jean Beleth expresses this very vividly in the *Summa de ecclesiasticis officiis*, written in 1160:

> "The matter [i.e. the rite of the mass] is arduous and quickly exhausts the powers of our mind. The priest, both representative and warrior willing to fight the old enemy, puts on paraments like armor. The sandals are worn as greaves to avoid getting stuck in dust or dirt. The outer garment protects his head like a helmet, he cloaks his body in alb like a breastplate, the cincture serves as a bow and the sub-cinctorium as a quiver. The stole covers his throat, he thrusts it like a javelin against him who wants to hold him back. He uses the maniple as club, the chasuble protects him like a shield; he holds the book like a sword in his hands."[10]

This allegory on the mass is given an even more specific form in Honorius Augustodunensis's *Gemma animae* from the 12th century, which probably served

---

7 In particularly, see Planchart, Origins, 324–325, who persuasively demonstrates that the chanson previously attributed to Robert Morton was composed by Guillaume Du Fays, also see van der Heide, New Claims, 10–11.
8 Prizer, Music and Ceremonial.
9 Linder, Raising Arms, 175–273.
10 Beleth, Summa, 61–62 (cap. 32).

as a model for Beleth. In this, all parts of the mass and all participants of the church service are interpreted in a military sense whereby singers and precentors function as war trumpeters, warriors and military leaders:

> "The singer, who intonates the chant, functions as trumpeter giving the signal to engage in battle. The precentors, presiding over both sides of the choir, are the generals, organizing the troops for battle. The singers cover their heads with caps and hold staffs or tables in their hands because warriors cover their head with helmets and protect themselves with weapons."[11]

In the 15th century this perspective intensified through various ceremonial practices, such as armoring priests during mass or placing military equipment on the altar.[12] The tradition of composing the *L'homme armé* mass cycles can be seen as a musical manifestation of interpreting the liturgy in this way as well. However, contemporary sources do not offer concrete proof for a connection of this kind.

But which courts appropriated this specific, musico-liturgical form of calling to the crusades? As mentioned above, in the early stages of this musical tradition the Burgundian dukes and possibly the French kings were the only ones to support compositions of *L'homme armé* masses and contributed to their dissemination. Subsequently, this tradition was continued and consolidated most permanently in the papal context. The *L'homme armé* masses of the members of the Papal Chapel, Josquin Desprez, Marbriano de Orto and Bertrand Vacqueras, were most likely composed at the Papal Court.[13] Therefore, the phenomenon of these masses can especially be associated with those centers of crusade propaganda originating from Burgundy through the Order of the Golden Fleece and the spiritual leader of Christendom. On the other hand, it seems that these masses had not been used by individual representatives in order to stylize their own military potential any more since the late 15th century. Evidently, the phenomenon of the *L'homme armé* masses is not determined by individual courts' aspirations to distinguish themselves, but rather marks a struggle for a concerted military effort. *L'homme armé*, the armed man, therefore represents the ideal *miles christianus*, a role model for every Christian ruler to whom the Burgundian dukes in their function as sovereigns of the order and the popes correspondingly appeal.

In conclusion, I would like to illustrate how composers specifically put this military codification of the ordinary text into practice and what semantic levels could be accessed in doing so. Josquin Desprez' *Missa L'homme armé sexti toni*,

---

11 Augustodunensis, Gemma animae, lib. I, cap. 74.
12 Warmington, Ceremony; for further aspects of the symbology of the armed man see Kirkman, Cultural Life, 98–134 and Wright, Maze.
13 On this tradition of musical settings, see Rodin, Josquin's Rome, 233–268 and passim.

composed around 1490 at the papal court,[14] will serve as an example for this. This piece is characterized through a subtle treatment of the melody: foregoing a Cantus firmus, the melody is split into small parts which are taken up in modified form. The effect of this is that only fragments of the otherwise so distinctive melody can be recognized when listening.[15] Two passages in the Credo are all the more expressive, in which the beginning of the song is clearly exposed. On the one hand, this concerns the text passage "Et unam sanctam catholicam ecclesiam," which is additionally highlighted from the preceding part through a clear cesura (cf. example 4). This is a rather unusual way of structuring the text musically within a Credo setting as these cesuras are commonly placed before "Et incarnatus est" or "Et in spiritum sanctum."[16] In this way the composer's strategy of highlighting the combination of the *L'homme armé*-melody with the mention of the catholic church becomes rather obvious to a contemporary listener.

Subsequently, the melody is replaced by new motifs and figurations but reoccurs towards the end with the words "et vitam venturi saeculi." The intention of this compositional strategy is obvious: text passages of the Credo referring directly to the main idea of a call for a crusade are set to the melody of the *L'homme armé* song. On the one hand it denotes "unam sanctam catholicam et apostolicam ecclesiam", and on the other it invokes "vitam venturi seculi," the promise of eternal life inherent to every crusade.[17] This musical message might well have been complemented by a sermon directly preceding the Creed in which the Turkish menace and the call for a crusade, addressed to Christian dukes, was stated explicitly – as many sermons of the time did.[18] Hence Josquin's musical mass setting utilizes the distinctive contour of the melody and its potential for military signification to comment on individual text passages of the Creed and deliver a reference to the crusades even comprehensible to a musically inept but attentive listener familiar with the *L'homme armé* song.

To conclude, military victories and defeats did not usually echo in courtly music of the 15th century – at least hardly any documents have been preserved

---

14 Following Jeremy Noble's unpublished considerations on the nature and extent of the sources Rodin assumes a composition date after Josquin departed from the Papal Chapel (Rodin, Josquin's Rome, 31 s.). However, Fallows considers it possible that Josquin composed the *Missa* during his time in Rome (Fallows, Josquin, 156).
15 Many studies are available on the compositional characteristics. For a summary, see Blackburn, Masses, 62–69.
16 Within Josquin's mass compositions a cesura of this kind before "Et unam sanctam" occurs only in the *Missa Gaudeamus,* which can be dated within the same creative period. (Rodin, Josquin's Rome, 31–32).
17 The conception of a crusade to be an armored pilgrimage with special clerical privileges was an a priori matter of fact for any crusade efforts. See e.g. Mayer, Kreuzzüge, 17–20.
18 As O'Malley has shown, the Turkish menace was indeed a popular subject in sermons of papal masses after Mohammed II. had conquered Otranto in 1480. O'Malley, Praise.

Example 4: Josquin Desprez, "Missa l'homme armé sexti toni", Credo

comparable to early modern compositions for similar festive and mourning occasions. Dufay's *Lamentatio*, one of the few exceptions, also transcends the sorrow and introduces a theological level from which a call to the crusades addressed to Christian rulers can be deduced. The same is true for the numerous musical mass settings of the *L'homme armé* song: they conceive the Sacrifice of the Mass as an armed engagement against Satan and exploit the intertextual possibilities of this compositional technique for an appeal to take the cross. However, the simultaneously promised victory is not primarily military in nature but rather spiritual.

Bibliography

Sources

Augustodunensis, Honorius, Gemma animae, ed. Jaques-Paul Migne (Patrologiae cursus completus. Series latina 172) Paris 1854. Patrologia Latina database: [http://gateway.proquest.com/openurl?url_ver=Z39.88-2004&res_dat=xri:pld&rft_dat=xri:pld:ft:all:Z400115573].
Beleth, Johannes, Summa de ecclesiasticis officiis, ed. Heribert Douteil (Corpus Christianorum Continuatio Mediaevalis 41), Turnhout 1976.

Guillaume Du Fay, Lamentatio Sanctae Matris Ecclesiae Constantinopolitanae, ed. Alejandro Enrique Planchart (Guillaume Du Fay Opera Omnia 01/21), Santa Barbara 2008.

Laubenthal, Annegret, L'homme armé in: MGG Online, ed. Laurenz Lütteken, 2016ff., first published 1996, published online 2016 [www.mgg-online.com/mgg/stable/15040].

Wiesenfeldt, Christiane, Art. Messe, Mehrstimmige Messvertonungen bis 1600 in: MGG Online, Laurenz Lütteken, ed., 2016ff., published Oktober 2017 [www.mgg-online.com/mgg/stable/47190].

Literature

Blackburn, Bonnie J., Masses on Popular Songs and Syllables, in: The Josquin Companion, ed. Richard Sherr, Oxford 2000, 51–88.

Fallows, David, Josquin, Turnhout 2009.

Finscher, Ludwig, Die Messe als musikalisches Kunstwerk, in: Die Musik des 15. und 16. Jahrhunderts, ed. Ludwig Finscher (Neues Handbuch der Musikwissenschaft 3), Laaber 1989, 193–275.

Gülke, Peter, Guillaume Du Fay. Musik des 15. Jahrhunderts, Stuttgart 2003.

Kirkman, Andrew, The Cultural Life of the Early Polyphonic Mass. Medieval Context to Modern Revival, Cambridge 2010.

Linder, Amnon, Raising Arms. Liturgy in the Struggle to Liberate Jerusalem in the Late Middle Ages, Turnhout 2003.

Marx-Weber, Magda, Art. Lamentatio in: MGG Online, ed. Laurenz Lütteken, Kassel, Stuttgart, New York 2016ff., first published 1996, published online 2016 [www.mgg-online.com/mgg/stable/16061].

Mayer, Hans Eberhard, Geschichte der Kreuzzüge, Stuttgart et al. [8]1995.

O'Malley, John W., Praise and Blame in Renaissance Rome: Rhetoric, doctrine, and reform in the sacred orators of the Papal Court, ca. 1450–1521, Durham 1979.

Pietschmann, Klaus, L'homme armé. Militärische Symbolik in der Ordinariumsvertonung um 1500, in: Zeichen des Militärischen am Fürstenhof im frühneuzeitlichen Europa, ed. Peter-Michael Hahn / Matthias Müller, Berlin 2017, 25–37.

Planchart, Alejandro Enrique, The Origins and Early History of L'homme armé, in: Journal of Musicology 20 (2003), 305–357.

Prizer, William F., Music and Ceremonial in the Low Countries: Philip the Fair and the Order of the Golden Fleece, in: Early Music History 5 (1985), 113–153.

Rodin, Jesse, Josquin's Rome. Hearing and Composing in the Sistine Chapel, Oxford 2012.

van der Heide, Klaas, New Claims for a Burgundian Origin of the L'homme armé Tradition, and a Different View on the Relative Positions of the Earliest Masses in the Tradition, in: Tijdschrift van de Koninklijke Vereniging voor Nederlandse Muziekgeschiedenis 55 (2005), 3–33.

Warmington, Flynn, The Ceremony of the Armed Man: the Sword, the Altar, and the L'homme armé Mass, in: Antoine Busnoys: Method, meaning, and context in late medieval music, ed. Paula Higgins, Oxford 1999, 89–132.

Wright, Craig, The Maze and the Warrior: symbols in architecture, theology, and music, Cambridge Mass. et al. 2001.

III The Culture of Dealing with the Vanquished

Thomas Scharff

Ad internitionem delevit. How Victorious Franks Treated their Defeated Enemies

In 841, the sons of Emperor Louis the Pious, who had died a year earlier, fought each other in the Battle of Fontenoy, near Auxerre on the border between Burgundy and Aquitaine. After a long and fierce battle, the two younger brothers, Louis the German and Charles the Bald, gained the victory. The eldest, Emperor Lothar, fled the battlefield together with his nephew and ally Pippin of Aquitaine and his entire army.[1]

What followed the younger brothers' triumph is described by Nithard in his 'Four Books of History'. Nithard, as the grandson of Charlemagne also a close relative of the princes involved, was in this conflict on the side of Charles the Bald. He personally fought during the battle and wrote his work on Charles' behalf.[2] On the immediate aftermath of the combat, he says:

> "The tough fighting over, Louis and Charles, still on the field of battle, began to discuss what ought to be done about those who were in flight. Some voices, motivated by anger, pressed for a pursuit; others, and especially the kings, having pity on their brother and his people, and desiring with their customary charity that the defeated, since they had been crushed by the Judgement of God and by the blow they had suffered, should now repent their wickedness and greed and with God's help, from now on be of one mind with them in their quest for true justice, they [the kings] urged their followers to put everything in God's hands. The rest of the army gave them their assent, and they halted the fighting and pillaging."[3]

---

1 For Fontenoy see Krah, Entstehung, 49–86; Dümmler, Geschichte, 139–162. For the actions and positions of the main protagonists see Schäpers, Lothar I., 345–449; Goldberg, Struggle, 86–116; Nelson, Charles, 105–131.
2 For Nithard and his account of the fratricidal war, see Nelson, Histories; Nelson, Knighthood; Clauss, Schlacht; Bachrach / Bachrach, Nithard; Airlie, World; Heinzle, Flammen.
3 Nithardi historiarum libri IV, III 1, 28: "Proelio quidem, uti prefatum est, strenue peracto, quid de palantibus peragere deberetur, Lodhuvicus et Karolus in eodem campo deliberare coeperunt. Et quidam ira correpti persequi hostes suadebant, quidam autem, et maxime reges, miserantes fratris plebisque et, ut iudicio Dei et hac plaga repressi ab iniqua cupiditate resipiscerent, et Deo donante deinceps unanimes in vera iusticia devenirent, piis visceribus solito more optabant. In quo negotio Dei omnipotentis misericordia ut prestolaretur, suadebant. Quibus cetera multitudo assentientes a proelio et praeda discesserunt et fere mediante die ad

In Nithard's account, then, the victorious kings stopped their men from pursuing, killing and plundering the members of the defeated army. Rather, they sought to restore unity and peace between the Franks on both sides. In doing so they opposed some of their own warriors, but acted as Christian kings were supposed to. According to Nithard's account, they thus also observed the norms for warfare as expressed in Carolingian mirrors for princes and episcopal letters of admonition. According to these, the rulers had, among other things, the task of preventing the warring nobility from assaulting and plundering and of leading them back to the right path of Christian charity. This is particularly important because the mirrors considered the king's right conduct to be the guarantee for the victory bestowed by God.[4]

But the peace sought by the victors did not last, and after a short time the war continued with even more cruelty and atrocities. Assuming that the historiographers on Charles' and Louis' side are telling the truth, Lothar, in search of new allies, formed an alliance with the enemies of Christianity, the Normans, and with the Stellinga, free Saxons, to whom he held out the prospect of revolting against the nobility and returning to paganism. At that time, the Christianisation of the Saxons had not been more than half a century ago.[5] But the Stellinga uprising was not crowned by success. Louis the German defeated and punished them severely. So reports Bishop Prudentius of Troyes, the author of the Annals of St-Bertin:

> "Louis marched throughout Saxony and by force and terror he completely crushed all who still resisted him: having captured all the ringleaders of that dreadful example of insubordination – men who had all but abandoned the Christian faith and had resisted Louis and his faithful men so fiercely – he punished 140 of them by beheading, hanged fourteen, maimed countless numbers by chopping off their limbs, and left no one able to carry on any further opposition to him."[6]

So here we have two examples of a great military victory and at the same time two examples of different ways of dealing with defeated enemies: mildness and charity on the one hand and deterrence and punishment on the other. This already shows that an answer to the question of this essay, how Frankish victors

---

castra redeunt, quid deinceps consultius acturum videretur, deliberaturi." Translation after Gillingham, Fontenoy, 252.
4 Scharff, Kämpfe, 15–29.
5 For the Stellinga see Goldberg, Revolt; Rembold, Conquest, 85–140.
6 Annales de Saint-Bertin, a. 842, 42f.: "Hludouuicus, peragrata omni Saxonia, cunctos sibi eatenus obsistentes ui atque terrore ita perdomuit ut, comprehensis omnibus auctoribus tantae impietatis qui et christianam fidem pene reliquerant et sibi suisque fidelibus tantopere obstiterant, centum quadraginta capitis amputatione plecteret, quatuordecim patibulo suspenderet, innumeros membrorum praecisione debiles redderet nullumque sibi ullatenus refragantem relinqueret." Translation after Nelson, Annals of St-Bertin, 54.

treated their defeated enemies, cannot be short and unambiguous. There was obviously a wide range of possible forms of dealing with defeated opponents, which depended on different preconditions. It is therefore worth discussing this question in a little more detail below.

War defeats have been an important topic of historical research for some years, including medieval studies.[7] The focus is usually on how the defeat is dealt with and how the defeated cope with it. While the victors – in the Middle Ages as well as in later epochs – were able to state that they had done everything right and had God on their side, dealing with defeat posed a much greater challenge for the vanquished and they were often forced to question their own previous views of history.[8] However, their interpretations often led to new and forward-looking explanatory models. A vivid example of this from the early Middle Ages is provided by Saxon historiography and hagiography from the hundred years after Charlemagne's conquest of Saxony. In the depiction of the Saxons of the following generations, annexation and forced Christianisation became the fusion of Franks and Saxons into one people and the gain of Saxony for the Christian faith.[9]

But before the defeated could worry about the interpretive sovereignty over their defeat, they were first in a highly critical situation in which they were more or less completely in the hands of their victorious opponents and at their mercy or disgrace. The two examples given show two extremes of the possible spectrum in the treatment of the defeated by the victors. From them it becomes clear that one must distinguish between different circumstances when discussing the behaviour of the Frankish victors. One must consider the different types of war, the quality of the defeated, the timing of their treatment and, of course, the different options the victors had for their actions.

To start with the last point: what were the options for dealing with enemies after defeating them? First, the victors could do what the warriors of Charles the Bald and Louis the Pious did at first, namely, pursue the vanquished who tried to flee the battlefield, slaughter and massacre as many as they could reach, and take their weapons and armour as booty. "Whom they seized, they killed, and cheerfully took the booty they had left behind them" is how the anonymous author of the 'Vita Hludowici' describes the behaviour of a marauding Frankish army detachment that had defeated Muslims who had followed them in Charlemagne's campaign in Spain in 810.[10]

If we look at the medieval historiography on the Battle of Fontenoy and its interpretations by the various authors, we can see that most authors, in contrast

---

7 For the Middle Ages see Clauss, Kriegsniederlagen; Scharff, Sinn.
8 In a broader context, see Koselleck, Erfahrungswandel.
9 Beumann, Hagiographie.
10 Astronomus, Vita Hludowici, c. 14, 324: "Quos adprehendere, necaverunt, et lęti ad praedas quas reliquerant redierunt."

to Nithard, record such a slaughter as the result of victory. They characterise the event as a slaughter or massacre with the terms *strages* or *caedes:* as *strages* or *strages magna* or even *innumera* they characterise the battle.[11] Non modicum ibi stragem dederunt, says the 'Chronicon Novaliciense'.[12] *Caedes magna, pessima* or *miserabilis* can also be found in texts.[13] The fact is that by no means all historiographers saw the reaction of the victors as generously as Nithard did.

Some authors who describe the battle of Fontenoy emphasise that the Christian people are killing or even annihilating each other in this struggle: *Christianus uterque populus mutua se caede prostravit.*[14] People who do not differ in arms or habits, as Ado of Vienne says.[15] The mutual killing thus takes place in the context of a civil war, a *bellum civile* or, even worse, a *bellum plus quam civile.*[16] According to Isidore of Seville's typology of war, this means a war waged not only against fellow citizens, but also against relatives or kin.[17] For this, the 'Annales Masciacenses' find the unique term *fraternum bellum.*[18] And this war is not only *dirum, crudelissimum* or *ingens*, but *infelix, lacrimabile, lamentabile, horribile.*[19] All these statements, however, are not directed exclusively at the behaviour of the victors, but they characterise the entire battle as a terrible killing.

The poem about the battle of Fontenoy written by Angelbert, a follower of Lothar, the 'Rhythmus de bella Fontanetica', evokes the bodies of the slain warriors lying on the battlefield only in their white undergarments, otherwise bereft of all things.[20] Literally looting the enemy to the hilt was quite normal behaviour in pre-modern warfare. Thus, we find in the 'Annales Fuldenses' on the Battle of Andernach in 876 that the victors from the army of Louis the Younger, after killing their enemies, took their gold, silver, clothes, weapons, armour, horses and other things.[21] According to the 'Annales Bertiniani', those defeated who were not killed by the victors were then finally robbed so com-

---

11 See Scharff, Gottesurteil, 228.
12 Chronicon Novaliciense, c. 28, 54.
13 See Scharff, Gottesurteil, 228.
14 Chronicon fani Sancti Neoti, a. 841, 131.
15 Ex Adonis chronico, 322: "non armis dissimiles, non habitu gentis distincti."
16 See Scharff, Gottesurteil, 228.
17 Isidori Etymologiarum libri XX, XVIII 1,4: "Plus quam civile bellum est ubi non solum cives certant, sed et cognati."
18 Annales Masciacenses, a. 842, 169.
19 See Scharff, Gottesurteil, 228.
20 Angelberti Rhythmus, v 10, 53: "Karoli de parte vero, Hludovici pariter / albescebant campi vestes mortuorum lineas, / velut solent in autumno albescere avibus."
21 Annales Fuldenses, a. 876, 88–89: "Hi autem, qui cum Hludovico erant, reversi ad caesorum spolia detrahenda, quantas ibidem praedas in auro et argento et vestibus et armis et loricis et equis variaque suppellectile tulissent, nullus valet edicere."

pletely by the rural population that they had to cover their nakedness with hay and straw.[22]

The defeated warriors who were not killed at Andernach were captured by the victors on the battlefield or in the nearby forest; the Annals of Saint-Bertin name the important personages among them.[23] Thus, another way of pursuing enemies was not to put them to death, but to lead them off captured. However, these prisoners could still be killed some time after the battle, as the example of the Saxon leaders of the Stellinga shows. Their execution, combined with the dishonouring punishment of hanging, or their mutilations can be seen as symbolic acts in a political context in which the victors wanted to show that the victory was a decisive one and that the opponents deserved such an ignominious death for certain reasons. It also belongs within this context when captured leaders were blinded after defeat and thus rendered incapable of ruling. This happened, for example, to the king of the Great Moravian Empire, Rastislav, who was captured by Carloman, the son of king Louis the German, and sent to his father.[24] Within Frankish society, such an act could also lead to sharp criticism, such as when Louis the Pious had Bernard of Italy blinded after the latter's revolt, from which he died three days later.[25]

It is reported in one case at least, that the king was urged by his army to execute enemy leaders. According to the 'Vita Hludowici', when Lothar I conquered the city of Chalon-sur-Saône in 834 during his uprising against his father, he had the counts Gauzhelm, Senila and the royal vassal Madalhelm beheaded at the call of his warriors (*adclamatione porro militari*).[26] However, the various historiographers weighted the responsibility for these executions and other atrocities in the context of the conquest of the city differently, so that it is difficult to say who was really the culprit here.[27]

Normally, however, the prisoners were not killed but later released; sometimes this happened after an oath of loyalty taken to the victor. Thus the 'Annales Bertiniani' say that in 844 Pippin completely defeated an army on the side of

---

22 Annales de Saint-Bertin, a. 876, 209: "Ceteri autem ita sunt a uillanis despoliati ut feno et stramine inuoluti uerenda celarent et nudi profugerent, quos insequentes occidere noluerunt."
23 Ibid.: "Fuerunt autem in ipsa congressione occisi Raganarius et Hieronimus comites et multi alii; capti autem in eodem campo et silua uicina fuerunt Ottulfus episcopus, Gauzlenus abba, Aledramnus et Adalardus, Bernardus et Eueruuinus comites et plures alii."
24 Annales Xantenses, a. 871, 30: "Rasticius rex Margorum a Karlomanno captus et in Franciam patri directus ibique postea luminibus privatus est."
25 Boshof, Ludwig, 141–147.
26 Astronomus, Vita Hludowici, c. 52, 469: "Adclamatione porro militari post captam urbem Gotselmus comes itemque Sanila comes necnon et Madalelmus vasallus dominicus capite plexi sunt."
27 See Schäpers, Lothar I., 291.

Charles the Bald. Only a few in the first line of opponents were killed, while all the others fled even before the battle broke out. Of those, however, only a few escaped; the rest were either held captive or robbed and sent home, bound by an oath.[28] We do not know who was held back and who was set free, but presumably it was the willingness to take the oath of allegiance that led them to freedom. In historiography we often read of oaths taken after a lost battle. These are probably oaths of allegiance. Sometimes this is the only statement about the outcome of a fight. Obviously, this reference was enough to make it clear to medieval readers what had happened.[29]

The victors could also release the captives after receiving a ransom. John Gillingham has recently discussed the question of whether we can observe a development in the second half of the 9th century and in the 10th century after Fontenoy from pursuit of the defeated enemy until death and plundering his camp to capture and ransom. He links this development to the rise of chivalry, which for him signifies a "code of conduct that encouraged high-status warriors to avoid killing each other". He sees plunder and oaths as the link between killing and ransom. That is an interesting idea that needs further consideration. The first example of ransom Gillingham has found in an intra-Frankish conflict is for the year 1020.[30]

Besides persecution or killing and imprisonment, a third option was to simply spare the vanquished and let him go out of charity or for other reasons. Nithard tells us, as we have heard, that the pious kings Louis and Charles stopped their warriors from pursuing Lothar's followers in order to avoid further inner-Frankish bloodshed. We often find such scenes serving as examples of the magnanimity of rulers. In the case of Fontenoy, according to Nithard's account, this royal clemency affected the entire enemy army. In other cases, it affected only a few ringleaders of such an army. In the battle of Andernach (876) already mentioned, Charles the Bald fought the son of his former allied brother. After the battle, the victorious Louis the Younger pursued his enemies and massacred many. On the other hand, he ordered many of the *optimates* to be taken prisoner and their lives spared "because of his humanity".[31] Proto-chivalric behaviour was

---

28 Annales de Saint-Bertin, a. 844, 46: "Pippinus ... exercitui ex Francia ad Karolum Tolosam ciuitatem obsidione uallantem properanti in pago Ecolisimo occurrens, ita breui et absque suorum casu eum profligauit, ut primoribus interfectis, ceteros fugam ante congressum etiam ineuntes, uix paucis euadentibus, aut caperet aut spoliatos sacramentoque adstrictos ad propria redire permitteret."
29 Scharff, Kämpfe, 162–165.
30 Gillingham, Fontenoy.
31 Annales Fuldenses, a. 876, 88: "Franci autem orientales ex utraque parte fortiter repugnantes ac signiferis Karoli occisis ceteros fugere compulerunt. Quos Hludowicus persecutus strages non paucas dabat; plurimos etiam ex optimatibus Karoli vivos comprehendit, quos propter suam humanitatem servari iussit incolumes."

thus, as in the High and Late Middle Ages, however, reserved for noble enemies. It was not normally owed to the common warriors.[32] It may be that Nithard did not even think he needed to elaborate on this fact.

As the examples show, the defeated could suffer various fates: they could be released or killed, they could be captured and later treated differently. Thus one has to do what historians should always do: one has to differentiate. The criteria for differentiation lie, as already said, in the time of treatment, the nature of the war and the quality of the opponents.

Obviously, the outcome of the battle must be clear before one can speak of victors and vanquished and the treatment of the latter by the former. But it is important whether one focuses on the moment shortly after the decision, when many are still fighting and some are taking a last stand, while others are already fleeing the battlefield, pursued by the victors, or whether one looks at the moment when everything is over, some have managed to escape, while the prisoners and wounded are awaiting their fate.

As for the first moment, it is a fact that the end of a battle has always been – and in every war – the most dangerous moment for a warrior. This is not only because of a period of fierce fighting, but because emotions were also so inflamed that, as Guy Halsall says, the attempt to "surrender immediately after close fighting was a risky business"[33]; one could not know whether the opponent would be merciful. During pursuit an individual warrior was often isolated from his comrades after the disintegration of his battle formation and was therefore at the mercy or disgrace of the sword blows of his pursuers. Therefore, losses during pursuit were usually the greatest. This can be said of the Battle of Fontenoy as well as of battles in later times. In battles of the early modern period, the fear of being killed while retreating or fleeing was often the only reason for experienced soldiers to hold their ground and remain in formation even under heavy enemy artillery fire.[34]

Therefore, the slaughters or massacres at the end of battles that we read about in the sources were not always the result of cool decisions but were due to the terrible and extreme situations to which the combatants on both sides were exposed. And it is not just that. A battle was also an extraordinary or exceptional experience that perhaps not so many of the early medieval warriors shared. Usually, Carolingian commanders tried to avoid battle because of its uncertain and unpredictable outcome. In this respect, they followed the Roman military writer Vegetius, who advised in his treatise 'De re militari' not to engage in battle if possible. Vegetius was widely known in the Carolingian Empire. We cannot say whether he was actually read by many and served as a basis for warfare, but sieges

---

32 Strickland, War, 176–182.
33 Halsall, Warfare, 211; see also Gillingham, Fontenoy, 247.
34 Keegan, Antlitz, 225–228.

and raids (*vastatio*), the everyday business of warriors, were much more common than fighting in open battle.[35] Even for veterans among these warriors, a battle was anything but an everyday or even frequent experience; men could hardly develop a routine for behaviour during the battle and especially at its end.

It is thus difficult to speak of "normal" or "customary" forms for the treatment of defeated opponents during or directly at the end of a battle. Only the treatment of prisoners a few hours or days after the end of the battle can be seen as the result of rational considerations or discussions that were based on norms. The king or commander-in-chief and his advisers could now deal with the defeated in a more differentiated way than simply letting the slaughter and killing happen or trying to stop it in an improvised way. With some distance to the fighting, there was now the opportunity to publicly show mercy or even to set a deterrent example. Now was the moment to bind the loser by an oath and to dictate the terms of peace, all this accompanied by symbolic acts that were of great importance to a largely oral society. And because these actions were so significant and important in such a society, they eventually found their way into written tradition, where we can still sometimes find them today.

We do not know what the exact role of the captured enemies was in these acts. This is mainly because we hardly know what happened there at all. In the sources we often only read that the victorious king came home in peace and triumph (*in pace et triumpho*), or that services were ordered. What this means in concrete terms is often difficult to say in detail.

After the description of a battle, historiography often simply refers to the flight of the vanquished and the triumph of the victor. One example is from a Carolingian genealogy written between 840 and 884, the 'Francorum regum historia': "Hludovicus et Karolus, Hlothario fugato, triumphum adepti sunt. Post cruentissimum vero proelium pace inter eos facta, diviserunt inter se Francorum imperium."[36] Such accounts are obviously influenced by the 'Etymologiae' of Isidore of Seville. The latter explains that war consists of four components: the fight (*pugna*), the flight (*fuga*), the victory (*victoria*) and the peace (*pax*).[37] Keeping this in mind, reports like the one from the 'Historia' become clearer because terse references can thus be expanded into whole chains of action. Here we find all four components brought together in two sentences.

The triumph of the 'Historia Francorum' stands for victory or for its result. Isidore elaborates on the ancient Roman triumph in a separate chapter.[38] Reli-

---

[35] Scharff, Kämpfe, 138–146.
[36] Francorum regum historia, 324. The text is also referred to as 'Commemoratio genealogiae domni Arnulfi episcopi'.
[37] Isidori Etymologiarum libri XX, XVIII 1, 11: "Quattuor autem in bellum aguntur: pugna, fuga, victoria, pax."
[38] Ibid. XVIII, 2, 1–8.

gious rituals significantly accompanied medieval victory celebrations and were also part of every Carolingian and every medieval battle. It was Michael McCormick who first emphasised the great importance of war liturgy for early medieval warfare and especially as an expression of the Franks' loyalty to the king. The invocation of God with the request for victory was just as important as the thanksgiving after the battle for divine help.[39]

Besides the prisoners, military insignia captured from the defeated apparently also played a role in the ceremonies. Perhaps they were laid down in important churches, as we know from later centuries. In 799, after a victory over Moorish 'pirates', Charlemagne was presented with their *signa*.[40] In the same year, margrave Wido sent him the swords of the Breton leaders he had subjugated, inscribed with the names of their former bearers.[41] Weapons and *vexilla* from the Normans were also sent by Count Robert of Anjou to Charles the Bald after a victory on the Loire in 865.[42] Following the triumph over the Normans at the Dyle in 891, 16 captured *regalia signa* were sent to King Arnulf. Perhaps they were part of the litanies or lauds that the monarch ordered for celebrating the victory and praising God.[43]

The treatment of the defeated opponents also depended on who they were, Franks or foreigners. Usually, unlike my first examples, they were not Franks. Janet Nelson has called Fontenoy the "trauma" of the Franks because for the first time after the Battle of Vincy (717) in the days of Charles Martel, Franks fought each other in a major civil war.[44] Although there had been repeated uprisings and rebellions since the beginning of Carolingian rule, they were not civil wars or even fratricidal wars.

In the war typologies of Stephen Morillo or Hans-Henning Kortüm, there is a basic distinction between intracultural and transcultural wars, i. e., wars between groups with the same cultural background and those between members of different cultures. The latter can be further subdivided into intercultural and subcultural wars. That means, on the one hand, there are transcultural wars that are

---

39 McCormick, Victory; Id., Liturgy; see also Bachrach, Religion, 32–63.
40 Annales regni Francorum, a. 799, 108: "Signa quoque Maurorum in pugna sublata et domno regi praesentata sunt."
41 Ibid.: "Wido comes … regi de Saxonia reverso arma ducum, qui se dediderant, inscriptis singulorum nominibus praesentavit."
42 Annales de Saint-Bertin, a. 865, 122: "Rodbertus autem de eisdem Nortmannis qui sedebant in Ligeri amplius quam quingentos sine dampno suorum occidens, uexilla et arma Nortmannica Karolo mittit."
43 Annales Fuldenses, a. 891, 120–121: "In eo proelio cesi sunt duo reges eorum, Sigifridus scilicet et Gotafridus; regia signa XVI ablata et in Baioaria in testimonium transmissa sunt. Eodem in loco … Kal. … letanias rex celebrare praecipit; ipse cum omni exercitu laudes Deo canendo processit."
44 Nelson, Years, 155.

fought between members of "really" different cultures, such as in the war of Christians against Mongols or in the Crusades, and, on the other hand, those that are fought between groups of the same nation or of the same country, but of different subcultures, who vie for supremacy, as was the case, for example, in the Albigensian Crusade or in civil wars in general.[45]

In this typology, the Frankish fratricidal war is a perfect example of a subcultural war, because members of the same culture but of different social subsystems fought there. This is of no minor importance, because the typology of war is justified by its representatives not least with the extreme ferocity and cruelty of the enemies in subcultural wars, which seems to be more like transcultural than intracultural wars.

Regarding the Carolingian wars, this would generally mean on the one hand, harshness or even cruelty against Normans, Avars, Saxons, Slavs, especially pagans, or against insurgents from within, on the other hand, leniency against Lombards, Bavarians or Bretons as "equals" (i.e., Christians) from "outside". Examples of all this can be found, that is true. But one can also bring a counterexample in almost every case, and often the early medieval warriors or historiographers obviously thought or argued more complexly than today's historians in search of clear classifications.

To give an example: during the reign of Louis the Pious, the Franks tried to subjugate Brittany. Every few years there was a military expedition that subdued the country "completely and definitively", at least until the next campaign.[46] The Bretons were Christians and we read nothing about Frankish atrocities or cruelty against their enemies. On the other hand, the best documented campaign of 818 was mainly justified with the allegedly unchristian behaviour of the Bretons. In the panegyric poem on the deeds of Louis the Pious from the pen of Ermoldus Nigellus, Count Lambert of Nantes says during an imperial assembly that Christianity was not deeply rooted in Brittany, that especially marriage laws were not observed, and that law was generally not accepted. And time and again, the Bretons raided Frankish territory and destroyed the churches there.[47]

When the Frankish army invades Brittany, the Breton king Morvan hides his troops and wages guerrilla warfare. As Ermold says, the king wants war (*bella*) and calls all Bretons to arms. At the same time, however, he plans to attack the Franks from ambush. The Bretons, therefore, try to avoid open combat, which Ermold comments on with the words: *bellum, Britto superbe, fugis*. And when the Franks come and ravage the land, the Bretons rarely appear and only fight with

---

45 Kortüm, Kriege, 56–65; Morillo, Typology.
46 See Annales regni Francorum, a. 786, 72; a. 799, 108; a. 818, 148; a. 824, 165.
47 Ermold, Poème, III, v. 1286–1311, 100/102.

words (*proelia voce gerunt*).⁴⁸ If you want to wage real war, Ermold is to be understood, you should offer open battle. Otherwise, you are cowards and what you do is not worthy of being called war.

A few verses later, Ermold refers to *bellum* and *proelia* again when he characterises what the Bretons do. They entrench themselves behind their walls and offer no battle (*proelia nulla dabant*). They fight only to attack the Franks on narrow forest paths. Ermold calls this *bella inproba*.⁴⁹ Twice *bellum*, twice *proelia*. This is obviously not a coincidence. Ermold says that what the Bretons do is not a battle. And so, logically, the war is not a war, it is *improbus*, bad, unworthy or dishonourable. The Breton method of warfare does not fit in with the Carolingian way of speaking of war in historiography. This warfare without battle can only be called *improbus*. The Frankish author goes to great lengths to prove the wickedness and otherness of the Bretons. He justifies the war against the Christians by denying their Christian faith and behaviour. This, by the way, is an often-used explanation for similar military actions. But this creation of an evil semi-pagan enemy does not lead to a special kind of treatment after the Frankish victory. Is this now an inter-, trans- or subcultural war? And what is the point of this classification in this case anyway?

But back to the subcultural wars. Just as Louis the German punished the Stellinga, so did other Frankish kings punish rebels and insurgents. While Louis beheaded and mutilated his enemies, others also had them blinded.⁵⁰ We might be inclined to see these as "normal" acts within a subcultural war. But for many contemporaries, they were also acts worthy of criticism. Charlemagne and Louis the Pious, for example, are explicitly defended by their respective biographers when they speak of their harsh treatment of internal opponents⁵¹. Obviously, these cases needed special justification.

The treatment of defeated enemies was thus different in each case and cannot be explained solely by the timing or by the nature of the war and the quality of the defeated. One must examine the whole context of each case. Let us look, for example, at Charlemagne's treatment of the Saxons during the 30-year war of conquest and Christianisation. The harsh legislation against them, possibly the executions at Verden or the forced relocations of large numbers of people, all this is unique in terms of Charlemagne's policy. And it is precisely this uniqueness that makes it worth explaining. Did all this happen because the Saxons were rebels in his eyes, because some of them submitted after the first campaign, or because Saxony, from Charlemagne's perspective, had belonged to the Frankish

---

48 Ibid., v. 1605–1609, 122.
49 Ibid., v. 1610–1615, 122/124.
50 Schaab, Blendung.
51 Scharff, Verden, 39.

Empire since the times of the Merovingians? So that he had to deal with internal enemies, with all the consequences for their treatment.

It is interesting in this context that the treatment of rebels in the Ottonian successor state to the East Frankish Empire in the 10th century differs greatly from what we have learned about the 9th century. It is common knowledge that the Ottonian kings and emperors since Henry I had a great many conflicts with their magnates. Hagen Keller and Gerd Althoff have analysed the largely non-violent forms of conflict resolution by the Ottonians that were accompanied by rituals such as the *deditio*.[52]

While pardon and reintegration were practised in dealing with internal enemies or rebels, the keywords for dealing with external enemies (Slavs, Byzantines) were *terror* and *vindicta* (revenge). In Ottonian historiography and hagiography, we often read about the killing of prisoners or their mutilation. This is always connected with the idea that it was revenge for slights suffered by the Ottonians and that the *terror regis* would keep them under control in the future.[53]

A comparison between the Carolingians and the Ottonians in the area of treating their enemies would be a complex matter. At this point, it should only be said that something obviously changed. While the terror of the Ottonian king was intended to control his enemies outside the empire, Nithard says in the time of the civil war that Charlemagne in the golden age used moderate terror (*cum moderato terrore*) to hinder Frankish magnates from acting against the common good (*publicae utilitati*).[54]

The treatment of enemies thus depends not only on the form of war (internal, intercultural, transcultural, subcultural), but also, or perhaps even more so, on the political, cultural and social conditions of the state. A ruler like Charlemagne may have had a different scope of action than the Ottonians, who ruled internally with the consensus of the *optimates*. This illustrates the different treatment of insurgents. But by defeating the Hungarians, Otto had proved that God's hand rested on him and that his reign was based on direct divine right. Thus, the terror against them is the terror that God himself brought upon them.

However, one should also be generally cautious about attributing a particular culture of war, manifested in the sum of knowledge, values, practices and ideas about war, to specific societies. For example, anthropologists studying frontier societies have shown that there are close links between and parallels in the behaviour of warriors on both sides in each case. In some respects, they have more in common with their opponents than with non-combatants in their own

---

52 Keller, Königsherrschaft; Althoff, Spielregeln.
53 Scharff, Herrscher.
54 Nithardi historiarum libri IV, I, c. 1, 1–2; IV, 7, 50.

societies.⁵⁵ In the Carolingian period, too, such similarities were reflected in the values of warriors from different cultures. In his historical poem about the siege of Paris by a Norman fleet, Abbo of Saint-Germain-des-Prés constructed a scene in which the Norman leader and the bishop of the city meet for negotiations at the beginning of the siege. Both the noble bishop and the pagan king are in complete agreement that the Frank, as leader, could not comply with the Norman demands for free passage without losing his honour and deserving death. And so, the battle begins after a thoroughly respectful opening.⁵⁶

After these glimpses of the late and post-Carolingian epoch, I would like to conclude with some remarks on the problematic nature of our sources. In my essay I have mainly cited historiographical texts. And historiographical evidence is the most important for this topic. Carolingian historiography, like any early medieval historiography, is primarily concerned with rulers and their deeds. If the texts contain information about the treatment of the defeated, it is probably very rarely in order to inform the readers about what happened to these people. As a rule, the author's aim was to characterise royal actions or the ruler himself this way.

This is not all that surprising at first. But if one takes this thought seriously, it has consequences for the work of historians. If the description of the way the defeated were treated characterises the king or his deeds, then they must be read in terms of the ruler and can sometimes be interpreted as ciphers or codes. Releasing enemies then means not only that enemies were released, but that the king acted according to the *clementia regis*, which characterises him as a good king. Taking an oath means that the enemy accepted and admitted defeat. That defeated enemies were pursued to destruction or that all but one who could report it home were killed marks a complete victory and not the fact that literally everyone was killed.⁵⁷

One example of the significance of this statement is the "massacre of Verden". Since the 19th century, historians have debated whether Charlemagne really had 4500 prisoners executed in Verden after a Saxon uprising in 782, as the Frankish Imperial Annals seem to say.⁵⁸ A positivist examination of the entire written tradition does not ultimately lead to a conclusion about the truth of this pas-

---

55 Turner, Gewaltträume.
56 Abbon, Siège, v. 36–60, 16/18.
57 For an example with both phrases in one sentence see Annales Fuldenses, a. 883, 110: "Heimricus ... cum Nordmannorum manum validam Prumiam venire cognoscit, usque eos, ut dicunt, nullo evadente cum suis ad internitionem delevit."
58 Annales regni Francorum, a. 782, 62: "Tunc omnes Saxones iterum convenientes subdiderunt se sub potestate supradicti domni regis et reddiderunt omnes malefactores illos, qui ipsud rebellium maxime terminaverunt, ad occidendum IIII D; quod ita et factum est, excepto Widochindo, qui fuga lapsus est partibus Nordmanniae."

sage.[59] But if you ask what all the sources have in common, it is the statement that Charlemagne won a tremendous victory against the Saxons, after which he made their defeats clear to them in a symbolic manner. This says nothing about the actual events, but it should warn against postulating a great massacre by the Franks or even placing it in a series with similarly poorly documented mass executions.[60] Perhaps it is precisely the extremes in dealing with the defeated that need to be scrutinised particularly critically in general.

Bibliography

Sources

Abbon, Le siège de Paris par les Normands. Poème du IXe siècle, ed. and trans. Henri Waquet (Les classiques de l'histoire de France au Moyen Âge 20), Paris 1964.

Angelberti Rhythmus de pugna Fontanetica, in: Nithardi historiarum libri IIII, ed. Georg Heinrich Petz / Ernst Müller (Monumenta Germaniae Historica; Scriptores rerum Germanicarum in usum scholarum separatim editi 44), Hannover 1907, 51–53.

Annales Fuldenses sive Annales regni Francorum orientalis, ed. Friedrich Kurze (Monumenta Germaniae Historica; Scriptores rerum Germanicarum in usum scholarum separatim editi 7), Hannover 1891.

Annales Masciacenses, ed. Georg Heinrich Pertz (Monumenta Germaniae Historica; Scriptores 3), Hannover 1839, 169–170.

Annales regni Francorum inde ab a. 741 usque ad a. 829, qui dicuntur Annales Laurissenses maiores et Einhardi, ed. Friedrich Kurze (Monumenta Germaniae Historica; Scriptores rerum Germanicarum in usum scholarum separatim editi 6), Hannover 1895.

Annales de Saint-Bertin, ed. Félix Grat / Jeanne Vielliard / Suzanne Clémencet, Paris 1964.

Annales Xantenses, in: Annales Xantenses et Annales Vedastini, ed. Bernhard von Simson (Monumenta Germaniae Historica; Scriptores rerum Germanicarum in usum scholarum separatim editi 12), Hannover / Leipzig 1909, 1–33.

Astronomus, Vita Hludowici imperatoris, in: Thegan, Die Taten Kaiser Ludwigs – Astronomus, Das Leben Kaiser Ludwigs, ed. and trans. Ernst Tremp (Monumenta Germaniae Historica; Scriptores rerum Germanicarum in usum scholarum separatim editi 164), Hannover 1995, 279–555.

Chronicon fani Sancti Neoti (Asser's Life of King Alfred, together with the Annals of Saint Neots erroneously ascribed to Asser), ed. William Henry Stevenson, Oxford 1904.

Chronicon Novaliciense, ed. Georg Heinrich Pertz (Monumenta Germaniae Historica; Scriptores rerum Germanicarum in usum scholarum separatim editi 21), Hannover 1846.

Ermold le noir, Poème sur Louis le Pieux et épitres au roi Pépin, ed. and trans. Edmond Faral (Les classiques de l'histoire de France au Moyen Âge 14), Paris 1964.

---

59 Scharff, Verden, 25–36.
60 Ibid., 37–46.

Ex Adonis archiepiscopi Viennensis chronico usque ad a. 869, ed. Georg Heinrich Pertz (Monumenta Germaniae Historica; Scriptores 2), Hannover 1829, 315-323.

Francorum regum historia, ed. Georg Heinrich Pertz (Monumenta Germaniae Historica; Scriptores 2), Hannover 1829, 308-09; 324-25.

Isidori Hispalensis episcopi etymologiarum sive originum libri XX, ed. Wallace Martin Lindsay, Oxford 1911.

Nithardi historiarum libri IV. Accedit Angelberti Rhythmus de pugna Fontanetica, ed. Ernst Müller (Monumenta Germaniae Historica; Scriptores rerum Germanicarum in usum scholarum separatim editi 44), Hannover / Leipzig 1907.

The Annals of St-Bertin, trans. and annotated Janet Nelson (Ninth-Century Histories 1), Manchester / New York 1991.

Literature

Airlie, Stuart, The World, the Text and the Carolingian: Royal, aristocratic and masculine identities in Nithard's Histories, in: Lay intellectuals in the Carolingian world, ed. Patrick Wormald / Janet L. Nelson, Cambridge / New York 2007, 51-76.

Althoff, Gerd, Spielregeln der Politik im Mittelalter. Kommunikation in Frieden und Fehde, Darmstadt 1997.

Bachrach, Bernard S. / Bachrach, David S., Nithard as a Military Historian of the Carolingian Empire, c 833-843, in: Francia 44 (2017), 29-55.

Bachrach, David S., Religion and the Conduct of War c. 300-1215, Woodbridge 2003.

Beumann, Helmut, Die Hagiographie "bewältigt". Unterwerfung und Christianisierung der Sachsen durch Karl den Großen, in: Cristianizzazione ed organizzazione ecclesiastica delle campagne nell'alto medioevo: Espansione e resistenze (Settimane di studio del Centro italiano di studi sull'alto medioevo 28), Spoleto 1982, 129-163.

Boshof, Egon, Ludwig der Fromme, Darmstadt 1996.

Clauss, Martin, Kriegsniederlagen im Mittelalter. Darstellung – Deutung – Bewältigung (Krieg in der Geschichte 54), Paderborn 2010.

Clauss, Martin, Die Schlacht als narratives Konstrukt. 841: Zweimal Fontenoy, in: Kulturgeschichte der Schlacht, ed. Marian Füssel / Michael Sikora (Krieg in der Geschichte 78), Paderborn 2014.

Dümmler, Ernst, Geschichte des Ostfränkischen Reiches, 1: Ludwig der Deutsche bis zum Frieden von Koblenz 860, Leipzig ²1887.

Gillingham, John, Fontenoy and after: Pursuing enemies to death in France between the ninth and the eleventh centuries, in: Frankland. The Franks and the world of the early Middle Ages. Essays in honour of Dame Jinty Nelson, ed. Paul Fouracre / David Ganz, Manchester 2008, 242-265.

Goldberg, Eric J., Popular Revolt, Dynastic Politics, and Aristocratic Factionalism in the Early Middle Ages. The Saxon Stellinga Reconsidered, in: Speculum 70 (1995), 467-501.

Goldberg, Eric J., Struggle for Empire. Kingship and Conflict under Louis the German, 817-876, Ithaca / London 2006.

Halsall, Guy, Warfare and Society in the Barbarian West, 450-900, London 2003.

Heinzle, Georg Friedrich, Flammen der Zwietracht: Deutungen des karolingischen Brüderkrieges im 9. Jahrhundert (Libelli Rhenani 77), Cologne 2020.
Keegan, John, Das Antlitz des Krieges. Die Schlachten von Azincourt 1415, Waterloo 1815 und an der Somme 1916, Frankfurt / New York 1978.
Keller, Hagen, Ottonische Königsherrschaft: Organisation und Legitimation königlicher Macht, Darmstadt 2002.
Kortüm, Hans-Henning, Kriege und Krieger 500–1500, Stuttgart 2010.
Koselleck, Reinhart, Erfahrungswandel und Methodenwechsel. Eine historisch-anthropologische Skizze, in: Zeitschichten. Studien zur Historik, Frankfurt/Main 2000, ed. Reinhart Koselleck [First in: Historische Methode, ed. Christian Meier / Jörn Rüsen (Beiträge zur Historik 5), Munich 1988, 13–61].
Krah, Adelheid, Die Entstehung der "potestas regia" im Westfrankenreich während der ersten Regierungsjahre Kaiser Karls II. (840–877), Berlin 2000.
McCormick, Michael, Eternal Victory: Triumphal rulership in late antiquity, Byzantium, and the early medieval West, Cambridge / Paris 1986.
McCormick, Michael, The Liturgy of War in the Early Middle Ages: Crisis, Litanies, and the Carolingian Monarchy, in: Viator 15 (1984), 1–23.
Morillo, Stephen, A General Typology of Transcultural Wars: The Early Middle Ages and Beyond, in: Transcultural Wars from the Middle Ages to the 21st Century, ed. Hans-Henning Kortüm, Berlin 2006, 29–42.
Nelson, Janet L., Charles the Bald, London / New York 1992.
Nelson, Janet L., Public Histories and Private History in the Work of Nithard, in: Speculum 60 (1985), 251–293.
Nelson, Janet L., Ninth-Century Knighthood: The Evidence of Nithard, in: The Frankish World, 750–900, ed. Janet L. Nelson, London 1996, 75–87.
Nelson, Janet L., The Last Years of Louis the Pious, in: Charlemagne's Heir: New Perspectives on the Reign of Louis the Pious (814–840), ed. Peter Godman / Roger Collins, Oxford 1990, 147–189.
Rembold, Ingrid, Conquest and Christianization: Saxony and the Carolingian World, 772–888, Cambridge 2018.
Schaab, Meinrad, Die Blendung als politische Maßnahme im abendländischen Früh- und Hochmittelalter, Phil. Diss. Heidelberg 1955.
Schäpers, Maria, Lothar I. (795–855) und das Frankenreich (Rheinisches Archiv 159), Vienna / Cologne / Weimar 2018.
Scharff, Thomas, Gottesurteil oder Katastrophe? Zur Deutung militärischen Handelns im Frühmittelalter am Beispiel der Schlacht von Fontenoy, in: Politischer Deutungsraum Mittelalter, ed. Christoph Dartmann / Jenny Rahel Oesterle (Nova Mediaevalia. Quellen und Studien zum europäischen Mittelalter 22), Göttingen 2022, 211–231.
Scharff, Thomas, Der rächende Herrscher: Über den Umgang mit besiegten Feinden in der ottonischen Historiographie, in: Frühmittelalterliche Studien 36 (2002), 241–253.
Scharff, Thomas, Die Kämpfe der Herrscher und der Heiligen: Krieg und historische Erinnerung in der Karolingerzeit, Darmstadt 2002.
Scharff, Thomas, Der Sinn der Niederlage. Kriegsniederlagen und ihre historiographische Sinngebung am Beispiel der fränkischen Eroberung des Thüringerreiches, in: Die Frühzeit der Thüringer. Archäologie, Sprache, Geschichte, ed. Helmut Castritius / Die-

ter Geuenich / Matthias Werner (Ergänzungsbände zum Reallexikon der Germanischen Altertumskunde 63), Berlin / New York 2009, 457–474.

Scharff, Thomas, Verden 782. Krieg, Gewalt und das Bild Karls des Großen in der Historiografie, in: Perspektiven der Landesgeschichte. Festschrift für Thomas Vogtherr, ed. Christine van den Heuvel / Henning Steinführer / Gerd Steinwascher (Veröffentlichungen der Historischen Kommission für Niedersachsen und Bremen 312), Göttingen 2020, 21–46.

Strickland, Matthew, War and Chivalry. The Conduct and Perception of War in England and Normandy, 1066–1217, Cambridge 1996.

Turner, Bertram, Überlappende Gewalträume. Christlich-islamische Gewaltwahrnehmung zwischen Polemik und Alltagsrationalität, in: Gewalt im Mittelalter. Realitäten – Imaginationen, ed. Manuel Braun / Cornelia Herberichs, Munich 2005, 225–249.

Michael J. Decker

The Wars of John II Komnenos and the Decline of Byzantium in the East

"More than all others, he was a lover of glory, and bequeathing to posterity a most illustrious name, he was highly honored...He presented himself to public view as a model of every noble action...he has been deemed praiseworthy by all, even to our own times, the crowning glory so to speak, of the Komnenian dynasty".[1]

On 8 April, 1143, the emperor John II Komnenos died of an accidental wound sustained while hunting. On his deathbed, the fading emperor is said to have named his youngest son, Manuel, heir. Manuel, who often accompanied his father on campaign, fortunately happened to be on the spot. With the army at his back, the position of the presumptive heir was mostly secure, but he nonetheless acted with all due haste. Manuel dispatched the Turk John Axouch to Constantinople to announce the accession and remove his rivals, including his older brother, the sebastokrator Isaac, as well as his powerful uncle Isaac. John Axouch succeeded and thus began the rather flamboyant reign of Manuel I Komnenos. Subsequently, the death of his father John has been largely relegated to the margins of history, even if a scholar of the caliber of Robert Browning raised the possibility of the emperor's death as having been no accident.[2] While beyond the scope of this paper, the possibility of such intrigue colors the episodes of the emperor John's campaigns in the east and leads to further questions about John II's motives and strategy.

The eastern campaigns of John II Komnenos have been often discussed by historians, including Ralph-Johannes Lilie, Ioannis Karayannopoulos, Paul Magdalino, and more recently John Birkenmeier and Ioannis Stouraitis. Stouraitis provides a fine summary of views of John's eastern campaigns. All of these individuals of course assume different stances and different perspectives, which it is useful to briefly summarize here. Lilie viewed John's activity in the east as part of a larger whole; governing his actions were the ultimate goals of controlling Antioch and creating space for Byzantine domination of Cilicia and northern

---

1 Niketas Choniates, Historia ed. van Dieten, 46.63–47.83; tr. Magoulias, 27.
2 Browning, Death of John II Comnenus.

Syria through the creation of an appanage, whence its power could quite possibly extend – through Frankish proxies – to Jerusalem and the Holy Land itself.[3] Lilie's assessment is thus processual; the emperor's wider aims are what matters, even more than what he did or did not actually achieve. Magdalino navigates a similar course and emphasizes the cultural ingredients of Byzantine ideology and action, including religious antagonism, triumphalism, and glorification of bloodshed rather than focusing too sharply on John's specific strategic aims and successes, or lack thereof.[4] Birkenmeier and Karayannopoulos have, however, interpreted John's campaigns in the east within the framework of evaluating their outcomes in the longer term, for which Karayannopoulos has been criticized as anachronistic, interpreting with the benefit of hindsight what could not have been known to the emperor at the time.[5] In a similar sense, in considering John's objectives it is also helpful to examine the longer term view of Byzantine policy offered by Shepard, who argues for a Byzantine policy of relative quietism, especially vis a vis, the Fatimids and the Christians of the Levant more generally.[6]

It strikes me as interesting and even important that John, considered by Ostrogorsky as the greatest of the Komnenoi, acted so decisively in the Balkans while his eastern policies were far less successfully executed.[7] For example, John fought large-scale conflicts against both the Pechenegs in 1119–21 and the Hungarians in 1127–29. While the Pecheneg war was clearly defensive, the conflict with the Serbs and Hungarians was at least partly predicated upon Byzantine provocations, and the war ultimately involved imperial armies advancing deep into enemy territory in order to gain important victories. By contrast, John appears cautious and not terribly effective in his eastern affairs. Why was the turn of John to the east seemingly so tentative and, if we judge success by the recapture of former imperial territory, ultimately unsuccessful? Were the aims simply different and thus somewhat opaque to us? John's gains in Anatolia were measured and, at first blush, difficult to understand in the context of any overarching strategy. Indeed, it could rightly be said that they amounted to no territorial gain and no real scaffold for future success.

Before turning to the imperial campaigns of interest in Cilicia and Syria, it would be well to review the quite complicated contemporary political situation in Asia Minor and Syria. In Asia Minor, the empire maintained a tenuous grip over most of the western coastal cities and the river valleys which supplied these settlements. The Sultanate of Ikonion, a rump of the Seljuk Empire, held sway over the interior. At the time of John, its ruler was Mas'ud (1116–55), who in 1116

---

3 Magdalino, Empire, 521.
4 Stouraitis, Narratives of John II Komnenos' Wars.
5 Ibid., 32 on John as the idealized emperor.
6 Shepard, Holy Land.
7 Ostrogorsky, History of the Byzantine State, 377.

had deposed and killed his brother Shainshah upon the latter's serious defeat at the hands of the emperor Alexios Komnenos. Mas'ud established his capital at Ikonion (Konya); during his long rule he continued to firm up the foundations of the Seljuk state in central Anatolia.

To the north and east of the Sultanate of Ikonion lay the lands of the Turkish Danishmends, descended from their founding dynast, emir Danishmend Gazi, equated in later Turkish literature with early Arabic folk heroes.[8] In the wake of the battle of Manzikert (1071) the Danishmends seized great swathes of northern and central Anatolia. By the time the forces of the First Crusade arrived in 1097, emir Danishmend controlled Sebasteia (Sivas) and the Iris (Yeşilırmak) valley, Cappadocian Komana, as well as the cities of Amaseia (Amasya) and Gangra (Çankırı), some 200 km to the west of Sivas. In 1116 the emir Gümüshtegin used his Danishmendid troops to establish his son-in-law, Mas'ud (1116-56) on the throne of Ikonion at the expense of Mas'ud's brother, Malik Shah (1110-16) who had enjoyed Byzantine support. The Danishmendid-Konya alliance disaffected another brother of sultan Mas'ud, brother, 'Arab, who accused the former of treason against the family and raised a revolt which drove Mas'ud into the arms of the emperor John Komnenos. The Byzantine-Danishmendid-Rūm axis forced 'Arab from the field; he fled to Cilician Armenia and found shelter among the Roupenid Prince Toros I (1129-30) The move by Gümüshtegin into Cilicia seems aimed, as a punitive expedition to chastise the Armenian princes for sheltering the rebel 'Arab.[9] 'Arab captured Mohammad, the son of Gümüshtegin but the latter prevailed in the battle that followed.[10]

A Byzantine invasion of 1132, in which the emperor John seized Kastamon (Kastamonu) from the Danishmend Amir Ghazi (1104-34), ended in a Roman withdrawal. The emperor's action had likely been intended to punish the Danishmends for their support of the imperial pretender, Isaak Komnenons and the fractious imperial vassal, Leo I the Armenian (see below). Following the departure of the imperial army, Kastamon immediately fell back into the hands of the Danishmends. The precarious hold that the Romans held upon the ancestral home of the Komnenoi clan did not stop John from staging a magnificent triumph in Constantinople (in 1133). Upon the accession of the Danishmendid emir Malik Muhammad (1134-42) the Romans fared no better, as they took, then lost again Kastamon and Gangra. After the revival of the alliance with Mas'ud I of Ikonion in 1135, the emperor retook Kastamon and seized Gangra. Having thus settled affairs in Asia Minor to his liking, in 1136 John cemented an alliance with the German king Conrad III (1093-1152) against the Normans of Sicily. The latter

---

8 See Mélikoff, Le Geste de Melik Dānişmend, 71-102.
9 Cahen, Formation of Turkey, 18.
10 Michael the Syrian, Chronique, 3.224.

maintained claims on Antioch and thus trouble could be expected from this quarter. Once these careful diplomatic and military affairs were completed, the emperor turned eastward.[11]

While a contemporary letter from the Geniza (discussed below) mentions no Armenian pressure on the city of Seleukeia, the forces of the Rupenid prince, Leo I the Armenian, nonetheless represented a serious irritant to the empire. Even as Roman authority dissolved in the East, Constantinople had turned increasingly to migrant Armenian noble families to represent them and to maintain some measure of imperial interests in Cilicia.

To such an end Alexius had granted the *nakharar* Oshin, a Byzantine vassal, the land around the castle of Lampron as a hereditary fief. According to the 12th century chronicler, Samuel of Ani, in 1075/6 Oshin had left his ancestral lands, apparently in Caucasian Albania, travelled to Cilicia and captured the fortress of Lampon from the Muslims.[12] When he came into the service of Alexius is uncertain, but while Oshin and his immediate successors were loyal, they were generally ineffective, failing, for example, to hold Adana in the face of Frankish aggression.[13] The key to Het'umid power rested on their hold over the castle of Lampron, as well as that a Babaron in the foothills of the Bulgar Dagh. These strongholds gave Oshin and his successors, known as the Het'umids[14] control of the southern portion of the Cilician Gates and the mountain approaches to Tarsus from which traffic entered the Anatolian plateau. The Het'umids were sheltered in their powerful fortresses from attack over the Taurus, whence they could control the traffic from the Cilician Plain from Tarsus and menace the eastern portion then under the control of the Franks and contested by the upstart Rupenids under their newly crowned leader, Leo I (1129–37).

Leo I the Armenian,[15] had ascended to his position as ruler of the mountain Armenians in 1129 following the death of his brother Thoros.[16] According to Gregory the Priest, Leo the Armenian held the imperial title of *sebastos*, an honorific of the highest order for the Komnenoi.[17] The title carried clear implications: from the emperor's perspective, at least, that Leo was 'his man' and the exclusion of the Armenians of Cilicia from the Treaty of Devol (Diabolis) underscores the Byzantine view (see below). For his part, Leo could see no interest in maintaining the status quo, neither with the Franks nor with his nominal

---

11 Lilie, Byzantium and the Crusader States, 112–113.
12 MacEvitt, Crusades, 57.
13 Smbat the Constable, Chronique, 615.
14 Toumanoff, Kamsarakan.
15 Vučetić, Emperor John II's Encounters, 79, calls the prince 'Leo II' for reasons that are unclear to me.
16 Boase, Cilician Kingdom of Armenia, 10.
17 Matthew of Edessa, Chronicle, 260; Kazhdan, Sebastos.

Byzantine overlords; his mountaineers could not enrich themselves nor expand their domains, save the expense of the cities of the Cilician Plain which were claimed by both the empire the Principality of Antioch under Bohemond II (1119–30).

In 1129, Leo entered into an alliance with Il-Gazi, the Danishmend emir (1104–34). While the pact of Leo with the Turks certainly caused concern for the emperor, even more troubling was the hosting by Leo in the winter of 1130 of the imperial defector Isaac, John's brother and chief rival who was attempting to create an Anatolian alliance to install him on the Byzantine throne.[18] With his northern flank protected by his alliance with the Danishmends, in 1132, Leo moved against the towns of lowland Cilicia. If the Het'umids, loyal imperial vassals, offered any resistance, our sources make no mention of it, and Leo apparently operated without interference from his rival countrymen. Smbat the Constable has him seizing in 1132 the chief settlements on the eastern plain, Tarsus, Adana, and Mopsuestia (Msis, Frankish Mamistra).[19] The following year, Leo's forces ravaged the territory of the count of Marash and Kaysun, Baldwin.[20] The next target for Leo's attacks was Sarvantikar (Savuran Kale),[21] which he took in 1135.[22] At least some of these strongholds had been under the control of Antioch since their conquest under Tancred during the Byzantine-Norman war of 1108.[23] The aggressive stance of Leo thus ended nearly three decades of Frankish rule in lowland Cilicia.

There would be no Frankish recovery in lowland Cilicia, as the Turks under the powerful Danishmendid emir Gümüshtegin wished to inflict punishment on the Rupenids after the failure of their alliance of 1129. In 1136, Bohemond II of Antioch (1119–30)[24] attempted to restore the authority of Antioch over Anazarbos but his campaign ended in disaster. On the Cilician expedition of Bohemond II, our sources are ill-informed and confused. William of Tyre makes the Antiochene foray into Cilicia in response to an incursion by the Aleppan Ridwan, who had died in 1114 and who was an Arab, not a Turk whom William correctly records were responsible for the attack.[25] Emboldened by the death of Thoros and

---

18 Magdalino, Triumph of 1133, 63.
19 Smbat the Constable, Chronique, 615.
20 Smbat the Constable, Chronique, 616.
21 Sinclair, Eastern Turkey, 318–320.
22 Smbat the Constable, Chronique, 616.
23 Der Nersessian, Kingdom of Cilician Armenia, 349.
24 William of Tyre, History, 2.XIII.27, who mistakenly claims this was an invasion of Zengi or his Aleppan proxy Sawar into Antiochene territory, but the direction of attack (from the West) makes this extremely unlikely.
25 William of Tyre, History, 2.XIII.27, 43; Ibn Qutaiba passes over the event in silence, nor does Ibn al-Athir have any information, merely recording without further comment that Bohemond perished in 1130, see Ibn al-Athir, al-Kāmil fī al-tārīkh, 391.

their successes against 'Arab, Danishmendid forces invaded lowland Cilicia. There, by chance, the army of Gümüshtegin encountered the army of the Principality of Antioch led by Bohemond II, who, after the failed siege of Banias in Damascene territory, had hastened north in an attempt to drive Leo out of the key city of Anazarbos. If we consider that the combined Frankish-Armenian force of Leo, Antioch, Tripoli, and Edessa that confronted Bursuqi in 1125 at Azaz numbered only 1,100 knights and 2,000 infantry, the Antiochene force at Anazarbos must have been significantly smaller than this, perhaps 500 knights and 1,000 infantry.[26] Ghazi Gümüshtegin's forces must have been considerably more numerous, though none of ours sources offer any idea of the Turkish strength. The Franks were caught unawares as they advanced against Leo and a running battle ensued in which the Frankish knights were massacred by the Turks; the Christians fought their way to a hillock where the Danishmendid army surrounded them and cut them to pieces. Those few Frankish stragglers who attempted to escape to Antioch were cut down by Leo's men in the mountain passes, making the Principality's defeat total.[27] Gümüshtegin sent the head of Bohemond II to the caliph in Baghdad.

Following Ghazi Gümüshtegin's surprise victory at Anazarbos, Leo took advantage of the weakness of Antioch and marched against the lands of his rivals. While he failed to seize the prize of Seleukeia, which resisted his siege, the Armenian met success elsewhere on the Cilician Plain and amongst the lowland cities; His forays further rendered precarious the position of the Franks of Antioch already in turmoil following the death of their prince, a disaster that forced Baldwin II of Jerusalem to assume the regency there following the accession of Constance, daughter of Prince Bohemond II. Joscelin II of Edessa (d. 1159) took control of Antioch and faced the imminent danger of Zengi's invasion of Tell Bashir (Frankish Turbessel) and the Antiochene.[28]

In spring 1137, the imperial army assembled at Attalia (Antalya), where the emperor personally led the march overland along the coastal road that ran through Side, Anemurium, and thence to Seleukeia, the easternmost imperial redoubt and a salient point that the empire wished to maintain, in no small part due to its role as an important port on the Kalykadnos River. Seleukeia had been in imperial hands from the time of the First Crusade, when Alexius I had the citadel refurbished and placed in the hands of the *dux* Strategios Strabos.[29] Strategios Strabos garrisoned the city and stationed a squadron of the imperial fleet at nearby Korykos:

---

26 William of Tyre, History, 2.XIII.16, 24.
27 Michael the Syrian, Chronique, 3, 227.
28 Michael the Syrian, Chronique, 3, 230.
29 Hild / Hellenkemper, Kilikien 5, 402–6; Jeffreys et. al, Prosopography 'Strategios 1013', [http://pbw2016.kdl.kcl.ac.uk/person/Strategios/103/].

"So this *drungarios* of the fleet [Eustathios]...went forth, and anticipating Bohemond's intentions, repaired the town (Korykos) and restored it to its former condition.[30] He also rebuilt Seleukeia and made it surer by digging trenches all round, and left a good number of troops in each town under the *doux* Strategios. Finally, he went down to the harbour and left a considerable fleet in it according to the emperor's instructions and then returned to the capital [...]"[31]

A letter which comes down to us, dated 21 July 1137 is revealing. The writer is a Jewish physician engaged in gynaecology who has relocated to Roman territory where he reports a prosperous diaspora under Roman authority – this is somewhat of a surprise given the reputation of the Byzantine state in their dealings with non-Christians.[32] As part of his practice, the physician in Seleukeia engaged in the trade of *materia medica*, which were apparently relatively cheap and abundant in his adopted home city but fetched high prices in Fustat.[33] He knew of the movement of the imperial army into the Antiochene which he believed had already fallen into imperial hands. The doctor, who may well have been engaged in serving the army at this point, had asked the local Roman military officers, whom he refers to as 'our commanders' (*ru'asānā* – 'our heads') to acquire medical books which might fall into their hands from Aleppo (Halab) or from Damascus.[34] It is not out of the question that the emperor's ambition was not restricted to operations in Antioch and Aleppo only, but that even Damascus itself was a target of the expedition, a possibility bolstered by the writer's optimistic tone which likely reflected rumours then circulating, "According to what we have heard, they [the Romans] have already taken Antioch."[35]

Finally, in 1137 John marched to Cilicia, where the Rupenid prince Leo I (d. 1140) had raised the ire of the emperor by besieging the imperial city of Seleukeia, five days march from Antioch.[36] If, as Gregory the Priest maintains, Leo held the title of sebastos, this was a clear act of rebellion.[37] The Roman army invaded and attacked Tarsus, Adana, and Mopsuestia in the Cilician Plain, all of which fell rapidly to imperial forces. It should be noted that these operations possibly opened hostilities against the Franks of Antioch, as the sources are in

---

30 The drungarios in question is Eustathios Kymineianos, megas droungarios of the fleet, see Jeffreys, Prosopography, 'Eustathios Kymineianos, megas droungarios of the fleet', [http://pbw2016.kdl.kcl.ac.uk/person/Eustathios/15001/].
31 Anna Komnene, Alexias XI.x.9, 353.6-21.
32 Holo, Economic History of the Jews, 54.
33 Goitein, A Letter from Seleucia (Cilicia).
34 Ibid., 300. "I have asked our commanders to take along any medical books for me, from Aleppo or Damascus, which might fall into their hands. According to what we have heard, they have already taken Antioch."
35 Ibid.
36 Nersessian, Kingdom of Cilician Armenia, 637.
37 Gregory the Priest, Continuation, 260.

disagreement as to who controlled Cilicia in 1137. Based on his reading of Michael Italikos, Lilie argued that the Franks held Cilicia, but this is not sustained by the sources and Italikos, in fact, mentions only 'barbarians' and does not mention the Franks by name, nor does he name any Frankish leaders, whereas he does specifically name Leo the Armenian.[38]

The Armenian historians Gregory the Priest and Smbat the Constable, as well as the Muslim Ibn al-Athir (1160–1233) inform us that, at the time of the Roman expedition, Leo the Armenian still held Cilicia.[39] Thus, the situation was confused when the emperor and his army arrived on the scene, with the Franks of Antioch hostile to Leo who was also in conflict with the Danishmends, with whom he was recently in alliance. Having subdued most of the important places of lowland Cilicia, the Byzantines turned north and besieged Armenian Anazarbos, which resisted stubbornly and was only overcome after a determined investment that lasted thirty-five days.[40] During the same period, the emperor captured the fortress of Tell-Hamdoun (Toprakkale) and deported its inhabitants to Cyprus.[41]

While his grievances against Leo initially brought John to the East, his ultimate designs were on the greater prize of Antioch. Ibn al-Athir would assign the intervention of the Romans to the pleas for help dispatched to Constantinople by the Franks following their heavy defeat at Ba'rin (Montferrand) in July, 1137 at the hands of Zengi, but it is clear that John was already well into his campaign by the time news of the defeat would have reached him. No doubt the emperor found conditions favourable for his attaining control of Antioch, given the present weakened condition of the Crusader States.[42] By August, 1137, late in the campaigning season, John's army stood poised outside the walls of Antioch. Antioch, which had been in Frankish hands since its capture by Bohemond of Taranto in 1098, was the key to the Christian north. The value of the city went far beyond its prosperous Levantine trade and the taxes its seizure promised to the imperial coffers; Antioch had been a thorn in the side of Byzantine prestige since its capture by Bohemond of Taranto during the First Crusade. The Principality founded by Bohemond became an active foe of the empire and its continued independence threatened Roman ambitions on the eastern Mediterranean coast and Cilicia. Since the emperor Alexios' triumph over Bohemond of Taranto and his subsequent signing of the Treaty of Devol (September, 1108), Antioch was the

---

38 Lilie, Byzantium and the Crusader States, 118 and n. 89.
39 Gregory the Priest, Continuation, 241, 260; Smbat the Constable, Chronique, 615; Ibn al-Athir, al-Kāmil fī al-tārīkh, 424.
40 Ibid., 241; Hild / Hellenkemper, Kilikien, 178–185.
41 Ibn al-Athir, al-Kāmil fī al-tārīkh, 424.
42 Ibn al-Athir, al-Kāmil fī al-tārīkh, 422.

centrepiece of Byzantine ambitions in the east. With its seizure, the empire would have access to one of the largest and most prosperous cities of the Near East.[43]

Antioch was predominantly Christian, seat of the Patriarchate of Antioch, whose metropolitan had, in the period under discussion here, numbered some 50 suffragan bishoprics.[44] Despite a considerable presence of Syrian Jacobite and Armenian anti-Chalcedonians, whom the Byzantine authorities had actively encouraged to colonize the conquered territory in the tenth and eleventh centuries, the city remained spiritually vital. Antioch possessed numerous richly ornamented and endowed churches and pilgrim shrines which drew visitors from around Eurasia. One of the principal concerns of the emperor was that the patriarchal seat be held by a Chalcedonian bishop, something which bolstered imperial prestige, lent weight to the dealing of Constantinople with the rival church in Rome, and provided material support to the government. For these reasons, John II Komnenos worked hard to ensure that the patriarchate would leave Frankish hands.

Antioch was one terminus of the Silk Road and was a hub of the luxury textile trade; late in the 10th century, the brother of Sayf al-Dawla, Abu al-Hayja fled to Constantinople with the aid of an Antiochene silk merchant.[45] Antiochene merchants traded throughout Syria and were brokers in a thriving textile economy which may have included local silk production.[46] When the Franks violated the Byzantine agreement with Zengi in 1138, they seized the Muslim merchants and travellers from Aleppo, who were apparently sizeable in number.[47] The general prosperity of the city in 1049, when the Christian Arab physician Ibn Butlan visited and described in an epistle dated 1051:

> "Antakiyyah (Antioch) is an immense city. It possesses a wall and an outer wall. The wall has three hundred and sixty towers, and these are patrolled in turn by four thousand guards, who are sent o Antakiyyah every year, from the presence of the king in Constantinople, as warrant for the safe-keeping of the city, and in the second year they are changed. The plan of the city is that of a semicircle; its diameter lying along the mountain (Silphius) and the city wall climbs up over the mountains to its very summit; and further, the wall completes the semicircle in the (in the plain below). On the summit of the mountain, but within the wall, is a castle, which appears quite small from the city below, on account of its distance up; and this mountain shades the city from the sun, which only begins to shine over the town about the second hour of the day. In the wall surrounding (the city) and in the part not on the mountain, are five gates."[48]

---

43 For this campaign see Beihammer, Changing Strategies, 93–97.
44 Todt, Antioch in the Middle Byzantine Period, 189.
45 Zakkār, Emirate of Aleppo, 44.
46 Vorderstrasse, Trade and Textiles.
47 Ibn al-Adim, Chronicle, 675.
48 Le Strange, Palestine under the Muslims, 370–371; on the city see now, Todt / Vest, Syria, 539–663.

Ibn Butlan goes on to describe the rich array of churches in the city, all richly decorated with gold and silver; its gardens, the patriarchal hospital (Bimaristan), its many baths (including hot spring fed baths), the many mills on the Orontes River (Ar. Al-'Asi) which watered the many gardens and orchards of the city and its territory.[49]

In 1154, the prosperity of Antioch was on full display to the Muslim traveller Idrisi, who noted that the city wall extended 12 miles in circumference and had mills, orchards, gardens, and vegetable plots within, all watered in abundance. He added:

> "The bazaars of the city are thronged, and have splendid wares exposed here, and all necessary goods and needful merchandise. The good things of the place are innumerable, and its blessings manifold. They make here plain stuffs (not striped), that are renowned, of the sort known as *Al-'Attabi* (moire)."[50]

Much to the emperor's advantage, Antioch was under threat from the Islamic East, due to the unification by Imad al-din Zengi (1085–1146) of the emirates of Mosul and Aleppo in 1128, which enveloped the County of Edessa, the Christian outpost which was doomed to be the first to succumb to the Islamic counterattack. Zengi's operations exposed the frontiers of Antioch to persistent danger. More recently, the Crusaders had suffered setbacks at the hands of Zengi, atabeg of Mosul who had discomfited the Franks at Ba'rin in (Montferrand in the Homs gap of northern Syria, 38 km southwest of Hama) in 1137, after the capture and slaying of Pons, Count of Tripoli by Bazwaj of Damascus. Zengi subsequently trapped King Fulk of Jerusalem inside the castle of Ba'rin.[51] The intervention of the emperor into Outremer made matters worse for the Latins in the north, who were caught to the one side in the jaws of Zengi, and on the other, the Romans, who sought to squeeze every advantage from their erstwhile allies. In a short space of time the Franks had watched the approaches to Cilicia and Antioch fall to a powerful imperial force, suffered the capture of their king, and the dawning that no military power at their disposal was sufficient to deal with neither Zengi nor John.

The Byzantines set up siege engines and parried several sorties made by the Latins from the city. It seems that at this time Roman forces also seized the port of Iskenderun (Alexandretta), which the emperor is said to have refurbished at the time.[52] Byzantine attacks had also given them control of several seaports and

---

49 Le Strange, Palestine under the Muslims, 370–375.
50 A textile with a wavy appearance usually produced from silk.
51 William of Tyre, History, II.XIII.6, 56.
52 While Lilie doubts the testimony of Ibn al-Athir, who states that John refurbished the port of Iskanderum (Alexandretta), in my view this is most plausible. Since John clearly intended to intervene permanently in the affairs of Outremer, the use of a major Crusader port and

forts, namely those seized during the campaign in 1104 against Bohemond by Kantakouzenos and the Roman general Monastras, whose forces took most of the eastern Cilician Plain, including Longinias, Tarsus, Adana, and Mamistra (ancient Mopsuestia) on the Pyramos River.[53] The latter was a key fortress that controlled territories claimed by both Constantinople and Antioch, and while Roman authority there proved ephemeral, the eastern policy of the emperor Alexios I was pursued with a vigour that signalled that the Romans would not part with northern Syria without a serious fight. In fact, Alexios' claims were widely acknowledged in both Latin sources and in modern historiography, first with the oath of fealty that Bohemond certainly swore to the emperor in Constantinople in 1097, a stark reminder of which Anna Komnene put in the mouth of the Byzantine admiral Kantakouzenos during the latter's unsuccessful investment of Syrian Laodicea (Latakia)[54] in 1104:

> "You know that you all promised service to the Emperor and agreed in accordance with your oath to hand over to him the cities you took. Then you transgressed your oath, disregarded also the terms of peace and after taking this town and handing it over to us, you changed your mind and kept possession of it."[55]

William of Tyre excuses Frankish recalcitrance by using the arguments of the leading princes of Antioch; according to such views Alexios I had forfeited his claims because he was "a vacillating and unstable man, and had dealt fraudulently with them and had been the first to break his own pledges."[56]

However, the Treaty of Devol (Deabolis), signed in September 1108 by Bohemond following his decisive defeat at the hands of Alexius, proves decisive in this regard. While both Alexius and Bohemond agreed that their previous oaths to one another had been nullified by subsequent events, the terms of the treaty were now renewed and extended. Antioch was the centrepiece of the treaty, reflecting the tremendous investments the Byzantines had made in the city and its territory during the span of their rule from 969–1084, including repopulating the region, restoring the walls, churches, and public buildings, and ensuring security with a large military presence under high-ranking, capable commanders.[57] Under the terms negotiated at Devol, Bohemond agreed that he would be the emperor's man (*anthropos lizios*) and that after his death the territories that Alexius had given him as the emperor's agent would be returned to the empire

---

putting it in good repair where it could serve the needs of his own fleet and Italian allies seems likely. Given that, initially at least, John was in the region on the invitation of the Antiochenes, Roman appropriation of the port need not have been a hostile act.
53 Anna Komnene, Alexias XI.3–4, 354.48–64.
54 On Latakia (Laodikeia): Todt / Vest, Syria, 1429–1449.
55 Anna Komnene, Alexias XI.6, 355.82–86.
56 William of Tyre, History, XIV.24, 84.
57 Todt, Antioch and Edessa.

and to the governance of John II Komnenos. Bohemond received territories 'in the East', namely Aleppo, as well as Edessa then not under his or imperial control, which were to become his lands and further received 200 lbs of gold and an annual salary from the emperor. Antioch, the main bone of contention, was pledged by Bohemond to the emperor and the leading nobles of the city signed the treaty pact as well.[58] The Rupenid princes of the mountains were excluded from Devol, as the treaty claimed they had already become subjects of the empire. Tancred, naturally, as the successor of Bohemond and the princely authority in Antioch, rejected the treaty and thus his leading men never signed it;[59] they clung to the notion that Alexius had forfeited his rights when he abandoned the Crusading project at Antioch in the First Crusade. The subsequent agreement of Raymond with John at Antioch was based on the earlier (unenforced) Treaty of Devol, in which the Latins would receive unconquered eastern territories in exchange for Antioch, a situation which the Frankish nobility of the territory obviously found unacceptable.

The emperor found the Latins ready to resist and he ordered bombardment of the city with trebuchets and Frankish archers offered stout resistance.[60] Skirmishing continued over several days. With neither side wanting to decide the conflict through a decisive encounter, Antiochenes and Byzantines opened negotiations. According to William of Tyre, Raymond of Poitiers, Prince of Antioch (1136–49), agreed to become the vassal of the emperor. The terms were essentially those Bohemond I had agreed in the Treaty of Devol. Raymond would give John free access to Antioch. In return, the emperor would grant Aleppo, Shaizar, Hama and Homs.[61] Joscelin II of Courtenay, Count of Edessa (1131–50), apparently also offered his vassalage to John II. Together these two men were the most important leaders of the Franks in northern Outremer and their compliance was vital for any Byzantine-Crusader alliance to succeed.

Ibn al-Adim reports in more detail a series of exchanges, both violent and diplomatic, between the empire and Zengi late in the campaigning season of 1137.[62] John journeyed from Antioch to the fortress of Bagras (ancient Pagrae), on the 10 September 1137, the emperor dispatched an embassy to Zengi. We are also told that Sawar, Zengi's general, massacred a large detachment of the Byzantine army and sent the remainder captive to Aleppo, although this seems odd in light of the understanding at which the two rulers had arrived, namely that the emperor was moving against the lands of Leo of Armenia and not Zengi.[63] The

---

58 Anna Komnene, Alexias VIII.5–XI.7, 349–355.
59 Rowe, Papacy and the Greeks.
60 William of Tyre, History, 2.XIII, 92.
61 William of Tyre, History, 2.XIV.24, 93.
62 Ibn al-Adim, Chronicle, 674.
63 Ibn al-Adim, Chronicle, 674.

latter then moved south to attack the Syrian cities of Hama, Homs, and Ba'albek while the emperor marched back to Cilicia. From these manoeuvrings it is apparent that John's intention was the subjugation of Antioch and the final realization of the terms of the Treaty of Devol, not open war with Zengi in the first instance. Once the Byzantine, Antiochene, and what remained of the County of Edessa's forces were united, did the emperor likely intend to strike against Zengi (if ever), and it is quite likely that he hoped to avoid a general engagement but rather believed he could seize Aleppo and force the atabeg to accept the new political realities; after all, Zengi had come into possession of the city only ten years prior, and given the fractiousness of Aleppan politics, his hold there was not entirely secure.[64] It is interesting that John II left out many of the territories originally granted to Bohemond in the Treaty of Devol and these were numerous.[65] The vassalage of Joscelin II of Edessa to John II obviously complicated matters, since Edessa was among the cities the treaty had granted to Bohemond.

There, during the winter of 1137–38, from their base at Anazarbos, Byzantine troops attacked Armenian holdings and seized the fortress of Tell-Hamdoun (Toprakkale) and deported the inhabitants to Cyprus.[66] These operations culminated in the siege of the castle of Vahka (Feke), 120 km north of Adana. The unfortunate prince Leo was captured and sent, along with his family, to Constantinople where he died in 1140.[67] After the power of the Rupenid Armenians in Cilicia had been drastically weakened, John mustered his army in Cilicia at the start of 1138 and again marched on northern Syria, expecting to enforce the terms of the treaty with the Franks of Antioch on which the ink had only just dried. As a prelude to war, Raymond violated his agreement with Zengi by arresting the Muslim merchants present in Aleppo; no doubt their goods and money were seized and partly used to fund the campaign. At first, things seemed to progress smoothly enough for the uneasy allies. The Byzantine army was joined by the forces of Antioch and those of the County of Edessa under Joscelin. Ibn al-Athir notes that the Byzantine army was very large and comprised of Greeks, Franks and various other Christians. John's approach filled the Muslim inhabitants of northern Syria with terror.[68]

The target of the expedition was Aleppo, the key to northern Syria and a city which had defied Byzantine ambitions for more than a century. At the start of the campaign, the coalition sieged the town of Buza'a, 40 km east of Aleppo.[69] Ac-

---

64 Zakkār, Emirate of Aleppo details the ambitions of the Arab clans and Turcomens in the period just prior to the Crusades, and conditions had not changed that much fifty years later.
65 Todt, Antioch and Edessa.
66 Ibn al-Athir, al-Kāmil fī al-tārīkh, 424; Ibn al-Qalanisi, Damascus Chronicle, 240.
67 Matthew of Edessa, Chronicle 239; Boase, Cilician Kingdom of Armenia.
68 Ibn al-Athir, Tarikh al-bahir fi al-Dawlah al-Atabakiyah bi al-Mawsil, 98.
69 On Bu'za'a (ancient Beselathōn Kōmē): Todt / Vest, Syria, 1004–1007.

cording to Ibn al-Adim, the allied host arrived at the town on Easter Sunday, April 3, 1138 and took it on 8 April. The seizure of Buza'a indicates that the emperor and his allies were interested in securing the eastern approaches to the city whence trouble was expected from the Muslims of Upper Mesopotamia, especially Imad al-din Zengi, *atabeg* of Mosul. While encamped at Buza'a, Byzantine cavalry are said to have raided as far as Hama (ancient Epiphaneia).[70]

While the Latin and Byzantine forces moved on Aleppo,[71] which belonged to Zengi, the atabeg himself was occupied with the siege of Homs (ancient Emesa). As the dominant Muslim prince of the region, Zengi's timidity in the face of imperial aggression is revealing. Despite Ibn al-Athir's efforts to portray Zengi, whose propagandists portrayed him as a great ghazi fighting for the faith, it is clear that the atabeg did very little. Ibn al-Qalanisi reports that Zengi sent infantry, horsemen, and archers, but only those he felt he could spare as he continued to press the siege of Homs.[72] These reinforcements arrived in Aleppo on the 10th or 11th of April. The Byzantines and Franks bombarded the city with trebuchets and assaulted Aleppo, whose garrison mostly comprised the city militia, but after sustaining losses the allies broke off their attack. Seeing that Aleppo was not to be taken without a prolonged siege, John instead turned his army on al-Atharib (Atarib), 25 km west of Aleppo which he seized on 21 April. According to Ibn al-Athir, Emir Sawar, general of Zengi in Aleppo, attacked the Byzantine garrison at Atharib, massacred them and freed the prisoners held there.[73]

The campaign now turned to another one of the settlements on the Byzantine-Frankish treaty list: Shaizar.[74] The imperial army marched via the major north-south road that passed through Ma'arrat en-Nu'mān).[75] Along their route the Byzantines occupied the much-contested Frankish stronghold of Kafartab after the defenders abandoned it.[76] Shaizar (identified with ancient Larissa) sits on a crag astride the Orontes River at a strategic position on the route through the valley. Unlike Aleppo, it was not under the direct control of Zengi, but rather in the hands of the Ismaili clan of the Banu Munqid, who had come into the possession of the fortress in 1081 after purchasing it from the Byzantine bishop of al-Bara.[77] Shaizar had an upper and lower town, with a powerful citadel and a

---

70 Ibn al-Adim Chronicle, 675; Abu'l Fida, al-Mukhtasar, I.24; Ibn al-Qalanisi, Damascus Chronicle, 249–250.
71 Todt / Vest, Syria, 665–801.
72 Ibn al-Qalanisi, Damaskus Chronicle, 249.
73 Ibn al-Athir, al-Kāmil fī al-tārīkh, 339.
74 On Shaizar, see the recent study of Tonghini, Shayzar I, and Todt / Vest, Syria.
75 Ibid., Syria, 879–88.
76 Kinnamos' contention that John took Kefartab is correct (see Ibn al-Adim, Chronicle, 677), though his assertion that they seized Hama is quite unlikely: Ioannes Kinnamos, Deeds, Book 1 tr. Brand, 24. On Kafartab (ancient Kapharda): Todt / Vest, Syria, 1351–1356.
77 Mouton, Shayzar.

strong set of walls. On the 26th of April (a Tuesday)[78], the Byzantine-Frankish army established its encampment; the Byzantines and Franks of Antioch and Edessa all encamped in different spots. After resting for a couple of days, on Friday the Byzantines and Franks assaulted the lower city and there was a violent confrontation at the end of which the Christians were repulsed. The following day (Saturday), John set up his siege engines and proceeded to bombard it. According to both Ibn al-Adim and Ibn al-Athir, the emperor set up eighteen trebuchets – an astonishing number, considering that employing one or two such machines was usually enough to demolish many medieval fortifications.

The bombardment of the lower city must have caused terrible destruction of property and no little loss of life. Ibn al-Adim states that the artillery fire cut off access to water and William of Tyre notes, perhaps optimistically, that the Christians actually took control of the lower town, though if the lower city is, in fact, the *madina* of Hisn al-Jisr with its fortifications.[79] Choniates states that the emperor conquered a place called Nistrion, "a city of Mesopotamia, situated a little distance from Shaizar and most excellently fortified".[80] Scholars have identified Nistrion as the Hisn al-Jisr (Ar. 'Fortress of the Bridge') that controlled the crossing of the Orontes and where a settlement grew up, becoming the 'lower city' (al-Madinah, the Latin *suburbium, pars inferior civitatis*).[81] Then, when it seems that the inhabitants of Shaizar were most hard pressed and the ripe fruit was about to fall into the hands of the emperor, the Byzantines broke the siege and marched back to Cilicia and Constantinople in May, 1138.

There is considerable variance amongst the sources as to why this happened. Michael Italikos (d. 1157) overlooked the failure at Shaizar entirely.[82] Kinnamos states that John despaired of taking the place and instead accepted a large payment. The Byzantine court poet Nikephoros Basiliakes, who wrote quite close to the events of the Syria campaign in 1139 likewise omits the failure at Shaizar and instead stresses the rich treasures which the emperor carried away.[83] The account of the emperor John's departure provided by Choniates states that the Romans withdrew to Antioch upon hearing reports of an attack by the Turks on Edessa.[84] This roughly comports with that Ibn al-Adim claims that the emperor heard that

---

[78] There is some confusion among the historians as to the precise timing of the campaign, especially Ibn al-Adim, who states they arrived at Shaizar on the 26th, but later states they departed for Shaizar on 29th of April where they arrived below the town: Ibn al-Adim, Chronicle, 677.
[79] Ibn al-Adim, Chronicle, 677; William of Tyre, History, II.XV.1, 96.
[80] Niketas Choniates, Historia, 29 ed. van Dieten, 49–52; tr. Margoulias, 17; Todt / Vest, Syria, 1552–1553.
[81] Humphreys, Munkidh; Hitti, Arab-Syrian Gentleman, 6.
[82] Michael Italikos (or. 43), 262.
[83] Nikephoros Basiliakes, Gli encomî, 113–117, ll. 685–804, §§ 30–32; Maisano, 215–220.
[84] Niketas Choniates, Historia, 31, ed. van Dieten, 30; trans. Margoulias, 18.

the Artuqid leader Kara Arslan had crossed the Euphrates with 50,000 Turkomens.[85] This is extremely unlikely, as Ibn al-Athir explains in detail that Zengi expressly ordered Kara Arslan not to send troops or otherwise intervene. According to Ibn al-Athir and his follower Abu'l Fida (d. 1331), it was the timely arrival of Zengi and his boldness in confronting John that forced the Byzantine withdrawal.[86] This is equally unlikely, as the atabeg had refused to confront the Romans in the field, being merely content to shadow the imperial army and to harass it: neither the Romans nor Zengi wished to chance an all-out confrontation, which may speak to the parity of their forces. Surprisingly, William of Tyre lays the blame for the failure upon the shoulders of Raymond and Joscelin, both of whom undermined the project from the start, wishing for the doom of John's project in Syria.[87] Gregory the Priest notes laconically that the emperor was deceived by the Franks in his attack on Shaizar.[88] Michael the Syrian does not know why the Byzantines fled, but predictably he rejoiced at their discomfiture.[89]

Modern scholars have likewise attempted to understand why John, after his extensive preparations and strenuous efforts, broke off this campaign. Lilie argues that the emperor aborted his Syrian offensive at Shaizar due to his own lack of strength and the surprising tenacity of the Muslim defences, as well as the Seljuk attacks in Cilicia, and harassment by the cavalry of Zengi.[90] Overall, Lilie pays more attention to the retreat from the walls of Antioch at the end of the campaign, which he attributes to multiple concerns on the part of the emperor, namely his long absence from the capital; the lateness of the campaigning season and his inability to control Antioch without storming it; but especially a growing threat from the West, where the treaty signed in 1136 was unravelling in light of new developments.[91] In support of this latter assertion, he cites a letter from Innocent II of March 1138 in which he commanded Latin Christians not to cooperate with John in his attempted Syrian conquests.[92] Harris favours the western threat as playing a dominant role as well, although he notes that the Byzantine Greek sources are at odds with one another on the matter.[93] Parnell accepts the explanation of William of Tyre that the emperor ended his siege because of the faithlessness of his Frankish allies.[94] Before further discussion it is important, however, to understand whether John in fact went back to Roman

---

85 Ibn al-Adim, Chronicle, 678.
86 Abu'l Fida, I.24.
87 William of Tyre, History, 2.XV.2, 96–97.
88 Matthew of Edessa, Chronicle, 241.
89 Michael the Syrian, Chronicle/Chronique, 245.
90 Lilie, Byzantium and the Crusader States, 127–128.
91 Lilie, Byzantium and the Crusader States, 130–131.
92 Rowe, Papacy and the Greeks, 121.
93 Harris, Byzantium and the Crusades, 89–90.
94 Parnell, John II Comnenus and Crusader Antioch, 154.

territory via Antioch. The Byzantine historian John Kinnamos has the emperor marching straight to Constantinople. Choniates, however, has the emperor staying in Antioch, where he wrongly places at least portions of the hostile reception John would receive in his next expedition, the campaign of 1142. However, if we look at the Syriac sources, one can more readily discern why the emperor John II Komnenos ended the siege of Shaizar, for while he was engaged there, Mas'ud, the Seljuk Sultan of Ikonion, made a sudden attack on Adana. This assault is recorded in the wrong year by the Syriac sources, who place it in 1137 when John first invaded Cilicia.[95]

The *Chronicle of 1234* offers significant detail about the Turkish attack on Adana. The Byzantines were welcomed there and the Jacobite Christians, led by their patriarch John, were said to be happy with Greek rule and glad to be free of the heavy tributes of the Franks. This revelation is rather surprising, in light of the dim view that many Syriac authors took of the Romans and Chalcedonian Christians, generally. At dawn on a Sunday, the Turks arrived and launched a ferocious surprise attack. The level of detail provided by the chronicler suggests that he relied on an eyewitness account of the battle. After a sharp encounter the Turks managed to scale the walls and open the gates and a massacre ensued. The metropolitan John and his clergy were garrotted and the Turks thoroughly pillaged the city, withdrawing, we are told, with enormous riches and many captives, most of whom were sold in the slave markets of Melitene.[96]

Bad though the Turkish sack of Adana and the Seljuk threat to John's rear, it was only one symptom of a much greater set of ills. In 1130, during his initial forays into Anatolia, John's younger brother Isaac had attempted to seize power. Isaac's attempted coup failed but he travelled to Asia Minor and perambulated around the courts of various rulers in the east. Isaac made an alliance with the Danishmendid Amir Ghazi and Mas'ud as well as Leo the Armenian around 1132. We must add, I believe, Constantine Gabras, *dux* of Trebizond who ruled as an independent prince, to the alliance that threatened the emperor.[97] More than any other reason, the potential of this coalition to do great harm to John, likely compelled the emperor to go east, even if the thicket of political intrigues and tangled alliances had become even thornier by 1137.

---

95 Michael the Syrian, Chronique, 3, 245; Chronicle of 1234, ed. Chabot, 82; Gregory the Priest, Continuation, 264.
96 The fact that Melitene was the destination for the captives who were sold raises the possibility that the Turkish attack was a Danishmendid one: Lilie, Byzantium and the Crusader States, 134 n. 154 who notes "the sources may confuse the Seljuks of Iconium with the Danishmendids". It is difficult to separate the two at the time, since the two Seljuk powers worked closely together during the period of Amir Ghazi and his son-in-law Mas'ud; it seems this alliance broke down only upon the death of Ghazi's son, Malik Muhammad in 1142. Chronicle of 1234, ed. Chabot, 82.
97 Niketas Choniates, Historia, ed. van Dieten, 34, trans. Margoulias, 20.

Upon his return to Constantinople in 1138, John settled matters at court but did not wait for long; it was the internal threat to his throne that had taken him back to the capital. Around this time, Isaac and John were reconciled and the sons of Isaac rejoined the fold of the Komnenoi. However, John wanted to punish the Turks and, if we accept that Mas'ud and Malik Muhammad the Danishmendid ruler were in fact in alliance in 1138, as they appear to have been, then John's unduly swift departure from the capital on an ill-advised winter campaign in 1139, is understandable. John's campaign, which was aimed not only against the Danishmendids or Gabras, as it usually thought to be the case, but the whole of the enemy coalition is, I think, correct. Even if the expedition faltered outside Neocaesarea, Gabras was at least brought to heel. However, the defection of Isaac's son John in the midst of battle at Caesarea and his welcome by the Turkish enemy no doubt underscored to the emperor how precarious was his family network on which the dynasty was based. Certainly, the imperial dignity demanded that Gabras and the Turks be suitably punished, even if that punishment could not yield justice.

Matters closer to home kept the emperor occupied for the next three years. It was only in 1142 that he was able to return to Syria. Late in the campaigning season of that year, John led his army to Turbessel (Tell Bashir)[98], a major fortress inside the County of Edessa.[99] There the Byzantines surprised the alleged architect of the delaying tactics of the Franks of Antioch, Joscelin II, who was forced to hand over hostages, among them his daughter. William of Tyre emphasizes the fact that Raymond had repeatedly urged the emperor to come to Syria and had promised he would abide by the treaty.[100] John then marched on Antioch and demanded the city be handed over to him. He insisted, we are told, that Raymond allow him free access to Antioch to use as a base from which to prosecute a war against the neighbouring Muslims. John maintained that Cilicia was too distant to serve the purpose and, moreover, that his presence attested his willingness to act in upholding his part of the bargain, namely to deliver into crusader hands the lands which to compensate the Franks for their loss of Antioch. Thus pressed, we are told, Raymond stalled for time. According to William of Tyre, the leading notables of the city urged the prince to abrogate the treaty with the emperor.[101] The flimsy excuse that Raymond offered in refusing to give the emperor what he demanded was that Antioch belonged by right and custom to Constance, his wife. John thus had his answer; according to Choniates (who seems to have no knowledge of Antiochene perfidy, as he omits mention of it), the imperial troops

---

98 Todt / Vest, Syria, 1783–1789.
99 William of Tyre, History, 2.XV.19, 123.
100 William of Tyre, History, 2.XV.20, 125.
101 William of Tyre, History, 2.XV.20, 125.

plundered the suburbs of the city where they were billeted, then marched to winter quarters in Cilicia where shortly thereafter he suffered a hunting accident and died.[102]

Some window into John's thinking can perhaps be deduced from a letter he dispatched in the winter of 1142-43 to King Fulk of Jerusalem in which the emperor states he wished to visit Jerusalem to pray and to aid the king against his enemies.[103] Fulk replied that his land was unable to sustain such a large force as that which accompanied John, but that if the emperor would be pleased to visit with ten thousand men, he would happily receive him. It is difficult not to believe, along with Chalandon and Browning, that John's plans towards the Latin were sinister, and that his mind was made up. Had he lived, he would certainly have turned his army against Antioch and marched as far as it would have carried him. But of course, John did not live; he died in a hunting accident, or perhaps as Browning suggests, through murder, in the Cilician Plain on 8 April 1143.[104] In a most surprising turn of events, his youngest son Michael, acclaimed by the army and supported by the kingmaker John Axouch, acceded to the throne. As with many such affairs in the Crusades, the escape for the Latins was most improbable.

The dramatic climax of John's confrontation against the Crusaders leaves the historian with important questions. What were his intentions? Did John really have the forces at his disposal and the capability to sustain a long and bitter conflict against the Franks in Outremer? While the Byzantine historian Kinnamos tells us that John had planned to hand the empire over to his son Isaac and provide Cilicia and Antioch to Manuel as an appanage, we have no way of knowing if this is true. Certainly the experiences of 1137 and 1138 had taught the emperor that the Franks of Antioch could not be trusted and were therefore useless as allies, and one is well justified to consider that the emperor had his mind set on open warfare which his death prevented.

As for the question of John's military capacities in Syria, this will have to await further discussion.[105] The forces of John certainly were sizeable and were apparently larger than those which normally took the field in the Levant, which is understandable given the patchwork of petty princes which ruled there. Choniates mentions that there were contingents of Pechenegs included in the force; these most certainly fought as horse archers. Likely the force included contingents of Armenians, as one would expect that those vassals in Cilicia who remained loyal to the emperor would have mustered to his banner.

---

102 Niketas Choniates, Historia, ed. van Dieten, 39; trans. Margoulias, 23.
103 Chalandon, Jean II Comnène et Manuel I Comnène,191.
104 Browning, Death of John II Comnenus, 234.
105 On numbers of the Komnenian army, see Birkenmeier, Development of the Komnenian Army, esp. 62 and 138 where the field armies of Alexios I and Manuel I numbered up to 35,000 men.

Regarding the size of the army that marched to Syria, we have scant information. The *Chronicle 1234* makes the ridiculous claim that the Greek army numbered 400,000 men.[106] Ibn al-Adim states that at Shaizar the Byzantine force arrived at the city in the number of 1,000 horsemen and 5,000 cavalry.[107] Is this number of 6,000 the whole of the Byzantine army in the field in Syria? It seems unlikely, especially when one considers that King Fulk suggested that John come to Jerusalem with 'only' 10,000 soldiers.[108] If on occasion John campaigned with perhaps 20,000 men or more, how can we understand the imperial hesitation, almost timorous prosecution of the siege of Aleppo and his unwillingness to confront Zengi in the field? Beyond this, we return to the basic question – why did John want Antioch so badly to begin with? While the richness of the prize and the importance the empire placed on its possession has been noted above, there were surely worthy conquests to be made much closer to Constantinople; indeed, one wonders why the emperor would attempt his far off Syrian adventure when Ikonion remained a thorn in his side and one 500 km nearer to the capital than Antioch. This is to mention nothing of the Danishmends, and both Turkish polities would have had to be dealt with for the empire to successfully hold the Cilician Plain and with it, a land corridor to Antioch. While we may cite religious and cultural motives – imperial prestige and notions of universal empire, of glory and so forth, these ring hollow in the face of the pragmatism that John showed on many occasions, including his avoiding all-out war with Zengi.

What should be clear from this discussion is that, despite considerable internal and external tumult, John II maintained that his claim to Antioch was a priority. The care of his preparations in 1135–36, the putative size of his forces, and his determination to return in 1142–43 should make it clear that the emperor was not content merely with recognition of his imperial status, as Harris has recently argued.[109] If this were the case, then the campaign of 1137–38 would have fulfilled this desire, as Raymond had, nominally at least, submitted himself as the emperor's liege. It seems, rather, that John II was intent on enforcing what he believed to be the terms his father had laid down in 1108 in the Treaty of Devol. Moreover, it would be naïve to argue that John misunderstood his Crusader adversaries and simply believed that they were bound by the decisions of their predecessors to uphold the treaty. John did not himself hesitate to break treaties when *realpolitik*, in his estimation, demanded it. Magdalino's argument, that John was motivated by 'a strong desire for revenge' must be seen in the context of

---

106 Chronicle of 1234, ed. Chabot, 81.
107 Ibn al-Adim, Chronicle, 677.
108 William of Tyre, History, 2.XV.21, 126.
109 Harris, Byzantium and the Crusades, 29–30.

the other, complicated factors: Antioch was a valuable prize for the empire, both economically and especially in terms of imperial prestige.

The emperor's ambitions in Syria cannot therefore be seen as a mere distraction or of secondary interest. In Ikonion, some 500 km nearer Constantinople than Antioch, Mas'ud had proven himself a fickle ally at best, and potentially a sponsor of alternatives to John's rule at best. The Danishmend emirate arguably posed a more present danger to imperial interests, yet the emperor devoted considerable efforts in his efforts to gain authority over Antioch. The large numbers of Christians in the Antiochene, even if they were anti-Chalcedonian Syrians and Armenians, were nonetheless viewed as potential allies of the emperors. There was obviously no shortage of their co-religionists in imperial service in the 12th century, and Constantinople had long courted these communities in shaping their frontier policies.

Whatever the motivations, the campaigns of John ultimately failed. His expeditions neither staunched the bleeding of the neighboring Christian petty states amongst the Crusaders, nor did he bring the latter into the imperial fold. His son and successor, Manuel, took a much more hands-off approach to the Crusader states and never risked an intervention of the intensity that John had begun in 1137. Manuel had his own form of revenge on Raymond of Antioch, whom his forces inflicted a sharp, although no means crippling defeat. It was this Roman victory and the fall of Edessa which brought the Prince of Antioch to Constantinople in 1145 where he had to grovel to the emperor and submit to humiliating terms, including the installation of a Greek patriarch on the throne of Antioch.[110] Nonetheless, Manuel was never willing or able to impose direct imperial rule over Antioch, despite the opportunities which presented themselves in the wake of the seizure of Edessa in 1144 by Zengi. This catastrophe exposed the Principality to existential peril. While it could certainly be argued that the empire could not have sustained a protracted war with the powerful atabeg, the death of the latter in 1145 certainly opened the road to further Byzantine intervention. While Manuel adopted many of his father's policies, he was content to hold Antioch as an overlord, and certainly did not share John's ambitions in Syria, being satisfied with direct control over Cilicia. Of course, while not the historian's business, the great 'what ifs' remain, for example – what if John II was alive a mere three years later when, in 1147, the armies of the Second Crusade arrived in the East? In the final tally, the campaigns of John II in the East therefore were without victors or vanquished, unless one counts the designs of the empire to restore Syria and the Holy Land to the authority of Constantinople, which died in April 1143 in the forests of Cilicia with John II.

---

110 Magdalino, Empire, 42.

Bibliography

Sources

Abu'l-Fida', al-Mukhtasar akhbar al-bashar, ed. Muhammad Z. M. 'Azab / Yahya S. Husayn / Muhammad F. Wasif, Cairo 1998-1999.

Anna Komnene, Alexias =Annae Comnenae Alexias, ed. Dieter R. Reinsch, 2 vols. (Corpus Fontium Historiae Byzantinae 40), Berlin 2001.

Chronicle of 1234 = Anonymi auctoris Chronicon ad annum Christi 1234 pertinens, ed. Jean Baptiste Chaot (Corpus Christainorium Orientalium. Scriptores Syri, series tertia, 14).

Goitein, Shelomo Dov, A Letter from Seleucia (Cilicia): Dated 21 July 1137, in: Speculum 39 (1964), 298-303.

Gregory the Priest, Continuation, trans. Ara E. Dostourian, in: Armenia and the Crusades: Tenth to Twelfth Centuries. The Chronicle of Matthew of Edessa, Belmont, MA 1993, 241-280.

Ibn al-Adim, Chronicle = Bughyat al-talab fi Tā'rīkh Ḥalab, in: Recueil des historiens des croisades, Historiens orientaux 3, Paris 1884, 577-690.

Ibn al-Athir, al-Kāmil fī al-tārīkh, in: Recueil des historiens des croisades (Historiens orientaux 1), Paris 1872, 189-744.

Ibn al-Athir, Tarikh al-bahir al-Dawlah al-Atabakiyah bi l-Mawsil, ed. 'Abd al-Qadir Ahmad Tyulaymat, Cairo 1963.

Ibn al-Qalanisi, Damascus Chronicle, trans. H. A. R. Gibb, The Damascus Chronicle of the Crusades, London 1967.

Ioannes Kinnamos, trans. Charles M. Brand, The Deeds of John and Manuel Comnenus, New York 1976.

Matthew of Edessa, Chronicle, trans. Ara E. Dostourian, Armenia and the Crusades: tenth to twelfth centuries: The Chronicle of Matthew of Edessa, Belmont, MA 1993.

Michel Italikos, Lettres et discours, ed. Paul Gutier (Archives de l'Orient chrétien,), Paris 1972.

Nikephoros Basiliakes = Niceforo Basilace. Gli encomî per l'imperatore e per il patriarca, ed. Riccardo Maisano (Byzantina et Neo-Hellenica Neapoletana 5), Neapel 1977.

Niketas Choniates = Nicetae Choniatae Historia, ed. Jan-Louis van Dieten (Corpus Fontium Historiae Byzantinae 11), Berlin 1975 [Engl. transl. Harry Magoulias, O City of Byzantium. Annals of Niketas Choniates, Detroit 1984].

Michael the Syrian = Chronique de Michel le Syrien, Patriarche Jacobite d'Antioche (1166-99), ed. and trans. Jean-Baptiste Chabot, vol. 3, Brussels 1901.

Smbat the Constable, Chronique du Royaume de Petite Armenie (Chronicle of the Kingdom of Little Armenia 1), Recueil des historiens des croisades, Documents arméniens, ed. and trans. Edouard Dulaurier, Paris 1899.

William of Tyre, A History of the Deeds Done Beyond the Sea, trans Emily A. Babcock / August C. Krey, New York 1943.

Literature

Beihammer, Alexander, Changing Strategies and Ideological Concepts in Byzantine-Arab Relations in the Eleventh and Twelfth Centuries, in: Ambassadors, Artists, Theologians: Byzantine Relations with the Near East from the Ninth to the Thirteenth Centuries, ed. Zachary Chitwoood / Johannes Pahlitzsch (Byzanz zwischen Orient und Okzident 12), Mainz 2019, 85–101.

Birkenmeier, John W., The Development of the Komnenian Army, 1081–1180, Leiden 2002.

Boase, Thomas Sherrer Ross, The Cilician Kingdom of Armenia, Edinburgh 1978.

Browning, Robert, The Death of John II Comnenus, in: Byzantion 31 (1961), 229–235.

Cahen, Claude, The Formation of Turkey: The Seljukid Sultanate of Rum, Eleventh to Fourteenth Century, trans. P. M. Holt, Harlow 2001.

Chalandon, Ferdinand, Jean II Comnène 1118–1143, et Manuel I Comnène 1143–1180, New York 1912.

Der Nersessian, Sirarpie, The Kingdom of Cilician Armenia, in: History of the Crusades, vol. 2, ed. Kenneth M. Setton, Philadelphia 1969, 630–659.

Harris, Jonathan, Byzantium and the Crusades, London 2014.

Hild, Friedrich / Hellenkemper, Hansgerd, Kilikien und Isaurien (Tabula Imperii Byzantini 5), Vienna 1990.

Hitti, Philip Khuri, An Arab-Syrian Gentleman and Warrior in the Period of the Crusades. Memoirs of Usāmah-Ibn-Munqidh (Kitāb Al-I'tibār), New York 1929.

Holo, Joshua David, An Economic History of the Jews of Byzantium from the Eve of the Arab Conquest to the Fourth Crusade , PhD Dissertation, Chicago 2001.

Humphreys, R. Stephen, Munkidh, in: Encyclopaedia of Islam, Second Edition, vol. 7, 577–580.

Jeffreys, Michael, Prosopography of the Byzantine World, 2016. London 2017. [https://pbw2016.kdl.kcl.ac.uk/].

Kazhdan, Alexander P., Sebastos, in: The Oxford Dictionary of Byzantium, Oxford 1991, 1862–1863.

Le Strange, Guy, Palestine under the Muslims: A Description of the Holy Land from A.D. 650 to 1500, London 1890.

Lilie, Ralph-Johannes, Byzantium and the Crusader States, 1096–1204, Oxford 1993.

MacEvitt, Christopher, The Crusades and the Christian World of the East: Rough Tolerance, Philadelphia 2008.

Magdalino, Paul, The Triumph of 1133, in: John II Komnenos, Emperor of Byzantium: In the Shadow of Father and Son, ed. Alessandra Bucossi / Alex Rodriguez Suarez, London 2016, 53–70.

Magdalino, Paul, The Empire of Manuel I Komnenos 1143–1180, Cambridge 1993.

Mélikoff, Irène, Le Geste de Melik Dānişmend. Étude critique du Dānişmendnāme, Paris 1960.

Mouton, Jean-Michel, Shayzar, in: Encyclopaedia of Islam, Second Edition, vol. 9, 410–411.

Ostrogorsky, George, History of the Byzantine State, Oxford 1968.

Parnell, David Alan, John II Comnenus and Crusader Antioch, in: Crusades. Medieval Worlds in Conflict, ed. Thomas Madden, Farnham 2010, 149–160.

Rowe, John Gordon, The Papacy and the Greeks (1122-1153), in: Church History 28 (1959), 115-130.
Shepard, Jonathan, Holy Land, Lost Lands, *Realpolitik*. Imperial Byzantine Thinking about Syria and Palestine in the Later 10th and 11th Centuries, in: Al-Qantara 33 (2012), 505-545.
Sinclair, Thomas Alan, Eastern Turkey: An Architectural & Archaeological Survey, vol. 4, London 1990.
Stouraitis, Ioannis, Narratives of John II Komnenos' Wars. Comparing Byzantine and Modern Approaches, in: John II Komnenos, Emperor of Byzantium: In the Shadow of Father and Son, ed. Alessandra Bucossi / Alex Rodriguez Suarez, London 2016, 22-36.
Todt, Klaus-Peter, Antioch and Edessa in the So-Called Treaty of Deabolis (September 1108), in: ARAM Periodical 12 (2000), 485-501.
Todt, Klaus-Peter, Antioch in the Middle Byzantine Period (969-1084): The Reconstruction of the City as an Administrative, Economic, Military and Ecclesiastical Center, in: Topoi. Orient-Occident 5,1 (2004), 171-190.
Todt, Klaus-Peter / Vest, Bernd Andreas, Syria (Syria Prōtē, Syria Deutera, Syria Euphratēsia) (Tabula Imperii Byzantini 15), Vienna 2014.
Tonghini, Cristina, Shayzar I, The Fortification of the Citadel, Leiden 2011.
Toumanoff, Cyril, Kamsarakan, in: Encyclopedia Iranica, vol. 15/5, London 2010, 453-455 [www.iranicaonline.org/articles/kamsarakan].
Vorderstrasse, Tasha, Trade and Textiles from Medieval Antioch, in: Al-Masāq 22 (2010), 151-171.
Vučetić, Martin Marko, Emperor John II's Encounters with Foreign Rulers, in: John II Komnenos, Emperor of Byzantium: In the Shadow of Father and Son, ed. Alessandra Bucossi / Alex Rodriguez Suarez, London 2016, 71-90.
Zakkār, Suhayl, The Emirate of Aleppo 1004-1094, Beirut 1971.

Graham A. Loud

Victors and Vanquished in Norman Italy

The Norman takeover of southern Italy during the eleventh century was in many respects a peculiar form of conquest. This observation is particularly apt when one compares the conquest of southern Italy with the contemporary Norman conquest of England – although one should stress that such a comparison can often be overdone, and that the process of conquest in England is very definitely *not* a guide to what happened in the south. Nevertheless, the differences in chronology and speed are striking. Above all, while it may be an exaggeration to suggest that the conquest of England was entirely decided by, and was inevitable from, the great battle of 14th October 1066, it is only a slight exaggeration. Certainly, apart from in peripheral regions such as the far north and Wales, the process of conquest and the displacement of the Anglo-Saxon upper-class was largely accomplished within a decade from the Battle of Hastings.

By contrast, the conquest of southern Italy and Sicily was a much more protracted affair. From the probable first arrival of the Normans at Salerno c. 1000 until the final conquest of south-eastern Sicily took some ninety years. Even if one dates the *conquest* phase as beginning with the establishment of a permanent and independent Norman settlement at Aversa in 1030, this process still lasted for some sixty years, and none of those who joined Count Rainulf at Aversa in the early 1030s can have lived to see the surrender of Noto in 1091. Probably few or none of these early settlers were still alive when Salerno surrendered in December 1076, which marked the last stage of the conquest of the mainland. Nor indeed was that conquest ever quite complete. Several of the more important towns on the mainland were either never conquered by the Normans (Naples and Benevento) or were never settled by them and regained their independence after a period of Norman rule (Amalfi in the 1090s and Bari c. 1120).[1]

There were several reasons for the slow pace of the Norman takeover, but the most fundamental was the small number of the incomers. Even though these south Italian 'Normans' in fact included people from other regions of (primarily)

---

1 Oldfield, City and Community, 39–54.

northern France, and the emigration to the south lasted for almost a century – a few isolated newcomers can be attested even in the first years of the twelfth century – no more than a few thousand ever settled in the south. That explains a great deal, not just about the conquest, but also about the society of southern Italy in the wake of that conquest. For the Normans did not just conquer southern Italy by force of arms, but they also infiltrated their way into south Italian society and recruited and relied upon local allies just as much as they succeeded through their own prowess.[2]

This is not to deny that the Norman conquest was at times a bloody and violent process, nor to downplay the human misery that often followed in its wake. The chroniclers of the conquest, of course praised the valour and military skills of the Normans, and recounted their victories, usually (if we are to believe these chroniclers) against heavy odds, and the hordes of enemies whom they (allegedly) slew. Yet in fact, contemporary warfare was more often a matter of ravaging the countryside, destroying crops and carrying off foodstuffs and other resources than of encounters in the open field. The effects on the general populace might well be horrific. So, when the Norman Richard of Capua was besieging Aquino c. 1059 in an attempt to extort money from the local count: "he surrounded Aquino, doing the greatest possible damage. He cut down the trees and grain still growing in the fields and killed every man that he could find".[3] The historian of the monastery of Casauria in the Abruzzi recorded under the year 1064 that the Normans "were depopulating the whole land", and then – referring to events about thirty years later that they "ruled over and terrorised both [the monks] and the whole region through violence".[4]

Indeed, the chroniclers at times made the horrors of war graphically clear. There is, for example, Geoffrey Malaterra's description of the Calabrian famine in the spring of 1058, "the flail of God's wrath" as he described it: "People sold their weeping children from freedom into slavery for paltry sums, but then could not find anything which they might purchase for food".[5] One can compare with this the account by Amatus of Montecassino of the privations suffered during the siege of Salerno in 1076, which he compared to those suffered by the Jews during the Roman siege of Jerusalem in the first century.[6] For sheer nastiness few episodes can compare with Malaterra's story about Count Roger of Sicily sending captured carrier pigeons back to Palermo after the battle at Misilmeri in 1068, with the messages on their legs dipped in the blood of the slain to announce his

---

2 Loud, Migration, passim; von Falkenhausen, I Ceti dirigenti, 327, estimated that no more than 2.000/2.500 milites emigrated to southern Italy.
3 Amatus, Storia de' Normanni, IV.14, 193.
4 Chronicon Casauriense, I. 1087, 1100.
5 Malaterra, Histoire, I. 27, ed. Lucas-Avenel, 209–211.
6 Amatus, Storia de' Normanni, VIII.19–20; 358–359.

victory to his enemies: "The whole city was thunderstruck, the tearful voices of women and children rent the air and rose to the heavens", or so the chronicler claimed.[7]

Lest we think that such lurid accounts were simply the product of the vivid imagination of contemporary historians, we can also turn to the more prosaic documentary evidence for some mention of the human cost of the conquest. So, for example, in June 1045 a Lombard count at Benevento donated to the monastery of St. Sophia for the soul of his young and unmarried nephew who in that very month had been killed fighting against the "most wicked" (*nefandissimi*) Normans in the Caudine valley.[8] Some years later, in April 1063, a widow with three young children at Salerno was forced to sell her property because:

> "these children proclaim themselves to be dying of hunger and nudity because of the wicked race of the Normans who have plundered in this province, and these children have neither movable goods nor animals from which they can free themselves from hunger and nakedness".[9]

And in 1071 a patron of a Greek monastery in Lucania, which his father had founded, donated this, clearly badly dilapidated, house to a larger and more prosperous abbey. He recounted a tale of woe which explained his decision:

> "Our whole country was seized and occupied by heathen hordes, and everything came to complete ruin. And moreover they made a complete end of the army of the emperor and everything was chaos. ... And as time went by, and the disorder of the times increased and continued, the whole place became waste land".[10]

The terms of these charters are in themselves instructive. The "most wicked Normans", "the heathen hordes", were not just violent and rapacious, but clearly widely disliked. The indigenous inhabitants at times sought to hit back at their tormentors. Thus in 1045, when the Normans were seizing and plundering much of the land subject to the abbey of Montecassino, a small group of these Normans went to a church to pray and were pious enough – or foolish enough – to leave their weapons outside the door. The locals immediately locked them in the church, summoned help, broke in and massacred them as they sought sanctuary around the altar. With great difficulty, the monks managed to rescue the Normans' leader from the lynch mob. A few weeks later the inhabitants managed to

---

7 Malaterra, Histoire, II.42, ed. Lucas-Avenel, 371.
8 Pergamene Aldobrandini, Cartolario I no. 36 (formerly in the Biblioteca Apostolica Vaticana, now at the Villa Aldobrandini at Frascati): "declaro quam quondam Madelfrid comes nepote meo in predicta mense et indictione cecidit in bello a nefandissimis normannis unde de hoc seculo decessit et sepultus est in sepulchre ubi predictus suus genitor sepultus fuerit in monasterio beate sofie" [unpublished].
9 Codex Diplomaticus Cavensis, VIII. 217–221 no. 1349, at 217.
10 Robinson, Carbone (1929), 171–175 no. 8 (there erroneously dated to 1061).

recover one of the abbey's *castella* which the Normans had seized. The latter "surrendered themselves into the hands of the monks, who were only just able to protect them", and eventually sent them back to their settlement at Aversa, without horses, weapons or money.[11] In the circumstances, this second group of Normans appear to have got off lightly. Similarly, if we are to believe Malaterra, the murder of Count Drogo of Apulia in 1051 was part of a wide-ranging conspiracy which resulted in the deaths of many other Normans. The reaction of Drogo's brother and successor Humphrey, torturing the alleged conspirators to death, probably did little for the Normans' popularity either.[12] And in the early stages of the conquest of Sicily, the Greek Christians of Troina, who had at first aided the Normans, turned against them when Count Roger billeted his soldiers in their houses, which made them "fearful for their wives and daughters". They rebelled and joined the Muslims against them.[13]

Yet, hated as the Normans must often have been, certainly during the years when the conquest was at its height – on the mainland roughly 1041–76 – there was another side to the story. This is exemplified by an incident recounted by Amatus of Montecassino. Like much of his account, the story is undated, but seems to have taken place in the early to mid-1060s. It began with another popular insurrection, showing once again how much the Normans were disliked. The Norman garrison at Piedimonte, near Montecassino, which had been stationed there by William of Montreuil, the son-in-law of Richard, the first Norman Prince of Capua, was massacred by the local peasants. The local Lombard lords, Counts Atenulf and Pandulf of Aquino, took advantage of this setback to recover territory they had lost, and William in retaliation laid siege to Aquino. Eventually, a meeting was arranged to negotiate a peace:

> "Atenulf went without fear. William happily welcomed him, throwing his arms around his neck and kissing him on the mouth. When they were sitting together and William was reminding him of their early friendship and of the numerous victories they had won together, he reproved him for the Normans he had killed, and told him that their friendship, which had been broken, should be renewed".[14]

Atenulf was then reconciled with Prince Richard, and it was agreed that he and William should share lordship over the locality. The story clearly shows that some local aristocrats allied with the Normans and provided military assistance to them. This was of course in part, and probably largely, a survival mechanism, to join the winning side to avoid expropriation. The counts of Aquino were re-

---

11 Chronica Casinensis II.71, 309–312.
12 Malaterra, Histoire, I.13, ed. Lucas-Avenel, 171.
13 Malaterra, Histoire, II.29, ed. Lucas-Avenel, 315.
14 Amatus, Storia de' Normanni, VI.6, 265–266; English translation, The History of the Normans, 151.

markably adept at this. Some years later, when Robert Guiscard invaded the principality of Capua in 1073, two of the four brothers then jointly ruling at Aquino joined his invasion, the other two remained loyal to Prince Richard.[15] Whichever of the Norman rulers won, members of their family would be on the winning side. Furthermore, while the counts of Aquino did suffer some territorial losses – Prince Richard gave one of their *castella* to another of his Lombard allies in 1065 – they retained their lordship. In the years after 1090, when the rule of the Norman Princes of Capua weakened, they re-asserted their local dominance in the area to the north of Montecassino – and waged a series of increasingly bitter conflicts with the abbey, with very little interference from the princes.[16]

The counts of Aquino were by no means the only south Italians who assisted the invaders. When Robert Guiscard faced rebellion, largely from his fellow-Normans, in Apulia in 1072–73, one of his principal lieutenants in suppressing that revolt was one of the younger brothers of the Lombard prince of Salerno Gisulf II – who was Guiscard's brother-in-law.[17] Lombard churchmen were also prominent 'collaborators' with the new regime – and I use that loaded term advisedly, for in modern understanding that is what these people were. Thus Desiderius, prior of the monastery of St. Benedict, Capua – who was shortly afterwards chosen to be abbot of the mother house of Montecassino – left Capua when Richard of Aversa laid siege to it in 1057 and joined the attacking army – this even though his own father had been killed fighting the Normans a decade earlier.[18] Similarly, when Robert Guiscard besieged Salerno in 1076 the archbishop of the city, Alfanus, abandoned Prince Gisulf and went over to Robert's side.[19] For all the attempts of the Cassinese chroniclers Leo and Amatus, who inform us of these defections, to justify them in terms of abandoning wicked rulers to adhere to more virtuous ones, naked self-interest – or at least the interests of the institutions which they headed – seem to explain the actions of abbot and archbishop. And indeed, their defections were richly rewarded. Richard I of Capua granted the lands of several local nobles who had opposed him to Montecassino in 1065–66, considerably enlarging the *Terra Sancti Benedicti* and giving the abbey control of the lower Liri River, and thus direct access to the sea, which in turn facilitated the rebuilding of Montecassino after 1066.[20] Robert

---

15 Amatus, Storia de' Normanni, VII.11, 302.
16 A modern study of this family would be extremely useful; for the present we still have to rely upon Scandone, Roccasecca. The 1065 charter is edited there, 128 no. 29; Loud, Calendar, 121 no. 8.
17 Amatus, Storia de' Normanni, VII.3, 294–295.
18 Chronica Casinensis. III.8, 369. For his father, ibid., III.2, 364.
19 Amatus, Storia de' Normanni, VIII.17, 357–358.
20 Registrum Petri Diaconi, III. 1158–63 nos. 408–411 [Loud, Calendar, 120–121 nos. 5, 10, 12–13, 14, this last not in the Registrum]; Loud, Church and Society, 48–55.

Guiscard paid for the rebuilding of Salerno cathedral after 1077[21] and was also a generous donor to Montecassino. The abbey chronicle recorded a long list of his gifts to the monastery, in cash, precious metals and textiles, jewels and also churches made subject to it. Much of this portable wealth was derived from plunder and tribute from his conquests in Calabria and Sicily.[22]

Valuable as such high-profile defections as those of Abbot Desiderius and Archbishop Alfanus were, the Normans also relied on more widespread local support, above all to enhance the relatively small numbers of their own knights. Count Roger's use of Muslim troops from Sicily in campaigns on the mainland, first attested at the siege of Salerno in 1076, is a case in point.[23] (Roger also relied on Muslim defectors, as well as Greek Christians, to assist his conquest of Sicily).[24] The support of Amalfi – increasingly at odds with its neighbour Salerno – was important in providing naval aid to Robert Guiscard.[25] We are also told that, after his capture of Bari in 1071, Duke Robert enlisted the people of that town, and also Greek prisoners-of-war to help man the fleet with which he set off to capture Palermo later in that same year.[26] The Normans lacked the experience and expertise to conduct naval warfare, which they needed to do to capture coastal cities, without local assistance – and a previous attempt to capture Palermo without a fleet, in 1064, had failed.[27]

And for all the violence of the conquest, once in control, the new Norman rulers went to some pains to conciliate the local population. Hence the importance of Robert Guiscard's marriage to the Lombard princess Sichelgaita of Salerno c. 1058. In the words of his biographer William of Apulia:

> "A marriage of such grandeur much augmented Robert's noble reputation, and people who had previously had to be constrained to serve him now rendered to him the obedience due to his ancestors. For the Lombard people knew that Italy had been subject to his wife's grandfathers and great-grandfathers."[28]

After his capture of Salerno – from his brother-in-law Gisulf – Robert kept his wife very prominently at his side – several of his *diplomata* were issued jointly with her, or at her request, and in 1083 she presided personally over a high-profile

---

[21] Carmi di Alfano, 216 no. 53, which records the (still surviving) inscription above the main entrance to the cathedral.
[22] Chronica Casinensis, III.58, 438–9, discussed by Loud, Coinage, Wealth and Plunder, 821–825.
[23] Amatus, Storia de' Normanni, VIII.14, 354; Loud, Age of Robert Guiscard, 184; Becker, Graf Roger I, 126.
[24] Malaterra, De Rebus Gestis, III.12, 30, ed. Pontieri, 64, 75.
[25] Malaterra, De Rebus Gestis, III.3, ed. Pontieri, 58.
[26] Guillaume de Pouille, Geste Guiscard, III, lines 162–166, 187–188, 235–239, 172–176.
[27] Malaterra, Histoire, II.36, ed. Lucas-Avenel, 351; Loud, Age of Robert Guiscard, 158.
[28] Guillaume de Pouille, Geste Guiscard, II, lines 436–441; 156.

legal case in his absence.[29] He also endowed the archbishopric and (as we have seen) paid for the rebuilding of the cathedral.[30] He became a major benefactor of the prominent local monastery of Holy Trinity, Cava (previously favoured by the Lombard princes). And in his first two *diplomata* for Cava he tactfully styled himself "duke by the grace of God of the Normans, Salernitans, Amalfitans, Apulians, Calabrians and Sicilians".[31] The conquered, in other words, had a share in his rule. Later, his son and successor Roger Borsa, was criticised by the Norman chronicler Malaterra, for being too partial to the Lombards, whom he favoured because of his Lombard mother.[32]

The continued significance of the conquered becomes clearer if we examine the settlement and consolidation of 'Norman' Italy. This is not to deny the dominance of new territorial lordships held by Normans and Frenchmen – and at the top level seemingly by actual Normans. At the highest level of south Italian society in the late eleventh century the overwhelming predominance of a handful of Norman kin groups is manifest. Virtually all the new counts of Norman Italy came from no more than six extended families, of whom five were certainly Norman. Most significant of all were the Hautevilles, the family of Robert Guiscard. Apart from the dukes of Apulia and counts of Sicily, no less than four other comital dynasties in southern Italy derived from the numerous descendants of Tancred de Hauteville. Similarly, three further comital lines sprang from the junior branches of the family of the princes of Capua, who seem to have come from near Dieppe in the Pays de Caux.[33] (In the 1070s Richard I of Capua granted the duchy of Gaeta to another Norman family, the Ridels, also from the Pays de Caux). Another clearly Norman kin-group, often known as the "sons of Amicus", spawned several comital dynasties in northern Apulia – and perhaps also in the Abruzzi if the later counts of Manopello were related to this group, which they may well have been. If we are to believe William of Apulia, the "sons of Amicus" kin had been at least as wealthy and powerful as the Hautevilles during the early stages of the conquest, if not more so,[34] but their involvement in several of the revolts against Robert Guiscard seriously weakened their position, and led to some of their lordships being confiscated and added to the ducal fisc. Two of the other three comital families, those of the counts of Ariano and Boiano, were clearly Norman too – the latter from Moulins-la-Marche (département Orne).

---

29 Codex Diplomaticus Cavensis, XI.140–145 no. 51; Ménager, Actes des Ducs Normands, 136–141 no. 43.
30 Ménager, Actes des Ducs Normands, 108–13 nos. 34–35.
31 Codex Diplomaticus Cavensis, X.286–8 no. 119, 331–333 no. 138; Ménager, Actes des Ducs Normands, 95–97 no. 27, 105–108 no. 33.
32 Malaterra, De Rebus Gestis, IV.24, ed. Pontieri, 102.
33 Ménager, Inventaire, 302–307.
34 Guillaume de Pouille, Geste Guiscard, II, lines 28–32; 132.

The origins of the counts of Sarno cannot be identified, although this family used French personal names.[35]

Alongside these kin groups there were many other new lordships held by incomers – some of which may indeed have been almost as substantial as those held by men with a comital title. Nor, at this stage, before the creation of the new kingdom of Sicily in 1130, was there any significant legal distinction between seigneuries held by counts and those held by those who lacked a comital title. Indeed, several other Norman / French families who held territorial lordships in the late eleventh century subsequently acquired comital titles in the time of Roger II.[36] One of these was the de Medania family from Anjou – lords of Acerra in the principality of Capua and subsequently counts of Buonalbergo in Apulia in the mid-twelfth century.[37] And while the counts of the ducal period seem to have been largely or exclusively Norman, a number of non-Norman French families can be identified at the next level down; lords of smaller, but still quasi-autonomous seigneuries, and as vassals of great lords. An example of the former was the Chiaromonte family in Lucania – originally from Clermont-en-Beauvaisis in the Île-de-France. And as an interesting corrective to the evidence for tension between invaders and indigenous inhabitants cited earlier, just three years after the complaint about "heathen hordes" in a charter from the Greek monastery of Carbone, Hugh of Chiaromonte and his wife donated to that same house, "knowing the monastery to be full of good and religious monks". Indeed, the Chiaromonte were to be major patrons of this Greek abbey over more than half a century.[38] Thus, even in the period of conquest relations between newcomers and natives were more complex than simply antagonism.

This is abundantly clear when one considers the continued significance of the indigenous inhabitants within the 'establishment' of 'Norman' Italy. Admittedly, at the highest level, that of territorial lords, the continuance of native families was primarily in marginal regions – such as that of the counts of Aquino on the northern border of the principality of Capua, and the Borell family in the upper Sangro valley, along the frontier between the principality of Capua and northern Apulia. Both these families had already established themselves by the later tenth century – both survived into the thirteenth. By 1100 the senior branch of the Borells had adopted the title of "count of Sangro", seemingly on their own

---

35 Loud, Age of Robert Guiscard, 246–253. For the origins of the counts of Boiano, Ménager, Inventaire, 332–336.
36 Loud, Age of Robert Guiscard, 253–255.
37 Ménager, Inventaire, 370–1; Cuozzo, Catalogus Baronum, 81–83.
38 Robinson, Carbone (1929), 176–178 no. 9; Ménager, Inventaire, 275–84, who gives a full list of this family's donations. Ménager, Pesanteur et étiologie, 204–205, suggested (somewhat tentatively) that between a quarter and a third of the immigrants were non-Norman Frenchmen.

initiative. Like the counts of Aquino, they were sometimes in alliance with the Normans during the period of conquest and like them they seem to have found a *modus vivendi* with them, which allowed them to preserve their hegemony in a relatively remote and marginal region.[39]

Two members of this family, probably brothers, were trusted members of the entourage of Roger I of Sicily and received lordships in southern Calabria and on the island of Sicily respectively.[40] Similarly, further north in the Abruzzi, while there was Norman penetration of the region, and bitter complaint about Norman violence and "tyranny", especially in the chronicle of the great local abbey of Casauria, the native aristocracy were never completely displaced. Indeed, Casauria's problems in the early twelfth century – and they were considerable – stemmed just as much from its (still-powerful) Lombard neighbours as from the Normans.[41]

Elsewhere, while the conquest led to the settlement of the victors and their establishment of territorial lordships, this still did not entirely displace or marginalise the locals. In some areas this is explicable by the nature of the conquest. In Calabria the small towns of the region submitted to the Norman conquerors, but usually this submission comprised an agreement to pay tribute to them – sometimes, but by no means always, also the construction of a citadel with a Norman garrison. Quite how extensive the new Norman lordships were in Calabria is a good question – the survival of contemporary documentation for this province is very limited – but there were probably fewer than in other regions. The urban élites of the Calabrian towns remained in place, and probably retained all or most of their extra-urban property. In some districts, as for example Stilo and Rossano, they were still effectively in control of the locality. When, for example, Duke Roger Borsa sought to impose a Latin archbishop at Rossano after the death of the Greek incumbent in 1093, he was forced to give way to the opposition of the Greek inhabitants and agree "that they might freely elect an archbishop from their own Greek race". It also seems probable that much of the property now held by the duke and counts of Sicily, and perhaps other Norman lords, had belonged to the former Byzantine fisc.[42]

The survival and continued prosperity of urban élites was notable over most of southern Italy. Major towns such as Amalfi, Bari and Salerno on the mainland, and also Messina and Palermo, were relatively unchanged after the Norman conquest. There were, as said, only a relatively few Normans, and fewer still

---

39 Jamison, Significance, especially 55–60; Cuozzo, Normanni, 163–174.
40 Becker, Graf Roger I, 96–99.
41 Feller, Casaux et castra, 155–161, 181–182; Feller, Abruzzes Médiévales, 725–763.
42 von Falkenhausen, I Gruppi etnici, 142–144; Peters-Custot, Les Grecs, 401–414. For the archbishopric, Malaterra, De Rebus Gestis, IV.22, ed. Pontieri, 100; Peters-Custot, Les Grecs, 257.

settled in the towns.⁴³ When such major towns had surrendered to the Normans it was usually by agreement. Robert Guiscard had facilitated the surrender of Bari in 1071 by cultivating one party among the citizens who favoured making a deal with the assailants.⁴⁴ When Palermo had surrendered a year later it was on terms, with the Muslim inhabitants being guaranteed the exercise of their own faith, and (in Malaterra's words) "that they would not be oppressed with new and unjust laws".⁴⁵ Towns subsequently conquered by the Normans in Sicily also surrendered on terms, notably Trapani in 1077, Jato in 1079, and Syracuse and Castrogiovanni in 1086.⁴⁶ There were still Muslim property owners in Sicily, landed proprietors and not mere peasants, well into the twelfth century, and while we have examples of these Muslims then selling their property, a number of these sales were to Arabic-speaking Christians.⁴⁷ Indeed, at Palermo during the second half of the twelfth century about a third of property was still in the hands of Arabic speakers – probably mainly still Muslims.⁴⁸

Furthermore, the new rulers of southern Italy derived many of their officials from this urban-dwelling indigenous patriciate. We can see this most clearly among the entourages of the provincial rulers. Thus, one of the earliest diplomas granted by Robert Guiscard after the capture of Salerno, and perhaps significantly at the request of his wife Sichelgaita, granted a house in the city to his *vesterarius* Gratian.⁴⁹ Almost fifty years later one of the witnesses at the deathbed of Guiscard's grandson, Duke William, was his seneschal, Alferius son of Count Adoaldus, who remained thereafter as a landowner in the principality of Salerno.⁵⁰ One of the most prominent figures in the charters of the first two Norman princes of Capua was a certain Pandulf son of Guala, and in the early 1070s he was joined by Cedrus *viceprinceps*.⁵¹ From their names all of these men were Lombards. Cedrus eventually became a monk at Montecassino, and the monastery chronicle preserves a long list of very valuable commodities that he gave to the abbey before he assumed the habit, which suggests quite how lucrative the per-

---

43 von Falkenhausen, Il Popolomento, 72–73; Oldfield, City and Community, 23–39.
44 Guillaume de Pouille, Geste Guiscard, II, lines 531–539, 160–162.
45 Malaterra, Histoire, II.45, ed. Lucas-Avenel, 385: "si certi sunt quod non cogantur ullis injustis et novis legibus."
46 Malaterra, De Rebus Gestis, III.11, 21, IV.2, 6, ed. Pontieri, 63, 70, 86, 88.
47 Bresc, La propriété foncière des Musulmans, passim.
48 von Falkenhausen, I Ceti dirigenti, 348–349.
49 Codex Diplomaticus Cavensis, X.297–298 no. 124; Ménager, Actes des Ducs Normands, 97–98 no. 28.
50 Guillaume, Essai Historique, XXXVIII–IX appendix I. Alferius was still alive in 1148 when he gave the abbey of Cava 13 villani in return for an annual pension. Loud, Pergamene scelte, 158–160 no. 42.
51 Pandulf, Loud, Calendar, nos. 4–6, 8, 10, 13, 16, 21; Cedrus, ibid., 16, 21. Fuller discussion, von Falkenhausen, I Ceti dirigenti, 332–338.

quisites of office might be.[52] Other territorial lords similarly relied upon local officials, at a variety of levels. In Calabria, for example, when King Roger's sister Maximilla, *domina* of Oppido, granted a fief to a certain William de Brix in 1138 – in a charter written in Greek – this property appears to have been administered by a Greek bailiff (*exousiastes*), in this case from a local peasant family.[53] We should hardly be surprised about this. Greek officials, clearly of a much higher status, had long been prominent at the court of the counts of Sicily, first at Mileto in Calabria under Roger I, and then at Messina and Palermo under Roger II.[54]

One final aspect to consider is the continuance of native nobles and knights as part of the landowning / military class after the conquest, not just in peripheral regions such as the Abruzzi, but in areas which were far more fully integrated into 'Norman Italy'. A particular case in point is the principality of Salerno, which became the core dominion of the Norman dukes of Apulia, where their authority remained unchallenged despite their increasing problems after 1085 in retaining control of coastal Apulia and Calabria. And after 1130 the principality was the base from which Roger II expanded his control over the continental mainland. Several powerful Norman seigneuries were established within the principality, notably that of the counts of the Principato (descended from Robert Guiscard's younger brother William), the lords of S. Severino (whose progenitor was a certain 'Turgisius the Norman') and the lords of Eboli – until that family died out in 1121.[55] Yet alongside these some Lombard families continued to hold lordships – even if less substantial ones – well into the twelfth century. Among these were relatives of the former princely family. Prince Gisulf II and (most of) his brothers had been expelled after the final surrender of the citadel of Salerno in 1077 – his brother Landulf had, for example, been forced to surrender his lordships at S. Severino and Policastro.[56] But other family members remained. Landulf's daughter (by then presumably elderly) was a nun at Salerno in 1136.[57] Even one of Gisulf's brothers, John, a cleric, was apparently allowed to remain at Salerno, and later acted as physician to his nephew Duke Roger Borsa, before another half-Norman nephew, Count Henry of Monte Sant'Angelo established a hospital under his direction on Monte Gargano in northern Apulia in 1098.[58] Most notably, the former prince's cousins, descended from the younger sons of Prince

---

52 Chronica Casinensis, IV.13, 482.
53 This text survives only in the record of a later court case in May 1188, Trinchera, Syllabus, 294–301 no. 225, at 296–9; Peters-Custot, Les Grecs, 323.
54 Becker, Graf Roger I, 110–122.
55 Loud, Continuity and Change, 327–330.
56 Amatus, Storia de' Normanni, VIII.30, 371.
57 Nuove Pergamene di S. Giorgio, 24–25 no. 11.
58 Glaze, Salerno's Lombard Prince, passim. For foundation of the hospital, Colonie Cassinesi II Gargano, 29–32 no. 1 [Registrum Petri Diaconi, III.1422–1426 no. 520].

Guaimar III (d. 1027), held lordships at Giffone (to the east of Salerno) and Capaccio (in the south of the principality). The last male member of the Giffone branch of the family died in 1114, the Capaccio branch were still going strong in the 1130s, although by then they had begun to divide their holdings.[59]

These Lombard nobles seem to have made the transition from being princely relatives before the Norman takeover to becoming ducal relatives after it – several of them were expressly identified as such in the record of a court case, held in the presence of Duke Roger Borsa, in May 1089.[60] Other Lombard lords, albeit of minor seigneuries, included, for example Lampus of Fasanella, who married a daughter of one of the lords of Capaccio, and became a royal justiciar during the 1140s.[61] During the mid-twelfth century two of the brothers of Archbishop Romuald II of Salerno (1153–81), and two of his cousins, also acquired minor territorial lordships within the principality (one of the cousins was a long-serving royal justiciar – his father had been Duke William's chamberlain in the 1120s). Romuald's family, Lombard nobles who were part of the civic élite at Salerno – his father had been the city's *stratigotus* (mayor or governor) in 1124-5 – provide a classic example of indigenous social survival, and indeed upward social mobility in the Norman era. The chamberlain's grandson was made a count by Henry VI in 1195.[62] Other Lombards also found a role at a lower, but still not insignificant, level among the knightly vassals of Norman lords, and especially among the considerable following of the counts of the Principato. Several of these seem to have been based at Eboli, which the counts appear to have taken over after the death of the last male member of its previous Norman lords in 1121 – the assumption must surely be that the lords of Eboli too had had Lombard vassals. And, in addition, one of the vassals of the count, named in an admittedly problematic charter of 1141, was a Greek who later became a royal justiciar in northern Calabria.[63] He was not the only Greek to belong to the military class in southern Italy – there was, for example a knight (*cabellarios*) who left his property to the abbey of Carbone in his will of 1134.[64]

Space does not permit a more extensive examination of this theme. But enough has been said to show that, while the Norman conquest of southern Italy was undoubtedly traumatic and disastrous for some of the vanquished, and the

---

59 Loud, Continuity and Change, 324–326; Loud, Social World, 193–202.
60 Codex Diplomaticus Cavensis, XII.274–278 no. 103.
61 Cuozzo, Catalogus Baronum, 125–127.
62 Romualdi Salernitani Chronicon, introduction, V–X; Cuozzo, Catalogus Baronum, 128, 131, 150–152; Loud, Age of Robert Guiscard, 283. 305. For Philip Guarna as Count of Marsico, Archivio della badia di S. Trinità di Cava, Arm. Mag. M.4 (November 1195) [unpublished].
63 Cuozzo, Normanni, 103–115; for the Greek, Robert de Clea (Robertos Cletzes) 109; Pergamene Salerno, 195–199 no. 102, at 198. For him as justiciar, Robinson, Carbone (1930), 30–42 nos. 37–38.
64 Robinson, Carbone (1930), 9–12 no. 32.

violence of that conquest led the Normans to be hated by many locals, some among the vanquished adapted to the new order, and found a place in the new society. Other factors, and particular inter-marriage, were also significant here. And indeed, by 1130 – and perhaps somewhat earlier – by which stage emigration from Normandy and northern France had ceased, and inter-marriage had created an increasingly mixed-race ruling class – the distinction between Norman and non-Norman had, arguably, ceased to matter.[65] There were still divisions within the new kingdom of Sicily: religious, cultural and linguistic. But being Norman – or indeed not being Norman – was no longer one of them.

Bibliography

Sources

Chronica Monasterii Casinensis, ed. Hartmut Hoffmann (Monumenta Germaniae Historica, Scriptores 34), Hannover 1980.

Codex Diplomaticus Cavensis, vols. I–VIII ed. Michele Morcaldi / Mauro Schiani / Silvano De Stefano, Milan 1876–93; vols. IX–X, ed. Simeone Leone / Giovanni Vitolo, Badia di Cava 1984–90; vols. IX–XII, ed. Carmine Carlone / Leone Morinelli / Giovanni Vitolo, Badia di Cava 2015.

De Rebus Gestis Rogerii Calabriae et Siciliae Comitis, auctore Gaufredo Malaterra, ed. Ernesto Pontieri (Rerum Italicarum Scriptores, 2nd series), Bologna 1927–28.

Geoffroi Malaterra, Histoire du Grand Comte Roger et de son frère Robert Guiscard, I, Livres I & II, ed. Marie-Agnès Lucas-Avenel, Caen 2016.

Guillaume de Pouille, La Geste de Robert Guiscard, ed. Margueritte Mathieu, Palermo 196.

I Carmi di Alfano I, arcivescovo di Salerno, ed. Anselmo Lentini (Miscellanea Cassinese 38), Montecassino 1974.

Le Colonie Cassinesi in Capitanata ii Gargano, ed. Tommaso Leccisotti (Miscellanea Cassinese 15), Montecassino 1938.

Le Pergamene dell'archivio diocesano di Salerno (841–1193), ed. Anna Giordano, Battipaglia 2014.

Liber Instrumentorum seu Chronicorum Monasterii Casauriensis seu Chronicon Casauriense, ed. Alessandro Pratesi / Paolo Cherubini, 4 vols., (Rerum Italicarum Scriptores, 3rd series), Rome 2017–19.

Loud, Graham A., A Calendar of the Diplomas of the Norman Princes of Capua, in: Papers of the British School at Rome 49 (1981), 99–143.

Nuove Pergamene del monastero femminile di S. Giorgio di Salerno I (993–1256), ed. Maria Galante, Altavilla Silentina 1984.

Pergamene scelte della badia di Cava, 1097–1200, ed. Graham A. Loud, Ariano 2021.

Recueil des Actes des Ducs Normands d'Italie (1046–1127). Les Premiers Ducs (1046–1087), ed. Léon-Robert Ménager, vol. 1, Bari 1981.

---

65 Loud, Migration, 351–352.

Registrum Petri Diaconi (Montecassino, Archivio dell'Abbazia, Reg. 3, ed. Jean-Marie Martin et al., 4 vols., Rome 2015.

Robinson, Gertrude, The History and Cartulary of the Greek Monastery of St. Elias and St. Anastasius of Carbone, Orientalia Christiana 15 (1929), 121–276; 19 (1930), 5–200.

Romualdi Salernitani Chronicon, ed. Carlo Alberto Garufi (Rerum Italicarum Scriptores, 2nd series), Città di Castello 1935.

Amatus = Storia de' Normanni di Amato di Montecassino, ed. Vincenzo de Bartholomeis (Fonti per la storia d'Italia), Rome 1935 [Engl. transl. Prescott Dunbar / Graham A. Loud (ed.), The History of the Normans by Amatus of Montecassino, Woodbridge 2004].

Syllabus Graecarum Membranarum, ed. Francesco Trinchera, Naples 1865.

Literature

Becker, Julia, Graf Roger I. von Sizilien. Wegbereiter des normannischen Königreichs, Tübingen 2008.

Bresc, Henri, La propriété foncière des Musulmans dans la Sicile du XIIe siècle: trois documents inédits, in: Henri Bresc, Una Stagione in Sicilia, ed. Marcello Pacifico, Palermo 2010, vol. 2, 73–101.

Cuozzo, Errico, Catalogus Baronum. Commentario (Fonti per la storia d'Italia), Rome 1984.

Cuozzo, Errico, Normanni, nobiltà e cavalleria, Salerno 1995.

Feller, Laurent, Casaux et castra dans les Abruzzes: San Salvatore a Maiella et San Clemente a Casauria (XIe–XIIIe siècles), Mélanges de l'École Française de Rome: Moyen-Âge, in: Temps Modernes 97 (1985), 145–182.

Feller, Laurent, Les Abruzzes Médiévales. Territoire, Économie et Société en Italie Centrale du IXe au XIIe siècle, Rome 1998.

Glaze, Florence Eliza, Salerno's Lombard Prince: Johannes 'Abbas de Curte' as Medical practitioner, in: Early Science and Medicine 23 (2018), 177–216.

Guillaume, Paul, Essai Historique de l'Abbaye de Cava, Cava dei Tirreni 1877.

Jamison, Evelyn M., The Significance of the Early Medieval Documents from S. Maria della Noce and S. Salvatore di Castiglione, in: Studi in onore di Riccardo Filangieri, Naples 1959, Bd. 1, 51–80 [reprinted in Evelyn Jamison, Studies on the History of Medieval Sicily and South Italy, Aalen 1992, 437–66].

Loud, Graham A., Church and Society in the Norman Principality of Capua, 1058–1197, Oxford 1985.

Loud, Graham A., Continuity and Change in Norman Italy: The Campania During the Eleventh and Twelfth Centuries, in: Journal of Medieval History 22 (1996), 313–43 [reprinted in Loud, Graham A., Conquerors and Churchmen in Norman Italy, Aldershot 1999].

Loud, Graham A., Coinage, Wealth and Plunder in the Age of Robert Guiscard, in: English Historical Review 114 (1999), 815–843.

Loud, Graham A., The Age of Robert Guiscard. Southern Italy and the Norman Conquest, Harlow 2000.

Loud, Graham A., Migration, Infiltration, Conquest and Identity: The Normans of Southern Italy c.1000–1130, in: Settimane di Studio del Centro italiano per l'alto medioevo 66. Le migrazioni nell'alto medioevo (2019), 339–360.

Loud, Graham A., The Social World of the Abbey of Cava, c. 1020–1300, Woodbridge 2021.

Ménager, Léon-Robert, Pesanteur et étiologie de la colonisation normande de l'Italie, in: Roberto il Guiscardo e il suo tempo (Relazioni e comunicazioni nelle Prime Giornate normanno-svevo, Bari, maggio 1973), Rome 1975, 189–214.

Ménager, Léon-Robert, Inventaire des familles normandes et franques émigrés en Italie méridionale et en Sicile (XIe–XIIe siècles), in: Roberto il Guiscardo e il suo tempo (Relazioni e comunicazioni nelle Prime Giornate normanno-sveve, Bari maggio 1973), Rome 1975, 259–390.

Oldfield, Paul, City and Community in Norman Italy, Cambridge 2009.

Peters-Custot, Annick, Les Grecs de l'Italie Méridionale post-Byzantine. Une Acculturation en Douceur, Rome 2009.

Scandone, Francesco, Roccasecca. Patria di S. Tommaso di Aquino, in: Archivio storico di Terra di Lavoro 1 (1956), 33–176.

von Falkenhausen, Vera, I Ceti dirigenti prenormanni al tempo della costituzione degli stati normanni nell'Italia meridionale e in Sicilia, in: Forme di Potere e struttura sociale in Italia nel medioevo, ed. Gabriella Rossetti, Bologna 1977, 321–377.

von Falkenhausen, Vera, I Gruppi etnici nel regno di Ruggero II e la loro partecipazione al potere, in: Società, potere e popolo nell'età di Ruggero II (Atti del terze giornate normanno-svevo, Bari 23–25 maggio 1977), Bari 1980, 133–156.

von Falkenhausen, Vera, Il Popolomento: etnie, fedi, insediamenti, in Terra e uomini nel Mezzogiorno normanno-svevo, ed. Giosuè Musca (Atti del settime giornate normanno-svevo, Bari 15–17 ottobre 1985), Bari 1987, 39–73.

Thomas Dittelbach

The Acculturation of Conflict. The Norman Conquest of Islamic Sicily under the Rule of Homage and Fealty

Victimisation

The common understanding of the term 'victors' has been linked historically with the ideal image of a social, political or cultural majority. Victors are considered to be those who have greater numbers of people, soldiers, skills and weapons at their disposal, and consequently possess greater ethical legitimisation. Otherwise – so the reasoning goes – they would not be victorious.

On occasion, however, victors had fewer but better trained soldiers, fewer but more sophisticated weapons at their disposal; bronze blades defeated stone blades, iron defeated bronze, and so on. But in most cases victories gained from a position of disadvantage were not of long duration because the victors failed to embed a commonly accepted fundament in the vanquished population, deliberately neglecting to explain their own cultural rules with their different forms of behaviour and language to their new subjects. The changes ensuing from this kind of victory were thus less likely to be maintained in the long term. At the same time, these 'short-term' victors failed to implement the core issue of an enduring settlement of the territories they occupied, that is, to 'embroider' a framework of their own essential cultural needs on the cultural behaviour and customs of the conquered. They also failed to enrich the texture of their own cultural and technological achievements by drawing on the texture of the cultural and technological achievements of the vanquished. Indeed, the effect of interweaving both cultural layers would ideally lead to the vanquished becoming *un*chained and released from the burden of being victimised. It is precisely this effect that I refer to as a characteristic mark of an acculturation of conflict.

However, recent history has shown that victimisation has become the most popular instrument of political seduction, forcibly occupying the gap between victors and vanquished. Populism's demagogic ploy is to act from a highly privileged position while declaring itself to be victimised by an established elite. Populism aims at gaining an oligarchic status in a pluralistic society by fostering division and ensnaring democratically elected majorities in tactical coalitions.

Leaving aside the ambiguity of the concepts of 'victor' – 'victim' – 'vanquished', current developments show that the traditional dualism of victors and majorities on the one hand, and of the vanquished and minorities on the other, is losing its validity. What we have experienced over the past few years in European politics is the realisation that populist ideology lodges itself *in between* hitherto valid key concepts, finding its way into mainstream everyday language, with use of words such as 'tribe' and 'nation'. This is encapsulated in the concept of 'tribal nationalism' that was first unmasked by Hannah Arendt in 1948. And it was precisely this term that was cited by Homi Bhabha 2018 in an interview with the Italian newspaper *La Repubblica*.[1] Bhabha identified a new tribal nationalism in the political theory postulated by current populist leaders, a theory which emphasizes and ennobles the illusion of a divinely ordained majority presenting itself as an oppressed minority.

In order to discuss this theory from a historical and art-historical perspective I invite the reader on a journey back to the Sicily of the eleventh and twelfth century. If the historical rule of victorious majorities was valid in the past, medieval Sicily seems to represent an excellent example of the exception to this rule, since the Norman liege lords were always in the minority compared to the long-established Byzantine, Jewish and Muslim population. However, the Norman dynasty in Sicily was only temporarily in power, its rule lasting less than a century. Ultimately the last Norman kings failed to sustain their politics of acculturation, disregarding the increasing demand for a self-determined cultural identity on the part of the Byzantine, Jewish and Muslim population which in Sicily constituted the majority until the end of the twelfth century.

Starting from this premise, contemporary medieval historiography emphasizes a leitmotiv running through the description of the conquest of Islamic Sicily: the literary topos of the Norman presence as the presence of a minority. The Norman expeditionary force was indeed chronically – sometimes disastrously – undermanned and ill-supplied. On the other hand, the Normans had learnt very successfully from their career as mercenaries how to ally themselves with promising ethnic or political groups claiming to represent the majority in a particular region.

---

1 Arendt, Origins of Totalitarianism. Interview by Giancarlo Bosetti with Homi K. Bhabha, "Ibridi e cosmopoliti così sfideremo l'onda populista", in La Repubblica, 6 June 2018, 34–35.

The Sources

For the Norman conquest of Islamic Sicily, we have two main historiographical sources at our disposal: Amato di Montecassino and Goffredo Malaterra.[2] Both underline the utopian character of this enterprise and concur that extreme political confusion reigned in the south at that time. Nonetheless, they emphasize the fact that the tribal organization of this small number of Norman knights, foremost among them Duke Robert Guiscard and his younger brother Count Roger, paired with their rigorous feudal upbringing constituted the secret recipe of their success. They started to try out their system of feudal tenure in a region where, apart from the territorial claims to supremacy of the Holy Roman Emperor and the papacy, three very different major ethnic and political traditions still interacted and overlapped: the Muslims, the Lombards and the Byzantines. The Muslims arrived in Sicily in 827 and had invaded and occupied parts of the mainland well before completing their conquest of the island from the Byzantines. Throughout the ninth century they continued to represent a real threat of enduring conquest.

The Lombards had been established since the late sixth century in southern Italy, where they founded the duchy of Benevento. However, they had not succeeded in consolidating their political hold in Apulia and Calabria, or over the maritime cities of Campania in the duchy of Naples, nor had they crossed over into Sicily. All these territories had remained nominally subject to the Byzantine Empire. For their part, the Byzantines, under the Macedonian dynasty, supported all kinds of efforts to regain Sicily from the Muslims. In the late ninth century, after the loss of Sicily to the Muslims, the Byzantine government had provided for the administration of Greek churches in the south by creating metropolitan bishops who were under the authority of the patriarch of Constantinople. Subsequently, over the course of the eleventh century, the popes in Rome considered the establishment of the Muslims in Sicily as a lesser threat than Byzantine imperialism.

Homage and Fealty

In retrospect it can be stated that the increasing Byzantine influence in southern Italy was the key factor in the enfeoffment of Duke Robert Guiscard by Pope Nicholas II at the Synod of Melfi in 1059. This prompts the question of whether Robert at this early stage of the conquest had at his disposal French, Lombard or even Byzantine advisors, who would have been familiar with the diplomatic policy of the papal court. The investiture of the Norman leader was a political

---

2 Amato di Montecassino, Storia dei Normanni; Goffredo Malaterra, Ruggero I e Roberto il Guiscardo.

masterstroke which is documented by the complete text of Robert's oath of allegiance, preserved in the Vatican archives:

> *Ego Robertus Dei gratia et sancti Petri dux Apulie et Calabrie et utroque subveniente futurus Sicilie, ab hac hora et deinceps ero fidelis sancte Romane ecclesie et apostolice sedi et tibi domino meo Nicholao pape; in consilio vel facto unde vitam aut membrum perdas vel captus sis mala captione, non ero. Consilium quod mihi credideris et contradixeris ne illud manifestem, non manifestabo ad tuum dampnum, me sciente. Sancte Romane ecclesie ubique adiutor ero ad tenendum et adquirendum regalia sancti Petri eiusque possessiones pro meo posse, contra omnes homines. Et adiuvabo te, ut secure et honorifice teneas papatum Romanum; terramque sancti Petri et Principatus nec invadere nec acquirere queram nec etiam depredari presumam absque tua tuorumque successorum, qui ad honorem sancti Petri intraverint, certa licentia, preter illam quam tu mihi concedes vel tui concessuri sunt successores. Pensionem de terra sancti Petri quam ego teneo aut tenebo, sicut statutum est, recta fide studebo ut illam annualiter sancta Romana habeat ecclesia. Omnes quoque ecclesias que in mea consistunt dominatione cum earum possessionibus dimittam in tuam potestatem et defensor ero illarum ad fidelitatem sancte Romane ecclesie. Et si tu vel tui successores ante me ex hac vita migraveritis, secundum quod monitus fuero a melioribus cardinalibus, clericis Romanis et laicis, adiuvabo ut papa eligatur et ordinetur ad honorem sancti Petri. Hec omnia suprascripta observabo sancte Romane ecclesie et tibi cum recta fide, et hanc fidelitatem observabo tuis successoribus ad honorem sancti Petri ordinatis, qui mihi firmaverint investituram a te mihi concessam. Sic me Deus, et cetera.*[3]

The first part, consisting of the salutatory address, and the last part, the final corroboration clause, yield an interesting detail: Robert accepts the title of Duke

---

3 Liber Censuum, c. 163, I, 422, in: Das Papsttum, 17–18. "I, Robert, by the Grace of God and of St Peter Duke of Apulia and of Calabria and, if either aid me, future Duke of Sicily, shall be from this time forth faithful to the Roman Church and to you, Pope Nicholas, my lord. Never shall I be party to a conspiracy or undertaking by which your life might be taken, your body injured or your liberty removed. Nor shall I reveal to any man any secret which you may confide to me, pledging me to keep it, lest this should cause you harm. Everywhere and against all adversaries I shall remain, insofar as it is in my power to be so, the ally of the holy Roman Church, that she may preserve and acquire the revenues and domains of St Peter. I shall afford to you all assistance that may be necessary that you may occupy, in all honour and security, the papal throne in Rome. As for the territories of St Peter, and those of the Principality, I shall not attempt to invade them nor even to ravage them without the express permission of yourself or your successors, clothed with the honours of the blessed Peter. I shall conscientiously pay, every year, to the Roman Church the agreed rent for the territories of St Peter which I do or shall possess. I shall surrender to you the churches which are at present in my hands, with all their property, and shall maintain them in their obedience to the holy Roman Church. Should you or any of your successors depart this life before me I shall, having taken the advice of the foremost cardinals as of the clergy and laity of Rome, work to ensure that the Pope shall be elected and installed according to the honour due to St Peter. I shall faithfully observe, with regard both to the Roman Church and to yourself, the obligations which I have just undertaken, and shall do likewise with regard to your successors who will ascend to the honour of the blessed Peter and who will confirm me in the investiture which you have performed. So help me God and his Holy Gospels."

of Sicily. This means that he was enfeoffed with Sicily by Pope Nicholas even though the island had not yet been conquered. And Robert raises his stakes even higher: in the corroboration clause of the privilege, he lays down the reconfirmation of his investiture by all newly elected successors on the papal throne.

The only point that Robert was unable to secure at this time, despite the dilemma in which his papal overlords found themselves, was the confirmation of enfeoffment for his own successors or heirs in the case of his premature death. That this notion had certainly been considered as part of the agreement is revealed by the wording of a second document which must have immediately preceded the oath of fealty sworn in August 1059 concerning Guiscard's obligation to pay quit-rent to Pope Nicholas II. In the final passage of the document Robert pledges himself "et omnes meos sive heredes sive successores" to pay quit-rent to the pope and his successors.[4] This phrase is missing from Robert's oath of fealty – or at least it was not recorded in writing. One reason for this may be that the hereditary principle of *hominium* and *fidelitas* (homage and fealty) had not yet become established in mid-eleventh century Italy, particularly in the provinces under Byzantine control. Marc Bloch describes this development between the tenth and twelfth centuries as a dialectic process: "We shall see that in practice vassalage very soon became, in most cases, hereditary; but this *de facto* situation allowed the legal rule to remain intact to the end. It mattered little that the son of the deceased vassal usually performed this homage to the lord who had accepted his father's, or that the heir of the previous lord almost invariably received the homage of his father's vassals: the ceremony had none the less to be repeated with every change of the individual persons concerned."[5] During the eleventh century, the Roman Church also avoided legitimizing the hereditary claims of the Norman dukes, as expressed in the appellation *heres et filius*.[6] A survey of the history of Norman enfeoffments in the *regnum Siciliae* shows that only two generations later, in 1156, the tide turned in the concordat between William I and Pope Adrian IV: the directive that was still in force under Roger II in 1139 and which prescribed the renewal of *hominium* and *fidelitas* at the death of each liege lord or his vassal, was attenuated under Roger's son William I to such an extent that the *fidelitas*, the oath of loyalty sworn by the king's heirs to the pope, became the central part of the enfeoffment: "fidelitatem facere et quae praescripta sunt voluerint observare." With this, the obligation of the Norman ruler to demonstrate *hominium* faded into the background.[7]

> "Imagine two men face to face; one wishing to serve, the other willing or anxious to be served. The former puts his hands together and places them, thus joined, between the

---

4 Liber Censuum, c. 162, I, 421–422 in: Das Papsttum, 18.
5 Bloch, Feudal Society, vol. 1, 147.
6 Deér, Papsttum und Normannen, 128.
7 Siragusa, Il regno di Guglielmo I. Appendice 381–388; Dittelbach, Rex Imago Christi, 68–69.

hands of the other man – a plain symbol of submission, the significance of which was sometimes further emphasized by a kneeling posture. The superior party, whose position was created by this act, was described by the term of 'lord'. Similarly, the subordinate was often simply called the 'man' of his lord."[8]

Hence this ceremony was called *homage*. "The future vassal placed his hands in the lord's joined hands while repeating a few words promising loyalty, after which lord and vassal kissed each other on the mouth."[9]

Since the Carolingian era, with integration into a new kind of societal system came the necessity of divine legitimation in the form of a symbolic act. For this reason, since the eight century the ceremony of enfeoffment had been enriched by a second, fundamentally religious gesture: "laying his hand on the Gospels or on relics, the new vassal swore to be faithful to his master. This was called fealty, *foi* in French (in German *Treue*, and formerly *Hulde*)."[10] Unlike *hominium* (homage), the promising of *fidelitas* (fealty) could be repeated several times on various occasions, albeit only towards one and the same person. "The fealty of the vassal was a unilateral undertaking to which there was seldom a corresponding oath on the part of the lord. In a word, it was the act of homage that really established the relation of vassalage under its dual aspect of dependence and protection."[11]

Et nulli iurabo fidelitatem

Against the background of later developments, the two above-mentioned documents relating to Robert from 1059 already demonstrate clearly how well-schooled his chancellery was, and the kind of forward-looking dimensions in which it thought and planned. Let us take another look at Robert's oath of fealty in detail: there is a particularly striking sentence at the beginning of the second section following a reference to the (separately composed) statute of obligation to pay quit-rent:

> Omnes quoque ecclesias que in mea consistunt dominatione cum earum possessionibus dimittam in tuam potestatem et defensor ero illarum ad fidelitatem sancte Romane ecclesie, et nulli iurabo fidelitatem nisi salva fidelitate sancte Romane ecclesie.

In formal terms the text is notable for its rhetorical refinement. The key word is *fidelitas*, which is repeated three times. Concealed behind the rhythmical sonority and overt rhetoric is the core of the document: by leaving all the churches

---

8 Bloch, Feudal Society, vol. 1, 146.
9 Bloch, European Feudalism, 129.
10 Ibid., Feudal Society, vol. 1, 145–146.
11 Ibid., 147.

in his territory to the Holy See he becomes *liggius homo*, as Romuald of Salerno later calls him in his *Chronicle* written around 1178, that is, the pope's vassal.[12] However, there is absolutely no mention of *hominium* in the documents of 1059. Nor are the *beneficia*, the fiefs themselves, named. The register of the *beneficia* was the most delicate and consequential section in every feudal contract.

> "Seine juristische Form gab das Lehnrecht, in dem die Rechtstechnik des Mittelalters ihren Gipfelpunkt erreichte. Lehngut kann alles sein, was einen nachhaltigen Ertrag abwirft. Sachen, vor allem Landgüter, Burgen, ferner Rechte und Inbegriffe beider, also ganze Herrschaftsbezirke, aber auch Renten, öffentliche Einkünfte usw. Dienst und Treue werden auf Grund eines personenrechtlichen Vertrags geschuldet. Es sind also stets zwei Seiten im Lehnsverhältnis zu scheiden: die dingliche und die persönliche."[13]

Although the key sentence of our document initially concerns only *fidelitas*, between the lines Robert was obliged to cede to the Holy See all 'churches', that is, all the ecclesiastical demesnes including their assets. If in the case of the Calabrian *beneficia* this had referred to Latin foundations, we could understand the pope's demand. However, these *ecclesiae* were in fact exclusively Greek churches and monasteries. Nicholas II will have had his eye on the venerable and very powerful Basilian foundations in southern Italy and Sicily; the spectre feared by the pontiff was the Eastern Church, not Islam.

The *fidelitas*, the oath of fealty, was a central element of the feudal system imported from northern France in the eighth century, the tradition with which the Normans identified by virtue of their tribal identity. This system of organisation, which was to evolve into a societal model in the Middle Ages, was alien to the Byzantines and Lombards in southern Italy, and – as we shall see – to the Muslims in Sicily. This may have been due to their disparate political interests as well as deep-rooted cultural – religious and linguistic – differences. "Vassalage was the form of dependence peculiar to the upper classes who were characterized above all by the profession of arms and the exercise of command."[14] "But as a paramount social bond designed to unite the various groups at all levels, to prevent fragmentation and to arrest disorder, it showed itself decidedly ineffective."[15] Nonetheless, we can define the feudal system in its most mature form in the twelfth century as a successful societal model that left its decisive mark on civil law from penal law to asylum law. "In feudal society the oath of aid and

---

12 Romualdi Salernitani Chronicon, ad a. 1060, 185, in: Das Papsttum, 17: "Interea Robbertus dux ad Nicolaum papam perexit eiusque liggius homo effectus est, promittens se iureiurando fidem servaturum Romane ecclesie et eidem pape eiusque successoribus canonice intrantibus. Ipse autem papa Nicolaus statim investivit eundem Robbertum Guiscardum per vexillum de honore ducatus sui cum tota terra."
13 Mitteis, Die Entstehung des Lehnswesens, 79.
14 Bloch, Feudal Society, vol. 1, 147.
15 Ibid., Feudal Society, vol. 2, 445.

'friendship' had figured from the beginning as one of the main elements of the system. But it was an engagement between inferior and superior, which made the one the subject of the other. The distinctive feature of the communal oath, on the other hand, was that it united *equals*."[16]

The Islamic Counter-narrative

In the 1160s Sicily was marked by conflicts between three independent emirs. First there was a certain Ibn at-Tinnah, to all appearances a Berber, who controlled the south-east of Sicily, with major garrisons at Catania and Siracusa. Secondly there was Abdullah Ibn Haukal, dominating the north-western corner of Sicily from his palaces at Trapani and Mazara, and finally, between the two, was the Emir Ibn al-Hawwas, who operated from his base at the village of Enna in central Sicily. All three Muslim princes had by now shaken off their earlier allegiance to the Zirid caliph of Kairouan, a Berber, who had himself been dislodged from his capital a year previously and was now fighting for survival among the tribal factions of North Africa. During the eleventh century the Shiite tribe of Alì al-Kalbi ultimately prevailed over the Zirid dynasty. Initially the Kalbid emirs were vassals of the Fatimid Caliph, a fact which presented the Normans with a unique opportunity to increase their strategic and political power.

By the end of the eleventh century the Fatimid court in Cairo had become the main model for the Norman court chancellery. The Normans adapted Fatimid court ceremonies and courtly forms of address in their official documents and on their coins. However, the Normans did not imitate the Fatimids, practising instead a sort of eclectic emulation in a first step towards eventual acculturation. Likewise, they adapted acclamation forms from the late ninth century Abbasid court in Bagdad. A famous example of this occurs on a Norman gold tarì dating from about 1140 and minted in Palermo, as attested by the inscription on its border (fig. 1).

Weighing slightly more than an ounce, the tarì was a quarter of a North African gold dinar. It was originally introduced in Sicily by the Kalbid emirs, vassals of the Fatimid caliph in Cairo. Called 'ruba'i tarì' ("new quarter"), it became the new reserve currency in Sicily and later on in the Norman kingdom. The inscriptions are all in Arabic, except for the legend in the inner circle of the obverse which reads in Greek letters 'Ἰησούς Χριστός νικᾷ' ("Jesus Christ victorious"). This represents a traditional Byzantine acclamation formula which was adapted by the Normans from the emperor in Constantinople[17] and boldly combined with an

---

16 Ibid., 355.
17 Kantorowicz, Laudes Regiae, 7–12.

Arabic acclamation formula deriving from an Abbasid caliph in Bagdad who held the title "Strong in God". Other coins display similar Fatimid formulas. The obverse of the gold tarì of William I struck in the mint at Messina in 1155 shows the name of the king in Kufic script and the acclamation *al-hādī bi-amr allāh* ("the leader invested by God").[18]

Figure 1: Tarì, gold, c. 1140, Kunsthistorisches Museum, Vienna

Figure 2: Muqarnas ceilings, general view, Cappella Palatina

The Islamic muqarnas ceilings in the Cappella Palatina, the royal palace chapel in Palermo, reveal the same idea of eclectic emulation (fig. 2). The panels were painted around 1160 in a mixed Egyptian-Iraqi style, as revealed by comparison

---

18 Dittelbach, Rex Imago Christi, 68.

with eleventh century Fatimid wood sculpture originating from the former Fatimid Palace of Al-Fustāt to the south of Cairo (fig. 3–4).

Figure 3: Musician, Muqarnas ceilings, Cappella Palatina, Palermo

Figure 4: Wooden panel, 11th century, Al-Fustāt/Cairo

The Battle of Cerami

Before introducing other examples of Siculo-Norman art and craftsmanship it is worth taking a brief look at a significant historical event from the conquest of Islamic Sicily, an event that exemplifies the ultimate foundation of Norman acculturation strategies, that is, their tribal identity. It was this sense of their tribal origin that constituted the fundament of Norman success, underpinned by a deep-rooted belief in feudalism[19] and fiefdom. Robert Guiscard and his younger brother Roger were descendants of Tancred of Hauteville, the exiled second-born son of the count of Hauteville in northern France. In Sicily, about eight miles to the west of the mountain village of Troina, the earliest Norman base in Sicily before the conquest of Palermo, lies the little town of Cerami, in a fold of the hills above the river that shares its name.

"Africani igitur et Arabici cum Siciliensibus, plurimo exercitu congregato, ut bellum comiti inferant, advenire nuntiantur, anno Verbi incarnati MLXIII."[20] The Norman historian Goffredo Malaterra gives the date of the battle of Cerami as 1063. Once again the Normans were heavily outnumbered. Count Roger and his nephew Serlo had at their command one hundred and thirty-six knights. We do not know the exact size of the Muslim army. Malaterra estimates it "at three thousand, not counting the foot-soldiers, whose numbers were infinite". Presumably Malaterra is exaggerating, but a major force of this kind, gathered from all over Sicily and reinforced with important detachments from North Africa, must certainly have run into thousands. Assuming proportionate numbers of infantry, the Norman army in its entirety cannot have been more than five or six hundred strong.[21] However, the Norman army was reinforced by the east coast tribes of the Norman ally Ibn at-Tinnah, who had meanwhile been assassinated. In the last book of his *History* Malaterra himself gives us the evidence that Count Roger was in supreme command of thousands of Muslim soldiers who fought in his armed forces: "Comes vero multa milia Saracenorum a Sicilia et Calabria conducens, equitum quoque sive peditum Christianorum copias."[22] According to Malaterra the fighting at Cerami continued until the mangled, trampled bodies lay thick on the battlefield. Then suddenly, as evening wore on, the Muslims turned in flight. "Loaded down with booty, the Normans now installed them-

---

19 From the 1970s the debate about feudalism took a sharply polemical turn which eventually led to the term being banished from scholarly discourse. I suggest rehabilitating feudalism basically as "a method of government", cf. Coulborn, Feudalism in History, 4; See also Kuchenbuch / Michael, Feudalismus – Materialien, 9–10.
20 Goffredo Malaterra, Ruggero I e Roberto il Guiscardo, II/33, 140.
21 Norwich, Normans in the South, 157.
22 Goffredo Malaterra, Ruggero I e Roberto il Guiscardo, IV/22, 319; Chalandon, Histoire, II, 576.

selves in the tents of the Mahommedans, seizing their camels and all else that they found there."[23]

The Normans had prevailed for the same reasons as in earlier clashes: by a combination of belief in divine predestination, which was closely intertwined with their belief in oligarchic feudalistic structures, and their talent for recognizing and rapidly adapting foreign military, economic and cultural standards. By now this talent had reached the point where the historian Malaterra is able to record without apparent surprise how – just before the Normans rode into battle at Cerami – their ranks were joined by a fair young knight, mounted on a white stallion, in his hand a lance from which streamed a white pennant bearing a shining cross. The young knight was immediately recognized as Saint George himself, who had come to lead the soldiers of Christ to victory:

"Dum talia versus certamen properando perorantur, apparuit quidam eques, splendidus in armis, equo albo insidens, album vexillum in summitate hastilis alligatum ferens et desuper splendidam crucem, quasi a nostra acie progrediens, ut nostros ad certamen promptiores redderet, fortissimo impetu hostes, ubi densiores erant, irrumpens."[24]

Exemplifying the whole book, this passage shows how in the work of Malaterra – the annalist at the Norman court – the concepts of traditional piety and modern vassalage overlie one another. The entire book is a treasure trove of phrases and keywords dressed up in literary forms which are inserted seamlessly into the narrative of historical events and pay homage to the utopia of a modern feudal state with a feudal society. One of the leitmotivs is that of the knight with his steed, furnished with "knightly weapons", that is, lance and sword. In Malaterra's writings the knight is already stylised as a single noble figure through which "the chivalric ideal of standing, pride of rank and the class ideology of the nobility are only now developed, and precisely by means of knighthood".[25] The Church supported the development of this new chivalric nobility with all available means, cementing its social position through episcopal consecration and giving it the role of protector of the weak and oppressed. The Church declared the knight to be the "champion of Christ", "thus raising him to a kind of ecclesiastical dignity".[26] During the eleventh century, the knighthood established itself as a discrete social rank or "ordo". "A turn of phrase in use even before 1100 will help us to grasp its

---

23 "Nostri itaque, triumphalibus spoliis onusti, usque ad hostium castra regredientes, in eorum tentoriis hospitantur, camelos et reliqua omnia, quae invenerunt, sibi vindicantes." Goffredo Malaterra, Ruggero I e Roberto il Guiscardo, II/33, 146.
24 Ibid., 144.
25 "[...] weil das ritterliche Standesideal, das Standesbewusstsein und die Klassenideologie des Adels sich erst jetzt, und zwar gerade durch das Rittertum, ausbilden." Hauser, Sozialgeschichte, 214.
26 "ließ ihn als den Streiter Christi gelten und erhob ihn damit zu einer Art geistlicher Würde", ibid., 215.

significance. A knight was not merely 'made'; he was 'ordained'. An *ordo* was a division of society, temporal as well as ecclesiastical. But it was a regular, clearly defined division, conformable to the divine plan."[27]

Malaterra refers to the white banner of St George, which featured a shining cross and with which the saintly knight rode ahead of the Norman army, as a *vexillum* ("lance-pennon"): album vexillum in summitate hastilis. It is the same phrase used by the author in the next sentence but one to describe the lance-pennon of Roger, the military commander, "which was seen by several people": "Visum etiam fuit a pluribus in summitate hastilis comitis vexillum dependens, crucem continens, a nullo, nisi divinitus, appositum."[28] In this passage Malaterra is particularly concerned with authenticity, because he is making use of a rhetorical – one might say almost cineastic – trick: he 'fades' the scene of the vision of St George into the description of the actual scene of the onslaught: Roger becomes St George, and the lance-pennon in the hand of St George, the *vexillum*, is transformed in Roger's hands into a "Lehnsfahne" or banner of feudal investiture. More than the sword, it was the lance-pennon that had been the valid symbol of vassalage since the beginning of the Norman conquest in southern Italy. "The symbol used at enfeoffment also held the wider status of legal evidence, and to no lesser degree than a document."[29] This is attested by Amato di Montecassino in his L'Estoire de li Normant. Before the battle of Civitate against Pope Leo IX in 1053, that is, six years before the famous oath of fealty sworn by Robert Guiscard at Melfi, the Normans presented the "Lehnsfahne" with which they were invested by the Roman Emperor as proof of the legitimacy of their territorial possessions: "Et monsterent lo confanon coment il furent revestut de la terre … e coment lor estoit confermée."[30] The existence of numerous seals from the first quarter of the eleventh century depicting the Norman vassals with lance-pennons underlines the symbolism of feudal law and thus the juridical roots of Norman feudalism.[31] As Deér convincingly demonstrates, the use of the *vexillum*, with which the popes invested the Norman princes from 1059, can be traced back directly to imperial feudal practice.[32]

The painted muqarnas ceilings of the Cappella Palatina in Palermo provide us with an image which alludes to Malaterra's account of the battle of Cerami. St

---

27 Bloch, Feudal Society, vol. 2, 314.
28 Goffredo Malaterra, Ruggero I e Roberto il Guiscardo, II/33, 144.
29 "Das bei der Belehnung verwendete Symbol besaß nämlich auch sonst die Bedeutung eines Rechtsbeweises und zwar keineswegs in geringerem Maße als eine Urkunde." Deér, Papsttum und Normannen, 25.
30 Amato di Montecassino, Storia dei Normanni, 232.
31 Cf. the wax seal with the double image of Pandulf VI of Capua and his son John from 1023, cf. Deér, Papsttum und Normannen, 27, Taf. I, 2–3.
32 Ibid., 28.

George is represented on a horse slaying the evil dragon with his lance (fig. 5). We find him three times on the ceilings, clad in Eastern or Western costumes in each case, but not represented as a knight in armour. Around 1160 Norman iconographic eclecticism was at its peak. St George is the only Christian image in the Islamic iconographic programme of the ceilings. It is no coincidence that at the same time he was one of the most prominent saints in Byzantine hagiography. In both cultures, the Arabic and the Byzantine, the symbolic narratives of homage and fealty were widely unknown. In the Byzantine Empire the government "had preserved the great administrative traditions of the Roman period" and was "concerned to provide itself with a strong army, created tenements charged with military obligations to the State – true fiefs in one sense, but differing from those of the West in that they were peasant fiefs. Thenceforth it was a paramount concern of the imperial government to protect these 'soldier's properties' against the encroachments of the rich and powerful".[33] In the Byzantine world the traditional images of St George were those of a soldier and a martyr. The Norman world enhanced his powers and invented a new image representing him as the vassal of God.

Figure 5: S. George, Muqarnas ceilings, Cappella Palatina, Palermo

---

33 Bloch, Feudal Society, vol. 2, 444.

Exchanging Symbols of Allegiance

According to Goffredo Malaterra, many people later testified to having seen St George's cross also flying from the point of Roger's lance at the height of the battle. Roger is thus made the living counterpart of St George as well as his proxy and vassal. In recognition of these signs, Roger ordered a sumptuous present to be sent to Pope Alexander II: four dromedaries, the most precious part of the booty which Roger had taken from the vanquished enemy. This event might be reflected by a picture at the muqarnas ceilings in the Palatine Chapel which is not without humour (fig. 6). Pope Alexander must have been delighted with his present: quite apart from their exotic character, the dromedaries were a living indication to him that Roger was on his side and that he could probably look to the Normans for support, as and when necessary. In other words, Roger's gesture was that of a loyal vassal towards his liege lord. However, Roger's direct overlord was not the pope but his elder brother Robert Guiscard, whom he was thus "bypassing". The aim of this risky gambit was fuelled by the hope that Alexander would enfeoff him directly with the conquered territories in Sicily. The pope's reaction was prompt: he conveyed his apostolic blessing and a general absolution of all sins to Roger and the knights, who were his subvassals. Malaterra writes that he did this in gratitude for Sicily having been wrested from heathen hands. In reality the final conquest of Sicily was to take another thirty years. What is remarkable in our context, however, is that Alexander ordered Roger to send the papal "Lehnsfahne" with the insignia of St Peter to Rome: *mandat, vexillumque a Romana Sede, apostolica auctoritate consignatum*.[34] Like a document, the *vexillum* bore the insignia of apostolic authority. In this we can see not only the legitimation of Roger's military exploits but also his claims under feudal law. However, Roger's gift to the pope of four dromedaries was a masterly stroke: they were more than mere trophies – they were Trojan horses. Pope Alexander was unaware of the ingenious tactic concealed in this gift. Indeed, Roger could have sent him the best Arab horses, which were also part of his booty and which would have doubtlessly been more appropriate to the highest liege lord of the Western world. But Roger chose precisely the gift he would have given to his Muslim allies and their sovereign, the Zirid Caliph of Kairouan. A dromedary in the world of Berbers – and the Zirid tribes were Berbers, not Arabs – had an inestimably higher value than a horse. On the other hand, the precious gift could just as well have been sent to the pope as a vassal's offering by the Muslim rulers. In other words, Norman diplomacy was acting more for the benefit of the Muslim tribesmen than the highest Christian authority in Rome. Considering the fragile pact with his new, culturally diverse allies, Roger was playing for high stakes. The

---

34 Goffredo Malaterra, Ruggero I e Roberto il Guiscardo, II/33, 148.

historical sources and even the *Liber Pontificalis* maintain diplomatic silence on the background to this event. We can therefore only surmise the reasons for it.

Figure 6: Dromedaries with riders, Muqarnas ceilings, Cappella Palatina, Palermo

One reason was certainly the deep distrust by Western clergy of foreign cultural influences and artisan objects from the Islamic world. In 1068, only five years after the battle of Cerami, the treasuries and famous libraries of the Fatimid caliph palace in al-Fustat had been looted by a marauding band of soldiers. Subsequently precious Islamic objects such as rock crystal vessels and delicately carved ivory boxes reached Western courts, usually having been transformed or adapted into receptacles of Christian relics along the way. Even if the Norman Duke Robert and his youngest brother Roger were obviously not the instigators of the organized looting in Egypt and Ifriqiya, they participated very early in the establishment of a flourishing 'art market'. Their hubs were Rome, Palermo, Constantinople and – following the first crusade – Antioch. Their network of educated Byzantine and Arab consultants and contacts with experienced Jewish and Muslim merchants and skilled craftsmen were immensely efficient. The Western clergy feared this ability to create a cultural network that was based on evenly balanced exchange and mutual acceptance. In the second half of the eleventh century, only one generation before the Council of Clermont (1095), the spectre of a new feudal hierarchy with a new socio-economic order was haunting

Europe. In the beginning, when the exiled second-born sons of Tancred of Hauteville quit their father's county, they left with the experience of an inequitable and corrupt feudal system in which the landed gentry prevailed over their liege lords by controlling and occupying their land. In other words, when they left Normandy the Hauteville sons bore a stigma on their name; it was the ancient brand of Cain, the mark of being *victimised*. This is the reason why no contemporary sources, no document from the eleventh or the twelfth century, mentions kinship ties with their Hauteville ancestors. Later on, the Norman kings went so far as to trace their descent right back to the Old Testament. In the late eleventh century, the Norman historiographer William of Apulia calls the Tancred sons *homines boreales*, describing them as the icy north wind which was invading southern Italy. From this point on the Normans pursue a sole objective: to acquire land in order to establish their own feoff. In doing so they upended the old feudal order which was formerly regulated by the liege lord. It was he who decided on the convenient time and the extent of the enfeoffment on the base of the vassal's 'existing' property, and not the vassal, on the base of property still to be acquired in the future. The early exiled Normans pursued the idea of a broad tribal network. Only after the complete Norman conquest of Sicily did Count Roger, or more precisely his wife Adelasia del Vasto, conclude the establishment of a new feudal order by creating a permanent residence and transferring the ruler's throne from Troina to Palermo with its predominantly Muslim population which had wholly divergent socio-economic ties and hierarchies. Now the city came into play as a fixed point of reference of feudal society, and with it the privilege of immunity as an integral constituent part of the feudal system.[35] Only now did the Normans set about transforming their former hermetic system of tribal identity ("Stammesbewusstsein") into an open system of class consciousness ("Standesbewusstsein"). The utopian character of this system was to create social cohesion amongst the four ethnic and faith groups in Sicily, giving rise to a cross-cultural social utopia which was to fail only 80 years later with the death of the last legitimate Norman king William II.

Another reason for the silence of contemporary ecclesiastical sources after the battle of Cerami was the moral condemnation of plundering. Malaterra provides us with an explanation between the lines. Following a detailed description of the victory and the capture of plentiful booty he gives a gruesome account of the merciless extinction of the defeated fleeing army:

> "Then, on the morrow, they left to seek out those twenty thousand foot-soldiers who had fled to the mountains for refuge. Many of these they killed, the remainder they took captive and sold as slaves, receiving for each a great price. But after a little time, the

---

35 Wunder, Einleitung, 27.

contagion which arose from the rotting corpses on the battlefield drove them away and they returned to Troina."[36]

The State of (the) Art

The images and inscription on the so-called coronation mantle of Roger II can only be seen in their entirety when the garment is spread out in a semi-circle, as it is displayed today in the Secular Treasury of the Vienna Hofburg (fig. 7).[37] This is important for understanding that it was probably not conceived as a piece of clothing to be worn. At all events, it was not worn by Roger II at his coronation. Instead, I surmise that it was exhibited in the palace chapel on special occasions or at audiences and paraded in public processions. The unworn mantle represented *pars pro toto* the claim to power that expressed itself in the physical absence of the monarch. It was the narrative symbol that created the image, not the physical body of the king.

Figure 7: So-called coronation mantle Roger's II, Kunsthistorisches Museum, Vienna

The Arabic inscription running from right to left along the lower border of the mantle ends with the place and date of its making: the capital Palermo and the Islamic Hegira date of 528, corresponding to 1133/34.[38] The palace workshops are extolled and associated with the wish that their marvellous artefacts be appreciated. This is the desire of the author of the inscription, who was certainly also the person who commissioned the mantle. At this point the indicative mood changes to the subjunctive or optative. The addressee of the mantle, that is, Roger II, is not

---

36 Goffredo Malaterra, Ruggero I e Roberto il Guiscardo, II/33, 146.
37 Bauer, Mantel Rogers II., 114–123.
38 Johns, Die arabischen Inschriften, 48.

mentioned. Instead, the individual who commissioned it expresses concrete expectations towards the king that are coupled with his gift: rich rewards, generosity, reputation, and above all the fulfilment of his vows and hopes: "May he enjoy a good reception there, rich profits, acts of generosity, splendour, reputation, magnificence, and the fulfilment of [his] vows and hopes."

The mantle is made of kermes-dyed silk brocade and embroidered with gold thread and hundreds of small pearls. The semicircle of the mantle is bisected vertically by a date palm, which when the mantle is worn, aligns exactly with the wearer's spine. The left and right quadrants contain a pair of addorsed lions facing outwards crouched over dromedaries and holding them fast with their claws. The master-narrative is evident: the Norman lion dominates the desert animal of the Berbers and Arabs, Christianity dominates Islam. If the narrative had stopped at this point, with this message, the mantle would have constituted an egregious insult for the Muslims at court and in the city. But the story also contains a counter-narrative: everyone who saw the mantle spread out would recognize that the dromedaries are depicted wearing bridles and saddle cloths, that is, they are domesticated animals (fig. 8).

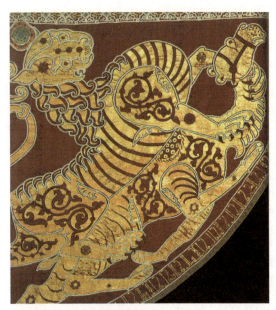

Figure 8: Lion and dromedary, so-called coronation mantle Roger's II, Kunsthistorisches Museum, Vienna

This will have been clear to Christians, Muslims and Jews alike. Nevertheless, the message remained implicit, rather like an accidental footnote. And everyone had the option of accessing this footnote and its additional level of interpretation.

This is what makes a good acculturation strategy: messages are transformed without being substantially changed; it is only the context that changes. The context becomes de-constructed before being re-constructed in an altered interpretation. Regarding the interpretation it is crucial to remember that images and texts were mostly conveyed orally to the medieval beholder, a task that fell to courtiers or clerics depending on content.

One of the interpretations was the narrative of the most important event in the history of Muslim and Norman Sicily: the battle of Cerami as related by Goffredo Malaterra, court historiographer to Roger II's father, Count Roger the Great. In the light of this great epic of homage and fealty the fundamental meaning of Count Roger's gift to Pope Alexander becomes clear in the image on Roger's mantle: the lions and the dromedaries were symbols of his own vassalage and the allegiance of his Muslim vassals. The image of two pairs of domesticated animals reminded the beholder that the communal oath of fealty united *equals*.

The Christian commissioner of the mantle representing lions and dromedaries not as victors and vanquished but as two equal parts of a common narrative was concerned to avoid victimising the other ethnic and religious population groups in the Norman realm.

Conclusion

The remarkable exchange of gifts between the pope and the Normans following the battle of Cerami in 1063 was both a symbolic and a juridical act that renders visible the original reason and motivation for the enfeoffment of Robert Guiscard with Islamic Sicily in 1059: the agreement concluded between the Norman and his papal liege lord was intended to legitimate the creation of a modern feudal state on Islamic soil. However, to achieve this Duke Robert and Count Roger needed the help of the Muslims themselves. Contemporary sources – historiography as well as Islamic and Christian works of art – provide information about the Normans' efforts to impose their *ordo*, a feudal pyramid with Christ at the apex, on the Muslims in Sicily, who only knew the system from the outside. Ultimately it took the Normans thirty years to realize this project. Viewed from the perspective of the victors and the vanquished, the events of Cerami tell the story of an alliance of a wholly new kind in the West – the birth of a closed and yet multicultural feudal society in the Middle Ages. It differed substantially from the idea of an open society of the kind familiar since the Enlightenment. Nonetheless, in the creation of a Norman feudal state in Sicily lay the key for a utopian Golden Age that was intended to last forever. The ultimate failure of this utopia in the beginning of the thirteenth century had its roots in the hierarchy of the victors and the vanquished, which lost the fascination of a clearly defined 'juridical' relationship of dependence and protection.

In September 1206 Pope Innocent III sent a letter to the insurgent Muslim rulers in Sicily admonishing them - albeit in vain - for maintaining their homage and fealty towards the young king of Sicily, Frederick II.[39] After four generations, the social and psychological traumas that a war of conquest always causes resurfaced, leading to the corrosion of an initially successful model of state. Despite cultural and technological progress, history has a tendency to repeat itself.

Bibliography

Sources

Amato di Montecassino, Storia dei Normanni, ed. Giuseppe Sperduti, Cassino 1999.
Chalandon, Ferdinand, Histoire de la Domination Normande en Italie et en Sicile, 2 Bde., Paris 1907 (reprint New York 1960).
Das Papsttum und die süditalienischen Normannenstaaten 1053-1212, ed. Josef Deér (Historische Texte / Mittelalter 12), Göttingen 1969.
Romualdi Salernitani Chronicon (A. m. 130 - A. C. 1178), ed. Carlo Alberto Garufi (Rerum Italicarum scriptores. Raccolta degli storici italiani dal cinquecento al millecinquecento, ordinata da L. A. Muratori, T. 7, Pt. 1), Città di Castello 1935.

Literature

Abulafia, David, The End of Muslim Sicily, in: Muslims under Latin Rule 1100-1300, ed. James M. Powell, Princeton 1990, 103-134.
Arendt, Hannah, The Origins of Totalitarianism, New York 1951.
Bauer, Rotraud, Der Mantel Rogers II. und die siculo-normannischen Gewänder aus den königlichen Hofwerkstätten in Palermo, in: Nobiles Officinae: Die königlichen Hofwerkstätten zu Palermo zur Zeit der Normannen und Staufer im 12. und 13. Jahrhundert. Eine Ausstellung des Kunsthistorischen Museums Wien und der Regione Siciliana, ed. Wilfried Seipel, Vienna 2004, 114-123.
Bloch, Marc, Feudal Society, vol. 1-2, trans. L. A. Manyon, London 1965.
Bloch, Marc, European Feudalism, in: Feudalismus. Zehn Aufsätze, ed. Heide Wunder, Munich 1974, 125-139.
Coulborn, Rushton (ed.), Feudalism in History, Princeton 1956.

---

39 Cf. Tramontana, Ceti sociali, gruppi etnici e rivolte, 151-166; Abulafia, The end of Muslim Sicily, 103-134.

Deér, Josef, Papsttum und Normannen: Untersuchungen zu ihren lehnsrechtlichen und kirchenpolitischen Beziehungen (Studien und Quellen zur Welt Kaiser Friedrichs II. 1), Cologne 1972.

Dittelbach, Thomas, Rex Imago Christi – Der Dom von Monreale. Bildsprachen und Zeremoniell in Mosaikkunst und Architektur, Wiesbaden 2003.

Goffredo Malaterra, Ruggero I e Roberto il Guiscardo, ed. Vito Lo Curto, Cassino 2002.

Hauser, Arnold, Sozialgeschichte der Kunst und Literatur, Munich ²1987.

Johns, Jeremy, Die arabischen Inschriften der Normannenkönige Siziliens: Eine Neuinterpretation, in: Nobiles Officinae: Die königlichen Hofwerkstätten zu Palermo zur Zeit der Normannen und Staufer im 12. und 13. Jahrhundert. Eine Ausstellung des Kunsthistorischen Museums Wien und der Regione Siciliana, ed. Wilfried Seipel, Vienna 2004, 36–59.

Kantorowicz, Ernst H., Laudes Regiae: A Study in Liturgical Acclamations and Mediaeval Ruler Worship, Berkeley / Los Angeles 1946.

Kuchenbuch, Ludolf / Michael, Bernd, Feudalismus – Materialien zur Theorie und Geschichte, Frankfurt a. M. 1977.

Mitteis, Heinrich, Die Entstehung des Lehnswesens: Die Immunität, in: Feudalismus. Zehn Aufsätze, ed. Heide Wunder, Munich 1974, 79–86.

Norwich, John Julius, The Normans in the South 1016–1130, London 1967.

Siragusa, Giovan Battista, Il regno di Guglielmo I in Sicilia: Illustrato con nuovi documenti, Palermo ²1929.

Tramontana, Salvatore, Ceti sociali, gruppi etnici e rivolte, in: Potere, società e popolo nell'età sveva. Atti delle seste giornate normanno-sveve (Bari-Castel del Monte-Melfi, 17–20 ott. 1983), Bari 1985, 151–166.

Wunder, Heide, Einleitung: Der Feudalismus-Begriff. Überlegungen zu Möglichkeiten der historischen Begriffsbildung, in: Feudalismus. Zehn Aufsätze, ed. Heide Wunder, Munich 1974, 10–76.

List of Figures

Dittelbach

Figure 1: Tarì, gold, c. 1140, Kunsthistorisches Museum, Vienna (KHM Wien).
Figure 2: Muqarnas ceilings, general view, Cappella Palatina, Palermo (photo Swiridoff), aus: Dittelbach, Thomas, Die Capella Palatina in Palermo. Geschichte, Kunst, Funktionen, Künzelsau 2011, Tafel S. 300–301.
Figure 3: Musician, Muqarnas ceilings, Cappella Palatina, Palermo (photo T. Dittelbach).
Figure 4: Wooden panel, 11th century, Al-Fustāt/Cairo west palace at Al-Fustāt, Fatimid, 11th century, Museum of Islamic Art, Cairo (aus: Hattstein, Markus / Deliuss, Peter, Islam, Kunst und Architektur, Köln 2000, S. 156–157).
Figure 5: S. George, Muqarnas ceilings, Cappella Palatina, Palermo (photo T. Dittelbach).
Figure 6: Dromedaries with riders, Muqarnas ceilings, Cappella Palatina, Palermo (photo T. Dittelbach).
Figure 7: So-called coronation mantle Roger's II, Kunsthistorisches Museum, Vienna (KHM Wien).
Figure 8: Lion and dromedary, so-called coronation mantle Roger's II, Kunsthistorisches Museum, Vienna (KHM Wien).

Pietschmann

Example 1: Biblioteca del Seminario maggiore di Aosta, Codex 15, fol. 95v–96r, concessione alla riproduzione su autorizzazione dell'Ufficio Beni Culturali Ecclesiastici – Diocesi di Aosta.
Example 3: Beinecke Rare Book and Manuscript Library, Yale University, General Collection MS 91 (Mellon Chansonnier), fol. 44v and 45r (https://collections.library.yale.edu/catalog/2008083).

Vukovich

Figure 1:   Iaroslav I (1019–1054), Silver Coin, find location: unknown, Staatliche Museen zu Berlin, no. 18216120.
Figure 2:   Seal of Isaac I Komnenos (1057–1069), © Dumbarton Oaks, Byzantine Collection, Washington, DC (BZC.1955.1.4319).
Figure 3:   Nomisma histamenon of Isaac I Komnenos (1057–1059), © Dumbarton Oaks, Byzantine Collection, Washington, DC (BZC.1948.17.2961).
Figure 4:   Cathedral of Saint Demetrios, Façade (https://commons.wikimedia.org/wiki/File:Vladimir_StDemetriusCathedral_6875.jpg).
Table I–VI: Author.